BACK
TO
CORREGIDOR

Also by Gerard M. Devlin

Paratrooper!: The Saga of U.S. Army and Marine Parachute and Glider Combat Troops During World War II

Silent Wings: The Saga of the U.S. Army and Marine Combat Glider Pilots During World War II

BACK
TO
CORREGIDOR

AMERICA RETAKES THE ROCK
Gerard M. Devlin

ST. MARTIN'S PRESS NEW YORK

940.5426
D

Editor: Jared Kieling
Copyedited by W. L. Broecker
Design by Judith Christensen
Maps by Paul Costa

Library of Congress Cataloging-in-Publication Data

Devlin, Gerard K.
    Back to Corregidor : America retakes the rock / Gerard K. Devlin.
        p.   cm.
    ISBN 0-312-07648-7
    1. World War, 1939–1945—Campaigns—Philippines—Corregidor
Island.   2. Corregidor Island (Philippines)—History.   I. Title.
    D767.4.D47   1992
    940.54'26—dc20   92-2995
                                                                      CIP

First Edition: June 1992
10 9 8 7 6 5 4 3 2 1

For the intrepid General George M. Jones and all who served as members of his Rock Force during the battle to liberate Corregidor.

and

For my son Michael; my daughters Deanna-Lyn and Patricia; Patricia's husband, Captain Robert S. Petree, Jr., U.S. Air Force; and my adorable grandchildren Michelle, Little Robert, Ann, and Joseph.

CORREGIDOR

Silver moon softens shattered walls,
Only the ghosts remain,
And the winds howl down the lonely halls
The tales of blood and pain.

And chutes sigh, like long lost souls,
Stranded in lifeless trees.
Death lurks in the cavelike holes
That gape at the lonely seas.

O Lord, consecrate and bless
The loved ones who must rest,
Who bore your cross and gave their all
In this their final test.

Written on Corregidor by Sergeant Gertus H. Jones of Battery
B, 462d Parachute Artillery Battalion during a lull in the battle
to liberate the island.

CONTENTS

FOREWORD

Gerard Devlin's *Back to Corregidor* is the history of a place known as the Garden Isle of the Philippines prior to World War II. It was lost to the Japanese in May 1942 and recaptured by U.S. military forces in February 1945.

Corregidor's spectacular recapture by the Rock Force involved the 503d Parachute Regimental Combat Team as the basic unit of Rock Force. I had the distinction of being commander of the combat team as well as the overall commander of Rock Force.

The 503d Parachute Infantry was America's oldest parachute regiment. The 2d Battalion of that three-battalion regiment was actually the first tactical parachute unit formed early in 1941; it was then known as the 501st Parachute Battalion.

The troopers of the 503d learned the art of tactical parachuting from scratch. With no prior experience to guide us, we had to learn by doing and trying new things as we went along in those early days. We experimented to find how to best get ourselves in sound physical condition, jump out of an airplane, and get on the ground with our weapons in our hands, ready to fight. This was a natural developmental process for the unusually aggressive and resourceful troopers of the 503d.

Another asset the 503d acquired was the knowledge of how to survive in the jungle. The jungle can be a very harsh environment. The regiment's junior officers and senior noncommissioned officers received training at the Australian Army's Jungle Warfare School at Conungra, Australia, while we were training at Gordonvale in 1942 and 1943. Our soldiers learned about edible wild fruits and plants and how to get water from the water vine. We learned how to make the jungle work for us. Our men could survive longer and better than the average soldier in the army. This gave all members of the regiment an unusually high degree of self-confidence.

Foreword

In Panama where the 501st Battalion trained for a year, and also in Australia, our units learned to jump into small, restricted and challenging areas. This capability served us well when we parachuted into the ultraforbidding areas of sheared-off trees and house-size bomb craters on Corregidor.

The 503d parachute team was experienced in making low-altitude combat jumps: 600 feet at Nadzab in New Guinea, and 400 feet at Noemfoor Island, Dutch New Guinea. At Noemfoor, on July 5, 1944, the first planeload jumped at an altitude of only 175 feet instead of the 400 feet scheduled for that mission. The pilot of the lead plane apparently failed to set his altimeter when we took off from a higher altitude at Lake Sentani in Hollandia, Dutch New Guinea. Nine out of the seventeen paratroopers who jumped from that lead plane suffered broken legs, ankles, backs, and other serious injuries. My enlisted aide, who jumped just ahead of me, had both legs broken. I had an extremely severe headache that lasted for at least a week after the jump. Possibly it was a concussion. But since I could still operate and had a great deal to attend to in the objective area, I did not have my condition medically recorded.

The 503d, with the rugged training it had received and its previous combat experience, was the proper unit to be assigned the mission of jumping onto Corregidor. The 3d Battalion, 34th Infantry Regiment, 24th Division, and other small units that were attached to the 503d Parachute Regimental Combat Team for that mission made us a relatively small but formidable fighting force. Every unit in the Rock Force, large or small, did an outstanding job.

My philosophy as a parachute commander was simple: Parachuting into combat is basically a poor means of transportation. There is always the very real possibility of jump injuries, loss or damage to weapons and supplies, and scattering of tactical units throughout the objective area and beyond. Parachute entry into combat should only be made when that mode provides a tactical advantage! This concept was the basis for delivery of the 3d Battalion of the 503d to Corregidor amphibiously instead of by parachute. In the previous Noemfoor Island operation the 3d Battalion had also been brought ashore by boat instead of by parachute. In our final combat operation after Corregidor, scheduled parachute jumps on Negros Island were canceled at my recommendation to Eighth Army. Air reconnaissance I made the day prior to the scheduled jumps indicated that all three initial objectives had been compromised: Two major river bridges were blown and a sawmill was on fire. As a result of that cancellation, the 503d was flown to Panay Island in the vicinity of Negros and we were brought to Negros by naval vessels.

It is interesting to recall that General Walter Krueger, the outstanding commander of Sixth Army, directed me to report to his headquarters on Goodenough Island to plan the Cape Gloucester Operation with the 1st Marine Division. When I reported to General Krueger, he asked me how I thought the 503d should participate. Having flown over Cape Gloucester only a few weeks before on an air force bombing mission during which we were on the receiving end of hostile antiaircraft fire, I already knew how the Japanese were defending that whole area. So I replied, "General, we ought to jump right on top of the Japs. It will be rough going for awhile, but we will win the fight." General Krueger looked at me with considerable consternation and said, "We don't fight wars that way!" I thought he was going to throw me out of his tent.

We fortunately did not participate in the Cape Gloucester Operation. General Krueger did not make the subsequent decision to jump on Corregidor. It was General MacArthur who directed that we jump.

Jump on top of the enemy was exactly what we did to overcome the force of 350–800 estimated by Sixth Army to be on Corregidor. We eventually took a toll of over 6,000 enemy during the operation; 4,500 Japanese dead were counted. Hundreds more were killed in caves and in Malinta Tunnel.

Troopers of the 503d were brave, determined, and always helpful to one another. Teamwork was evident in every one of our operations. The characteristic of helpfulness extended even to our enemy. We were informed that the Japanese wanted to die for the Emperor. The troopers of the 503d eagerly helped them achieve their goal.

Captain Itagaki, the Japanese naval commander of Corregidor, had been ordered by Imperial Headquarters to prepare a defense against an airborne landing attack. Captain Itagaki was killed during the first hour of the operation. We captured his enlisted aide who, under interrogation, reported that the captain had made a reconnaissance of the island with his staff as directed. Following that reconnaissance, and a detailed study of his existing defensive positions, Itagaki concluded that it would be impossible to land paratroopers on Corregidor. He therefore prepared no antiairborne defense plan.

So by at least one person's estimate, Rock Force did accomplish the impossible!

I trust that you will enjoy reading *Back to Corregidor*.

George M. Jones
Brigadier General, U.S. Army, Ret.
Tuscon, Arizona
June 1991

ACKNOWLEDGMENTS

Among the host of veterans who contributed to the book I would like to thank in particular the following: Howard Cary, Clifford Warren, and Lieutenant Colonel Jules D. Yates, all of whom defended Corregidor during the 1941–1942 siege and assault by Japanese forces and who subsequently endured three years as prisoners of war, for familiarizing me with the island's topography and its many military and civilian facilities; Brigadier General George M. Jones, who commanded Rock Force throughout the parachute assault and ground fighting that resulted in Corregidor's liberation, for providing me with copies of voluminous after-action reports prepared by his staff and company commanders who fought the battle; Lieutenant General John J. Tolson III, who as a major commanded a battalion in the 503d Parachute Infantry Regiment before being moved up to General Krueger's Sixth Army staff, for telephone interviews during which he provided detailed information concerning the regiment's early lineage and the planning that took place at Sixth Army for the Corregidor jump mission; Command Sergeant Major Leroy F. Tolson (no relation to General John Tolson), for allowing me to borrow the actual combat map he jumped with and carried during the fighting on Corregidor; Chief Petty Officer Millard Blevins and Keith E. Snyder, both of whom were aboard the destroyer *U.S.S. Fletcher* when she was struck by Japanese shells fired from Corregidor, for detailing the heroics of Watertender Second Class Elmer C. Bigelow, and for providing documents concerning their gallant ship's battle history; Lewis H. France, Norman H. Smith, James D. White, and O.D. Williford, Jr., all former PT boat sailors who were aboard the boats that rescued misdropped paratroopers, for explaining how those daring pickups were made under enemy fire. I owe Mr. France a special word of thanks for sending me a copy of PT 376's log for March 2, 1945, the day she transported General MacArthur from Manila to Corregidor for the historic flag-raising ceremony with the paratroopers and other members of Rock Force.

For sending me information about the many risks involved in making parachute jumps on Corregidor, I am most grateful to Colonel Ramon M. Ong of the Armed Forces of the Philippines who is himself a parachutist of considerable experience.

My thanks also go to these other contributors: Donald G. Rhodes, Executive Vice President of PT Boats Inc., and his staff in Memphis, Tennessee, for sending names and addresses of individuals who served aboard the PT boats that rescued paratroopers misdropped at Corregidor; Lou Varrone, who is a noted artist and writer of the airborne world and also a former paratrooper, for permitting me to use his rendering of Private Lloyd G. McCarter that appears in this book; Thomas P. Gaffney, a veteran of World War II service in the U.S. Navy who is a walking reference book relating to warships and naval personalities, for interviews at his home and allowing me to borrow books and photos from his private collection; Dennis Davies, an established authority on weapons and equipment carried by airborne troops of all nations, for answering my many questions about American and Japanese paratroopers of World War II; Lieutenant Thomas H. Costa who, while a cadet at West Point, took time from his busy academic schedule to research information for me that was only available in the academy's library; George "Pete" Buckley, a World War II combat glider pilot, for coming to my aid on several occasions with information I had requested concerning U.S. Air Force matters, and Anne Cloy, wife of my OCS classmate, Colonel Richard C. Cloy, who graciously sent me the names and addresses of several former residents of the Philippines who provided me with considerable information about Corregidor and Manila.

A great many other generous contributors took time to answer my requests for photos to accompany the manuscript. Space does not permit me to list all their names, but I am grateful to them all. Those who deserve special mention are Carl Kuttruff, this country's foremost authority on the history of Corregidor and all other islands located in Manila Bay; Command Sergeant Major

Acknowledgments

Leroy F. Tolson and Dominico Muzio, both veteran paratroopers of the Corregidor and other combat jump missions, who managed to carry cameras during the fighting on Corregidor; and Bennett M. Guthrie, a noted airborne author who also jumped on Corregidor as a member of Rock Force.

For continuous words of encouragement during the time it took me to write this book, my thanks to my son, Michael; my daughters, Deanna-Lyn and Patricia; Patricia's husband, Captain Robert S. Petree, U.S. Air Force; my grandchildren, Michelle, Robert, Ann, and Joseph, and my brother, Arthur, who is himself an author. My thanks also go to my agent, Paul Gitlin; and to Jared Kieling, senior editor at St. Martin's Press, for his patience and understanding of the difficulties that caused me to be tardy in submitting the completed manuscript. I must thank the eagle-eyed copyeditor W. L. Broecker for catching my spelling errors and word omissions, and for untangling my many garbled and verbose sentences.

Above all others who gave me encouragement and assistance stands Leona, my wife. She organized and collated material, typed much of the manuscript, and was my constant source of strength when the going was toughest.

As happened during the writing of my previous works on the airborne troops of World War II, there were a great many times when I was unable to think of the right words to complete an important paragraph. On each of those occasions, I put my pen down on my desk and prayed to the Almighty and the Blessed Mother for assistance. As before, they never let me down.

Finally, I also owe another special word of thanks to Saint Anthony, the worker of miracles, for my many requests that were all answered. I'll try not to be such a pest to him in the future.

BACK

TO
CORREGIDOR

OUTER MONGOLIA

U.S.S.R.

MANCHUKUO

PEIPING

CHINA

KOREA

JAPAN

HONSHU

TOKYO

HIROSHIMA

NAGASAKI

SHANGHAI

OKINAWA

IWO

FORMOSA

INDIA

BURMA

HONG KONG

FRENCH INDO-CHINA

THAILAND

LINGAYAN GULF

LUZON

CORREGIDOR

MINDORO

PANAY

SAMAR

LEYTE

PHILIPPINES

SAIGON

NEGROS

MINDANAO

MALAY

SARAWAK

NOEMFOOR

SINGAPORE

BORNEO

NETHERLANDS

NEW GUINEA

EAST INDIES

DARWIN

MILES

0   400   800

AUSTRALIA

PAUL L. COSTA

HOKKAIDO

JIMA

SAIPAN
GUAM

LAE
SOLOMON IS.

PORT
MORESBY

CAIRNS

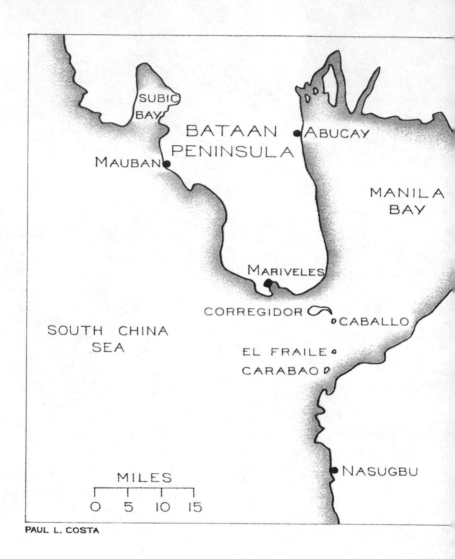

SUBIC
BAY

BATAAN
PENINSULA

● ABUCAY

MAUBAN ●

MANILA
BAY

MARIVELES
●

SOUTH CHINA
SEA

CORREGIDOR ⌒
ᴅ CABALLO

EL FRAILE ◦
CARABAO ᴅ

MILES

0   5   10   15

● NASUGBU

PAUL L. COSTA

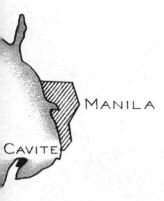

MANILA

CAVITE

TAGAYTAY RIDGE

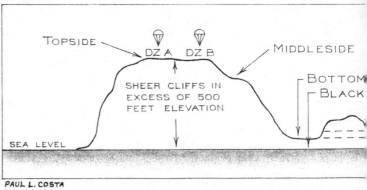

PAUL L. COSTA

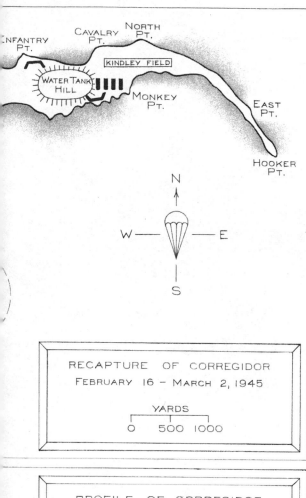

INFANTRY PT.

CAVALRY PT.

NORTH PT.

KINDLEY FIELD

WATER TANK HILL

MONKEY PT.

EAST PT.

HOOKER PT.

N
W — E
S

RECAPTURE OF CORREGIDOR
FEBRUARY 16 – MARCH 2, 1945

YARDS
0   500   1000

PROFILE OF CORREGIDOR
(NOT TO SCALE)

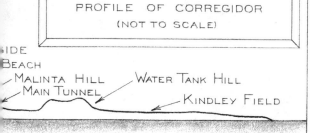

SIDE
BEACH
MALINTA HILL
MAIN TUNNEL
WATER TANK HILL
KINDLEY FIELD

1

ORIGINS OF FORTRESS CORREGIDOR

Looming like a half-surfaced sea monster whose head looks menacingly upon the South China Sea, Corregidor sits at the entrance to Manila Bay. Fortified with big naval guns, for centuries the island had guarded the seaward approaches to Manila, capital of the Philippine archipelago that stretches for more than a thousand miles north and south and as much as 600 miles east and west.

Collectively, the Philippines comprise a land area greater than that of the British Isles. Yet less than half of its over 7,100 islands are big enough to have formally recorded names, and only eleven of them can boast an area greater than 1,000 square miles. The largest and most important is Luzon in the north, where the capital city of Manila and the great harbor of Manila Bay are located. Next in size is Mindanao at the southern end of the chain. In between are the Visayas, a grouping of the large islands of Leyte, Samar, Negros, Panay, Cebu, and others.

Because of its extremely rugged terrain, and sea-monsterlike shape, the strategically located island of Corregidor appears forbidding, as well as far larger than it really is, to all who approach it from the open sea. From end to end it measures only three and one-half miles. Its imposing stature is considerably enhanced by the fact that the highest elevations are located on the large bulbous head of the monster, which is one mile in diameter and

1

is formed by jagged volcanic rock walls that rise straight up out of the water to a height of 628 feet. There the terrain levels off, forming a broad plateau that gradually tapers down in the east to the beginning of a second, lower plateau which in turn drops off sharply to the beginning of a long, narrow tail section trailing off toward Manila. Near the midpoint of the tail there is a single large hump that rises to an elevation of some 250 feet, known as Malinta Hill.

Corregidor was uninhabitated when European interest in the islands began in 1521 with the arrival of a three-ship expedition headed by Ferdinand Magellan, a Portugese in the service of Spain. Upon stepping ashore on the island of Samar, Magellan plunged a wooden staff bearing the flag of Spain into the sand and solemnly proclaimed all territory before him henceforth to be the property of the Spanish crown. According to the royal orders for this historic voyage, Magellan was to have ceased all exploratory operations immediately after discovering land in those uncharted waters and returned to Spain. However, he ignored those instructions in order to take a closer look at some of the other magnificent tropical isles that appeared to stretch endlessly north and south from where he had planted the Spanish colors.

Pausing only long enough to restock his ships with fruit and game found on Samar, Magellan proceeded on a meandering southerly course across Leyte Gulf—the future scene of the greatest naval battle of all time, between Japanese and American warships during World War II—to the islands of Cebu and Mactan. On Mactan Magellan provoked a skirmish with a band of native warriors who killed him and eight of his sailors. The remainder of his party fled the islands and returned to Spain.

Magellan's expedition was followed by others composed largely of heavily armed Spanish soldiers dispatched from Madrid with orders to establish firm military control at strategic points throughout the archipelago while missionaries who accompanied them went about their assigned task of converting the islanders to Christianity. The first such expedition was commanded by Ruy Lopez de Villalobos, who gave the name "Filipina" to a single island in honor of the Spanish crown prince who later became

King Philip II. Subsequently, the entire chain became known as the Philippine Islands. Despite unsuccessful attempts by Portugal and Holland to wrest control of the islands from her, and a brief British occupation of Manila in 1762–1764, Spain ruled the Philippines for 377 years after Magellan and his sailors met their deaths on Mactan.

During the early days of the Spanish occupation, defense works were constructed along the shores of the clamshell-shaped Manila Bay, at the base of which rests beautiful Manila, the Pearl of the Orient. Recognizing that Corregidor was the perfect site for an outpost to provide warnings to their shore-based defenses upon the approach of hostile vessels, the Spaniards emplaced three cannons on the island. Each had a range of about one mile and was supported with spacious underground ammunition bunkers and gun-crew quarters. Two of Corregidor's cannons were positioned to fire toward the Cavite shore that forms the southern shoulder of the bay. The third cannon was emplaced to fire toward the mountainous, jungle-covered Bataan peninsula that juts out into the bay to form its northern shoulder and is separated from Corregidor by only a two-mile expanse of water.

In addition to serving initially as a military outpost, Corregidor was also a relay station where semaphore flag messages were transmitted between skippers of galleons on patrol duty in the South China Sea and the commander of Manila's Fort Santiago. Later, in 1836, the Spaniards constructed a lighthouse on Corregidor to provide navigational aid to the many commercial vessels visiting Manila's expanding port facilities.

The event that marks the beginning of the end of Spanish rule in the Philippines occurred early in 1898: A still mysterious explosion sank the American battleship *U.S.S. Maine*, killing 260 of her 358 crewmen as she lay at anchor halfway around the earth from Manila in the harbor of Havana, Cuba, another of Spain's far-flung possessions. That incident, despite profuse Spanish apologies, hastened a break in the already strained Spanish-American relations and led to a declaration of war by the United States two months later.

The war with Spain was brief, ending in a lopsided American victory not quite four months after it began. Termed the Splendid

3

Little War by journalists of that period, it is a conflict best remembered by most Americans as the one in which Colonel Theodore "Teddy" Roosevelt and his Rough Riders made their much publicized charge up Kettle Hill (on the right flank of the general assault known as the Battle of San Juan Hill) near Santiago, Cuba, on July 1, 1898. But in reality, the most significant action of that war took place two months prior to the storming of San Juan Hill. In American military history it is known as the Battle of Manila Bay.

When the United States declared war on Spain, Commodore George Dewey was commanding the Asiatic Squadron anchored just off mainland China in Hong Kong's harbor. With his country at war, Dewey was forced by international law to leave Hong Kong within forty-eight hours. Just prior to his departure he received a coded message from Washington instructing him to capture or destroy the Spanish fleet in the Philippines. Under cover of darkness on the night of April 30, Dewey and his squadron of four cruisers and two gunboats steamed into Manila Bay, drawing light and ineffective fire as they passed barely out of range of Corregidor's guns. At dawn, Dewey gave his famous battle order to Captain Charles V. Gridley on the bridge of the flagship *Olympia*, "You may fire when you are ready, Gridley." The American warships steamed three times through a flat elliptical course, bringing deadly broadsides to bear on the numerically superior Spanish fleet which was cleverly positioned under the protection of Cavite's heavy shore batteries. By early afternoon all eleven Spanish vessels had been destroyed with a loss of 381 hands. Eight American sailors were slightly wounded; there was no damage whatsoever to Dewey's ships.

This remarkable naval victory was followed in August with a landing fifteen miles south of Manila by General Wesley Merritt's 10,000-man VII Corps, which had been hurriedly formed in the United States and shipped directly to the Philippines. Merritt's corps comprised four infantry brigades, one of which was commanded by Civil War Medal of Honor recipient Brigadier General Arthur MacArthur whose young son, Douglas, was then a cadet in his first year at West Point. Supported by Dewey's shipboard guns, Merritt's infantrymen marched on Manila and

4

overwhelmed the Spanish defenders. With the fall of Manila, the Spanish government sued for peace. At the signing of the treaty in Paris, Spain relinquished her sovereignty over Cuba, ceded Puerto Rico and Guam to the United States, and sold the Philippines to Uncle Sam for the modest sum of $20 million, about three times the price paid earlier for Alaska. Thus, America became a colonial power with an important stake in the Far East. The consequences of that real estate transaction have affected the course of world history for the past three-quarters of a century.

Following its acquisition of the Philippines, the United States began a long and costly construction program designed to defend the capital of Manila by sealing off the entrance to Manila Bay with firepower. Forts were constructed on Corregidor and its three satellite postage-stamp size islands of Caballo, El Fraile, and Carabao. By 1914 the task was completed and American defense experts began calling that area the Gibraltar of the East. Mirroring the military doctrine of that era, the forts were designed to withstand any attack from the sea by the heaviest of warships then afloat. Because of their location at the gateway to Manila, the finest natural harbor in the Orient, these four little islands would assume a strategic importance out of all proportion to their size during World War II. And since it was the kingpin of the bay defense works, Corregidor would become the scene of some of the most grueling battles fought anywhere during that terrible global conflict.

The rapid advancements in military aviation during the 1920s greatly reduced the effectiveness of America's expensive and skillfully wrought Gibraltar of the East. When those weaknesses became apparent to American military staff officers based in Manila, they were recorded and forwarded to Washington along with a request for funding to significantly upgrade the defenses to withstand attack by airplanes. But with the Philippines scheduled for full independence in 1946, Congress was loathe to invest large sums of money in property that was to be given away in the not too distant future. As a result, only limited funding was eventually granted for the installation of antiaircraft guns and the construction of reinforced concrete walls around some installations on the bay islands.

5

Even with its weaknesses in defense against attack by aircraft, on the eve of World War II Corregidor was still a mighty fortress. So much so that the men stationed there affectionately referred to their island home as the Rock. Scattered about the higher elevations of the Rock were fifty-six coastal guns positioned in twenty-three separate artillery batteries, many of them bearing names of Civil War and Spanish-American War heroes. The weapons with the longest range were two twelve-inch guns, one in Battery Smith, the other in Battery Hearn. Both batteries were on Corregidor's westernmost tip, facing out into the South China Sea. Each of those enormous guns could fire an armor-piercing shell weighing 700 pounds a distance of nearly seventeen miles with pinpoint accuracy. The only problem was that the twelve-inch guns were not mounted inside thickly armored turrets of the type found in European fortresses; instead, they were completely out in the open on circular concrete firing pads a thousand feet apart. To the pilots of passing airplanes each of these exposed positions looked exactly like the bull's-eye of a dive-bombing practice target.

Supplementing Corregidor's coast artillery were twenty-four antiaircraft guns and forty-eight .50-caliber machine guns. In addition to those land-based defenses, the waters around the island had been heavily mined by the Navy.

There were several bomb shelters on the Rock, but the only truly bombproof part of the island was an extensive network of tunnels that had been hewn out of volcanic rock under Malinta Hill by Army engineers who, because of fiscal constraints, had to utilize outdated mining equipment and prison labor to complete the vast project. Started in 1931 and finished only in 1938, the tunnel network consisted of three interconnected systems. Because the tunneling operations were conducted during the years that the restrictive Washington Naval Treaty was still in force, the Americans publicly stated that their purpose was to provide the crowded island with nothing more than some additional space for the storage of routine supplies required to feed and clothe the troops stationed there. However, the subterranean passageways had really been built to house far more important things.

The main system consisted of a huge tunnel 1,400 feet long and thirty feet wide that enabled vehicular traffic to pass east to west through Malinta Hill. Branching out at regular intervals from that throughway were twenty-five laterals, or wings, each 400 feet long and twenty feet wide. Most of those laterals were filled with wooden crates containing ammunition of all calibers, aerial bombs, torpedos, and huge amounts of canned food and fifty-gallon drums of gasoline. Other laterals were kept empty because they had been designated to serve as emergency command posts and living accommodations for American military and diplomatic staffs based in Manila, and for civilian members of the Philippine government, in the event it should ever become necessary to evacuate the capital.

To the north of the main system was another series of tunnels in which a 300-bed hospital and surgical unit had been established. Opposite the hospital, under the south side of Malinta Hill, was yet another pair of connecting tunnel systems known as the Quartermaster Area and Navy Tunnel. The Quartermaster Area had eleven laterals. Nine were filled with crated small arms ammunition and army combat uniforms. The remaining two were kept vacant for emergency use as storage vaults for the Philippine government's silver and gold bullion deposits. Navy Tunnel was quite small, consisting of two heavily guarded vaults where cryptographers worked in great secrecy decoding monitored Japanese radio transmissions. Fresh air was continually pumped throughout the entire tunnel network by an electrically powered ventilation system.

Some 5,000 American and Filipino troops were stationed on Corregidor, the majority artillerymen assigned to the gun battalions on the island. Most of the Americans were quartered in an enormous three-deck, hurricane-proof concrete building located up on Topside, the broad plateau stretching across the island's highest terrain. Because of that building's great length of 1,520 feet—equal to the height of New York City's Empire State Building, and the world's longest military bararracks—it was commonly (though inaccurately) known as Mile-long Barracks. Fronting the barracks was a grass-carpeted parade field beyond which stood the headquarters of Major General George F.

7

Moore, who commanded Manila's harbor defenses and all fortified islands in the bay. Each day, as he entered his headquarters
General Moore would throw a snappy salute to the large American flag fluttering atop the island's flag pole, which had formerly
been the main mast of a Spanish ship sunk in Manila Bay during
the Spanish-American War.

Corregidor's remaining American troops resided in sturdy concrete barracks located on Middleside, a slightly lower elevation
abutting the eastern slopes of Topside. Filipino troops of the 91st
Coast Artillery Battalion were also quartered on Middleside. All
other Filipino units were quartered in teakwood barracks down
on the tail of the island adjacent to Kindley Landing Field, a
2,000-foot airstrip that could accommodate only light aircraft.

The typical duty day for members of the Corregidor garrison
was both long and rigorous. It began with a 5:30 A.M. reveille
formation, followed by one hour of brisk callisthenics. After
breakfast, the troops drew rifles from the arms rooms to participate in an hour-long series of boring marching drills, which all
military leaders of that time felt would instill a sense of discipline
in their soldiers. From the drill fields, the troops marched to their
respective gun emplacements. There they spent the remainder of
the day going through repetitious mock firing drills using dummy
shells as large and cumbersome as the real ones, and relaying
the guns under the watchful eyes of strict sergeants. Officially,
the duty day ended at 5:00 P.M. with the bugle calls and pounding
drums of formal retreat ceremonies as the troops stood at attention on the parade field, saluting their flag as it was slowly lowered. Unofficially, the day did not end then, for the artillery
pieces had to be cleaned and there were dozens of sentinel posts
that had to be manned throughout the long tropical nights.

Realizing that duty on Corregidor was both stressful and mo-
notonous, the top command in Manila endeavored to provide all
who were stationed on the Rock with many of the same privileges
and recreational facilities that would be available to them on a
large stateside base. Some senior grade officers and sergeants
were permitted to have their families live with them on the island
in small, comfortable government housing. Separate clubs were
available for officers, noncommissioned officers, and enlisted

8

men. In addition to a grade school for dependent children and a fully staffed aboveground hospital, Corregidor also had a movie theater, library, commissary, and baseball diamond, plus four tennis courts, two swimming pools, and even a nine-hole golf course. Nearly all of those facilities were situated up on Topside, which had beautiful parklike grounds lined with palm trees and tropical plants of many varieties, plus well-tended roads and pathways that reminded visitors of a large university campus.

For those soldiers who preferred to swim in the warm waters of the surrounding sea, there were two scenic beaches located down on Bottomside, the low sandy waist section of the island between Middleside and Malinta Hill. One of those beaches was reserved for use by officers, the other for enlisted men. Since the waters of Manila Bay were known to be shark infested, both beaches were protected by steel wire nets which none of the bathers fully trusted. Bottomside was also the site of San Jose, a small village containing the island's post exchange and the homes of some 800 Filipino civilians employed by the Americans as cooks and general workers. Twice each day, a commercial ferry that served as a liberty launch left San Jose's south dock for the thirty-mile trip to Manila. Since the monthly salary of an Army private soldier was then only $21.00, the ferry was seldom crowded.

Some sixty-five miles of winding roads and trails provided easy access to all regions on the Rock. Another thirteen miles of electric trolley tracks connected seacoast gun batteries with the vast ammunition storage areas under Malinta Hill and with Kindley Field out on the tail of the island. That same trolley system was used as a commuter line for soldier and civilian passengers traveling to various points on the island. Large rail sections of the system had originally been laid in 1919 to transport heavy construction materials and newly manufactured artillery pieces from the Bottomside dock facilities up to firing positions then being constructed on Topside and Middleside.

Even with their long duty days, and the isolation of their position, the troops on Corregidor were well known throughout the Philippines for having high morale and total confidence in their ability to repel any invader. This air of heady optimism had been spawned by their belief that the Rock, with its vast array of lethal firepower, was a genuinely impregnable fortress, and their knowledge that they were soldiers of a nation that had never lost a war.

The supreme self-confidence of the Corregidor garrison remained unshaken through the first few months of 1941. By that time Hitler's Wehrmacht had already achieved domination over an incredible amount of territory and the Japanese armies campaigning in China appeared to be shifting gears for what American intelligence experts in Manila were openly predicting would be an attack aimed at the Philippines. But in April 1941, when the wives and children of American servicemen stationed in the Philippines were suddenly ordered back to the United States and all duty stations were placed on a low-level combat alert, there appeared the first hardly noticeable crack in the Rock's morale. Even though their country was not at war, some soldiers quartered in Mile-long Barracks began wondering aloud what might become of Corregidor if Japan ordered its veteran combat troops, who were located only 600 miles away in China, to invade the Philippines. The nearest American reinforcements were based in Hawaii, over 6,000 miles from Manila.

The answer to that thought-provoking question would not be long in coming.

2
DISASTER IN THE PHILIPPINES

For many years prior to the outbreak of World War II, military strategists in Washington had been giving considerable thought to what could be done in the event the Philippine Islands were ever attacked by the increasingly aggressive Empire of Japan. The result of all their planning was a two-inch thick top-secret document titled War Plan Orange, or WPO.

The preamble of WPO acknowledged that it would be impossible to prevent Japan from making a successful landing in the Philippines due to the paucity of American and Filipino forces there to defend them, their extreme distance from mainland America, and the complex geography of the islands. Accordingly, WPO stated that if Japan did invade the islands the defenders were to make an orderly withdrawal into the mountainous Bataan Peninsula, and to the island of Corregidor, where they were to conduct a determined defensive battle for six months, at the end of which time, it was estimated, a powerful American relief force would arrive by ship and expel the invaders.

The harshest critic of War Plan Orange was Lieutenant General Douglas MacArthur who, in July 1941, was stationed in Manila as the newly appointed commander of the U.S. Army Forces in the Far East. It was MacArthur's opinion that WPO was basically unsound because it would take the Americans far longer than six months to raise and ship to the Philippines a relief expedition that would be strong enough to evict an entrenched Japanese army. MacArthur's low opinion of WPO was shared by Admiral Thomas C. Hart, commander of the small Asiatic Fleet based in the Philippines. Hart knew that a Navy Department survey conducted in the late 1930s had glumly concluded that reinforcing the Philippines would take from two to three years.

More than anyone in the American military establishment, MacArthur knew and understood the Philippines and its people. Thus far in his illustrious career the general had served four tours in the islands, a total of thirteen years over four decades. His first tour began in 1903, the year he graduated first in his class at West Point with the highest academic record achieved there in a quarter of a century, and the year in which he underwent his baptism by fire. At that time he was a twenty-two-year-old second lieutenant assigned to an engineer battalion that was constructing dock facilities in the port city of Tacloban on the island of Leyte. When the more experienced officers in his battalion cautioned MacArthur that some of the local Visayan tribesmen could be openly hostile to the presence of American soldiers he airily brushed their warnings aside. Shortly thereafter he led a platoon of engineers into the jungle to cut timbers for piling and was ambushed by two guerrillas, one of whom fired a shot that knocked the disbeliever's hat off and buried itself in a tree behind him. In a lightning-fast move, MacArthur drew his pistol and shot both ambushers dead.

Since that dramatic event, MacArthur's other tours in the Philippines had been far more peaceful. This most recent one had begun back in 1935 when, just after completing a four-year assignment as Army Chief of Staff, he was invited to Manila by the President of the Philippine Commonwealth, Manuel Quezon, to organize and train native defense forces in anticipation of the Philippines being granted full independence in 1946.

The forces available to MacArthur in mid-1941 for the defense of the islands consisted of 19,000 U.S. Army troops, 12,000 Philippine Scouts (professional soldiers), and some 100,000 partially trained men of the recently mobilized and poorly equipped Philippine Army. Nearly all of those forces were positioned on the big island of Luzon where it was expected the Japanese would make their main effort when and if they ever decided to strike.

Just as the Americans suspected, Japan was in fact planning to widen the war it had been waging in China since 1931. But unlike the Americans, who thought that any new Japanese offensive would be limited in scope to perhaps an invasion of the Philippines, the militarists in Tokyo had much bigger plans. On September 6, 1941, the Imperial General Staff gave its approval to an exceedingly ambitious master plan that called for seizing not only the Philippines, but all of southeast Asia.

Japan's strategy for the Pacific War was simple in concept. It also shrewdly took advantage of the fact that the oil- and rubber-rich overseas colonies of European nations then occupied by German troops could be had simply for the taking. First, the Americans were to be simultaneously dealt two crippling surprise blows: one aimed at the Pacific Battle Fleet in its home port at Pearl Harbor, Hawaii; the other against MacArthur's forces in the Philippines. Then, while the Americans were still reeling from those blows, Japanese forces would quickly overrun the Philippines, Guam, Wake, British Malaya (including Singapore), Hong Kong, Siam, Burma, all of the Netherlands East Indies, and occupy French Indochina. With those areas under its control, Japan could cut all lines of communication between New Zealand and Australia, thus forcing the Anglo-American powers to sue for peace. Over half the earth's population would then be under Japan's economic, political, and military control.

Japan carried out the first part of its grandiose master plan of conquest with great stealth and devastating effect on Sunday, December 7, 1941, without first declaring war on any of its targeted victims. Shortly before 8:00 A.M. on that day planes from six carriers that managed to steam undetected to within 275 miles of Oahu came winging over Pearl Harbor. There they achieved total surprise, catching the Pacific Battle Fleet and nearby army, navy, and marine airfields completely unaware, enjoying a relaxed Sunday morning routine. Because it was then a navy custom to spend weekends ashore, most of the warships had only skeleton watch sections aboard. Elsewhere in the numerous antiaircraft battery positions defending the harbor all but a few of the artillerymen were still fast asleep while their ammunition was stored in locked bunkers. And only the duty officers—most of whom were away from their posts enjoying leisurely breakfasts—had the keys. A stouthearted defense was put up by the sleepy-eyed Americans. However, considering the tremendous shock effect the Japanese had achieved with their sneak attack, and the overwhelming firepower of their diving warplanes, the situation was hopeless.

Just before 10:00 A.M. the Japanese aircraft broke off the methodically executed attack and flew away to rejoin their homeward-bound carrier force, leaving in their wake a grotesquely impressive record of death and destruction. In less than two hours the vaunted Pacific Battle Fleet had been neutralized as a fighting force and over half of the aircraft on the island had been destroyed. Some 2,400 Americans had been killed and almost half as many wounded. Japanese losses were extremely light: twenty-nine airplanes, four midget submarines, and 100 men.

When news of the Pearl Harbor attack reached his headquarters in Manila, General MacArthur was stunned. Both he and Admiral Hart had been forewarned as early as November 27 by the War Department of the possibility of an attack by Japan but he really did not think it would occur until some time in April of the coming year. MacArthur and his staff were still discussing the Pearl Harbor attack when, shortly after 8:00 A.M. Manila time (five hours after Pearl Harbor had been bombed), a radar operator on the west coast of Luzon picked up signals indicating the approach of a large formation of unidentified aircraft heading south over Lingayen Gulf in the direction of Manila.

What the radar operator had just sighted was the other half of Japan's well-planned surprise strike at America's overseas bases. The rapidly approaching aerial attack force was composed of some 200 airplanes that had taken off from bases on Formosa with orders to attack American installations throughout the Philippine archipelago. This second attack was supposed to have occurred at exactly the same time Pearl Harbor was being hit, but bad weather on Formosa that morning had delayed the takeoffs for several hours.

Disaster in the Philippines

Although it penetrated Philippine air space with much less surprise than had been achieved at Pearl Harbor, Japan's Formosa-based strike force still managed to speedily inflict considerable damage on American bases scattered throughout the islands. Hundreds of neatly parked bombers and fighters at Clark, Nichols, and Iba airfields were destroyed. American and Filipino casualties amounted to 50 killed and 150 wounded. And once again, Japanese losses were extremely light: seven fighters. Although it had come through the attack virtually unscathed, the U.S. Asiatic Fleet was ordered south that same day, to be followed the next day by the surviving aircraft of MacArthur's miniature air force.

Having thus skillfully isolated the battlefield with paralyzing air strikes, the Japanese proceeded with their plan to seize control of the Philippines. On December 10, they initiated preliminary invasion operations by putting ashore on northern Luzon two small amphibious infantry detachments that quickly captured small airfields at Appari and Vigan. Supplies and reinforcements coming from China were still being landed at those airfields when, on December 23, some 43,000 troops of Japan's powerful Fourteenth Army delivered the main hammer blow by storming ashore in Lingayen Gulf, only ninety-five miles northwest of Manila.

Commanding the invading land forces was fifty-four-year-old Lieutenant General Masaharu Homma, a veteran of numerous hard-fought campaigns in China where he had earned the reputation of being one of the finest combat leaders in the entire Japanese Army. Ironically, during World War I Homma had served as an observer of British forces in France. While there he also witnessed some of the battles fought by then Colonel MacArthur and his American 42d Infantry "Rainbow" Division. Homma was a man of many virtues, but humility was not one of them. Long before embarking from Japan on this campaign he had boasted to the Imperial General Staff that it would take him only eight weeks of light skirmishing to capture the Philippines. Homma's optimistic outlook was reassuring, especially to logistics planners on the General Staff, who were depending on him to quickly subjugate the Philippines so that Manila's extensive port facilities might be utilized to support other vital Japanese operations planned for that region.

Homma relentlessly drove his troops inland from the invasion beaches where they easily swept aside MacArthur's defending forces. Fearing a complete rout of his shattered battle formations, MacArthur decided on a phased withdrawal to the Bataan Peninsula and Corregidor much in accordance with War Plan Orange. MacArthur's fervent hope was that this series of delaying actions would buy enough time for the expected reinforcements to arrive and help him drive out the invaders.

Homma's advancing land units were still some eighty miles from Manila when, on the day before Christmas, he confidently left his command ship anchored in Lingayen Gulf to establish his battle headquarters ashore in the village of Santiago. Later that same evening, MacArthur secretly abandoned his headquarters in downtown Manila and moved out to the island of Corregidor along with his staff and several key Filipino leaders. Two days later, MacArthur declared Manila an open city so as to prevent it from destruction by the approaching Japanese. Each passing day brought more tactical reverses for the American-Filipino forces streaming into the Bataan Peninsula. On January 2, Homma's troops triumphantly entered Manila unopposed.

Although he had seized the treasured Pearl of the Orient and all of its excellent port facilities in only eleven days after his main landings in Lingayen Gulf, General Homma was not yet able to notify Tokyo that he had achieved victory in the Philippines. MacArthur's American and Filipino forces out on the Rock and on Bataan still held the key to strategic Manila Bay.

The forces defending Bataan were under the command of Major General Jonathan M. Wainwright, a leathery cavalryman who was a descendant of a line of distinguished naval officers. His most famous relative was an uncle, Richard Wainwright, who had been aboard the U.S.S. Maine when she was blown up in Havana Harbor but survived to become an admiral and superintendent of the Naval Academy at Annapolis. Like his boss, General MacArthur, Wainwright had fought in France during World War I and was a veteran of previous service in the Philippines. A

16

keen tactician, Wainwright took maximum advantage of Bataan's naturally rugged terrain by deploying his troops along a partially prepared defensive line running across the jungled, twenty-mile-wide neck of the peninsula from Moron to Abucay. With his own artillery and Corregidor's big guns backing him up, Wainwright's position was formidable. But the already noticeable food and ammunition shortages were indeed ominous. At the time of the Japanese strikes at Pearl Harbor and the Philippines, an American supply convoy bound for Manila was diverted to Australia by shocked naval planners who had already conceded the ultimate loss of the islands. MacArthur's forces were now totally isolated.

Heavily armed Japanese occupation forces had been patrolling the streets of Manila for exactly one week when, on January 9, General Homma launched an all-out attack against the Moron-Abucay line on Bataan. There followed ten days of continuous fighting during which the Japanese achieved a breakthrough near Moron, forcing the defenders to withdraw to a shorter Orion-Bagac line. Two Japanese attempts to amphibiously land troops behind this new line ended in failure. Undeterred, Homma launched another major offensive on January 27, again penetrating the American-Filipino lines. Homma's tactical success was shortlived, however, for a heroic counterattack by the Philippine Army's depleted 41st Division resulted in all lost ground being regained. Unable to get his stalled attack rolling again, Homma was forced, on February 8, to suspend ground operations and sit in utter ignominy until reinforcements could be sent from China.

By this time Corregidor's population had swollen to over 15,000 and Japanese bombing attacks were a daily occurrence. Everything from living space to such basic requirements as food and ammunition was in short supply. And with no sign of reinforcements coming to the rescue, tempers were also very short.

At his headquarters deep inside Malinta Hill's Lateral No.3, MacArthur still had good communications with Washington. Through a series of increasingly discouraging communiques from the War Department he had been tracking the progress of Japan's war machine, which seemed to be almost effortlessly steamrolling its way across Asia. At this early stage of the war Japanese forces had already invaded the Philippines, occupied French Indochina, captured Wake Island, Hong Kong, and the "impregnable" fortress of Singapore (the loss of which Churchill likened to the fall of France), and were well on their way to other easy victories in the Java Sea, Siam, Burma, Borneo, New Guinea, the Celebes, Bismarks, Gilberts, Solomons, and Dutch East Indies.

As MacArthur correctly saw, the only place the rampaging Japanese had been stopped cold was in the Philippines. This fact caused him to repeatedly send cables to Washington pleading for everything from carrier-launched air strikes against the halted Japanese troops on Bataan to relief convoys of reinforcements and supplies so that his beleaguered forces might actually drive the invaders back into the sea.

MacArthur's pleas fell on deaf ears. Unknown to him, a decision had already been reached in Washington between the American and British Combined Chiefs of Staff to first send the majority of available troops and supplies against Germany and Italy, then retrieve all lost territories in the Far East. In other words, the Philippines had already been officially written off as lost. Yet despite that command decision having already been made, it is a condemning fact that all of MacArthur's superiors, from President Franklin D. Roosevelt on down to Secretary of War Henry L. Stimson and Army Chief of Staff General George C. Marshall, kept sending him cables containing assurances that immediate relief was on the way. Convinced by those promises of forthcoming help, MacArthur and his hard-pressed troops on Bataan and the Rock grimly held on to what little ground they had left to defend.

As the war entered its third month the encouraging messages from Washington stopped. Meanwhile, the appalling food and ammunition shortages of the American and Filipino forces were becoming more acute. Having already been on half-rations since January 11, MacArthur had lost twenty-five pounds and many of his troops who had lost even more weight were becoming ill from the effects of malnutrition. The shortages were more pronounced on Bataan where there were no underground storage tunnels to draw from and the soldiers had been reduced to slaughtering their horses and mules for food. But the heroic defenders doggedly held on in the belief that a mighty relief armada would appear on the horizon within a few days at most.

MacArthur had by now recognized the hopelessness of his tactical situation and that he was being cruelly deceived by Washington. He was fully prepared to die fighting on the Rock with his gallant troops rather than surrender one square inch of Philippine soil to the Japanese. But Washington had other plans for his future. As he had already demonstrated, MacArthur was the only Allied commander who knew how to fight the Japanese. Much like England's Lord Gort who was pulled out of Dunkirk in June 1940 before he could be captured by the invading Germans, and Germany's renowned Field Marshal Rommel who would later be extracted from North Africa to prevent advancing British forces from taking him prisoner, General MacArthur was far too valuable to be allowed to fall into captivity. He was also the obvious choice to serve as commander of the forces that would one day fight to reclaim lost territories in the Far East.

It took a direct order from President Roosevelt to make him do it, but under cover of darkness on March 11, MacArthur finally left the Rock aboard a PT boat skippered by Lieutenant John D. Bulkeley on the first leg of a hazardous journey to Australia. With his departure, command of all the remaining American-Filipino forces passed to General Wainwright, who had been summoned to the Rock two days previously. Upon his arrival in Adelaide, MacArthur made a short but powerful speech, the last three words of which echoed around the world. "The President of the United States ordered me to break through the Japanese lines and proceed to Australia for the purpose, as I understand it, of organizing the American offensive against Japan, a primary objective of which is the relief of the Philippines. I came through and I shall return."

MacArthur had been in Australia not quite three weeks when, on March 31, General Homma launched the anticipated assault on the Bataan position using newly arrived tank and infantry reinforcements. A ferocious battle raged for a full week during which the Japanese shelled field hospitals filled with Filipino and American wounded as their tanks achieved breakthroughs at several points along the front. It soon became apparent that the half-starved defenders were no match for the onrushing hordes of well-supplied Japanese. The Bataan garrison was forced to surrender on April 9 as its ruptured defenses finally collapsed from sheer exhaustion and lack of ammunition.

The forsaken captive defenders were still in the midst of their infamous Death March on Bataan when General Homma turned the full weight of his pent-up fury against the one remaining thorn in his side: Corregidor. Some 400 artillery pieces gathered from all over Luzon, plus six superheavy sixteen-inch siege guns brought in from Japan, were wheeled into positions along Bataan's southern shore where they would be protected against counterbattery fire from Corregidor's guns. By May 4 a steady drumbeat of Japanese shells was falling on the Rock at the rate of one every five seconds, knocking the big American guns out of action one by one and burying many defense works under landslides. Throughout this terrifying saturation bombardment the Japanese were able to achieve pinpoint accuracy with nearly every round because their artillery spotters were located in a gondola suspended from a hot air balloon tethered to a hilltop on Bataan; they could see all of Corregidor except for its southern shoreline. The Japanese Army had learned this very accurate fire-direction technique from the Americans during the Civil War, when several of its officers witnessed balloon-stationed Union artillery spotters in action against entrenched Confederate troops.

During the afternoon on May 5 the deafening roar of exploding artillery rounds subsided slightly, giving the shell-shocked defenders of the Rock a brief respite during which the wounded were hurriedly carried into the already overcrowded tunnels beneath Malinta Hill and the dead were buried in shallow graves. But at 8:30 that same night the shelling resumed with an even greater intensity. Most of the incoming rounds were directed at the north shore and tail of the island where they killed dozens of troops manning the beach defenses, severed telephone lines leading to Wainwright's command post, and detonated all of the protective minefields that had been so methodically sown in the sea and along the shoreline.

From experience he had acquired during the trench warfare

of World War I, and more recently on Bataan, Wainwright knew that the intensified artillery barrages signaled an impending infantry assault. His worst fears were realized at 11:45 that same night when a runner dashed into the east end of Malinta Tunnel between shellbursts and shouted, "Boatloads of Japs from Bataan have just come ashore down by Kindley Field . . . and they've even brought tanks with them!"

As captured Japanese documents would reveal in postwar years, General Homma had launched 2,000 of his soldiers in small wooden boats to attack the Rock that night. This amphibious assault force was supposed to land in the vicinity of Malinta Hill, where it was to quickly seize the hill and its many tunnels to force a quick surrender of the dazed defenders. But in the darkness and confusion created by their own fierce artillery preparatory fire, the boat crews became disorientated and allowed the swift-flowing current to carry them down to the tail of the island. There they were sighted while still some 500 yards from shore and came under intense rifle and machine-gun fire. The result was that over 60 percent of the landing craft were sunk and less than 800 of the Japanese made it to the beach. Once ashore, however, the survivors organized into small groups, overpowered the defenders, and began a cautious advance toward Malinta Hill. They soon ran headlong into a mixed detachment of Filipino and American troops who engaged them at very close quarters with hand grenades and bayonets. That halted the bulk of the advancing Japanese, but some of their smaller platoon-size units skirted around the edges of that bottleneck and continued to inch toward their assigned objective under the cover of darkness.

At dawn, a vigorous counterattack by Wainwright's Beach Defense Reserve Battalion and Batteries B and C of the 59th Coast Artillery drove the Japanese back almost to where they had come ashore the previous night. Just when the counterattacking force was achieving its greatest success it was destroyed almost to a man by a tremendous artillery barrage from Bataan. Dust from that barrage was still swirling in the air when the Japanese resumed their advance.

Having already committed his reserve, Wainwright knew he had thrown his one remaining punch and that it had failed to halt the attackers. He was frantically trying to think of what else he could do to stop them when, at 10:00 A.M., his orderly handed him an extremely discouraging message from Colonel Samuel L. Howard whose decimated 4th Marine Regiment was still manning the beach defenses. Howard's hastily scribbled note stated that the Japanese were landing more tanks and fresh infantry down on the tail of the island. Knowing full well that he did not have the resources available to prevent those tanks from rolling right up to the entrance of Malinta Tunnel and firing shells that would massacre his helpless wounded lining its walls, General Wainwright decided to surrender the Rock and all forces in the Philippines. It was the greatest surrender in American history, not excepting Appomattox. So ended the enormously humiliating debacle which the U.S. Army historians discreetly choose to call "the fall of the Philippines" when they got around to writing the official history of that disastrous campaign.

General Homma received no promotion or medals for having achieved his belated victory. Instead he was relieved of his command one month after the fall of Corregidor and recalled to Japan. There he was censured by the Imperial General Staff for failure to achieve a speedier, less costly triumph and was forced into an early retirement.

Homma had not, however, seen his last of the Philippines. After the war he would be returned there as a prisoner of the Americans to stand trial for the many hideous war crimes committed by troops he commanded.

In the vacuum created by the capitulation of the American-Filipino forces there soon grew a number of guerrilla bands comprised of patriotic civilians and soldiers whose units had been overrun during the chaotic withdrawal into the Bataan Peninsula. For raw courage and sheer audacity the escapades of those bands were on a par with—and in many cases superior to—the brazen French Maquis units that brought so much grief to the German occupation troops.

From the very start of the Japanese occupation, General Homma's conquering soldiers meted out brutal punishment to all islanders they suspected of being guerrillas or of providing them any form of assistance. In central Luzon, a Japanese district commander ordered the execution of ten Filipinos each time one of his soldiers was killed by guerrillas. Other district commanders held public beheadings of guerrillas to discourage members of the local population from taking part in such activities.

Despite the barbaric end that awaited them if they were caught, the Filipinos continued supporting the resistance movement that flourished with each passing week. By the time the Philippines were liberated in 1945 the number of guerrillas exceeded 250,000. Although there were some inevitable rivalries and disagreements between the many bands, they were united in their trust of General MacArthur whom they knew so well because of his long service in the islands. And they firmly believed his solemn pledge, constantly beamed to them by a California radio station: "I shall return."

3
A PROMISE KEPT

When General MacArthur made his pledge in the dark days of the futile Bataan and Corregidor struggles to return to the Philippines his words seemed little more than the courageous utterances of a defeated general. No one in Tokyo took him seriously. And only a few of his closest friends in Washington felt he could ever do it. The road back to Corregidor, MacArthur acknowledged, was both long and strewn with obstacles. But the general's iron will became a driving force, and within two and a half years the Americans actually were ready to return to the Philippines.

In July 1944, General MacArthur and Admiral Chester W. Nimitz—the U.S. commanders in chief for the Pacific theater— were called to Hawaii for a crucial meeting with President Roosevelt. By that point in the war MacArthur's Southwest Pacific Forces, and Nimitz's Pacific Ocean Area Command had fought their separate ways up from Australia and the Solomons to a point some 300 miles from Mindanao, the southernmost island of the Philippines, where they were poised to either wrest control of Formosa from the Japanese, or liberate the Philippines. It was no secret in Washington that MacArthur strongly favored a return to the Philippines, and that Nimitz, along with his boss, Chief of Naval Operations, Admiral Ernest J. King, were equally as strong in their desire to seize Formosa as a base for future operations.

A Promise Kept

The president had called this Hawaiian meeting to have it out face-to-face with his subordinates and settle the simmering dispute concerning where the next step should be taken on the road whose ultimate end was Tokyo. During that meeting the eloquent MacArthur opened his remarks by stating that American honor and prestige in the Far East demanded the liberation of the long-suffering Filipinos and thousands of Americans still being held captive in the islands. At the conclusion of his presentation the general had converted not only the president, but Nimitz as well to his strategic concept for winning the war in the Pacific: Move as quickly as possible to liberate the Philippines, transform Luzon into the "England of the Pacific" with massive troop and supply bases, then strike out at the Japanese home islands.

MacArthur's dramatic return to the Philippines occurred on October 20, 1944, only a few hours after American assault troops landed on Leyte, the first island to be liberated. Wearing a freshly pressed khaki uniform and accompanied by a horde of high-level officers and media representatives, the general waded ashore at Red Beach where he briskly strode up to a special truck-mounted loudspeaker. The sound of Japanese rifle and machine-gun fire could be heard only a few hundred yards away as MacArthur cleared his throat and took hold of the microphone. A light drizzle was falling as he spoke these memorable words:

"People of the Philippines, I have returned. By the grace of Almighty God, our forces stand again on Philippine soil. . . . Rally to me! Let the indomitable spirit of Bataan and Corregidor lead on. As the lines of battle roll forward to bring you within the zone of operations, rise and strike. . . . For your homes and hearths, strike. . . . Let no heart be faint. Let every arm be steeled. The guidance of God points the way. Follow in His name to the Holy Grail of righteous victory."

It took a long series of difficult land, air, and sea battles for MacArthur's forces to work their way up the 1,500-mile-long Philippine archipelago. By January 1945, MacArthur was simultaneously directing two major operations on Luzon. The largest involved the freeing of Manila by U.S. Army divisions attacking along the same routes used first in 1898 during the Spanish-

American war by American infantrymen, and again in 1941–1942 by the invading Japanese. The other operation had as its purpose the reopening of Manila Bay to allied shipping. To accomplish this latter task, MacArthur had begun a two-phased maneuver. Phase one involved clearing Japanese forces off the Bataan Peninsula so they could not interfere with phase two, retaking the Rock.

Responsibility for the clearance operations then in progress on Bataan, and for the eventual seizure of Corregidor, rested with Lieutenant General Walter Krueger and his Sixth Army. When he received the order to start planning for the Corregidor mission, Krueger instructed his staff to discuss the various ways the Rock could be attacked. They arrived at two options: a shore-to-shore amphibious assault to be mounted from Bataan as the Japanese had done, or a parachute assault.

After much consideration the staff officers recommended to Krueger that he combine the two by having paratroopers jump on Corregidor a few hours prior to a secondary amphibious assault just as the Allied armies in Europe had done so effectively only eight months previously during the gigantic Normandy landings. Krueger bought the recommendation, setting D day for Friday, February 16, by which time he expected his ground forces would have the Bataan peninsula swept clean of all Japanese forces.

In deciding to use parachute troops to spearhead an assault upon a fortified island, Krueger was setting out to do something that had been done only twice before in this war and at considerable cost to the attacking airborne force. Sending paratroopers to capture a distant island is a very risky undertaking. Especially when the target has extremely rugged terrain such as that on Corregidor. To achieve quick success the attacking airborne force requires a detailed knowledge of the enemy's strength and troop dispositions; complete cooperation of the air, sea, and land units supporting the mission; plus absolute secrecy during the planning and execution phases so as to achieve the critical element of surprise.

At the time the decision was made in late January 1945 to spearhead the Corregidor attack with paratroopers there were only two airborne outfits in all of the Pacific Theater of Operations. Both were in the Philippines under MacArthur's operational control. The larger of the two, Major General Joe Swing's 11th Airborne Division, was then committed on Luzon, fighting as a straightleg (nonjumping) infantry division attacking toward Manila's southern city limits.

The other airborne organization was a smaller bastard outfit known as the 503d Parachute Regimental Combat Team (RCT), which was being held in reserve some eighty air miles south of Corregidor on the island of Mindoro. The 503d was commanded by thirty-two-year-old Colonel George Madison Jones of Memphis, Tennessee. Jones was the grandson of a Confederate soldier and a graduate of West Point, class of 1935. Standing nearly six feet tall, this outwardly appearing southern gentleman was a physically rugged individual. In his plebe year at West Point he had gained a spot on the boxing squad and still thoroughly enjoyed a good fight, no matter what the odds were against him. Prior to volunteering for parachute duty he had been a military police officer at Fort Benning, Georgia. Because of his background with the military police, and his firm application of discipline, Jones was known to his troops, semiaffectionately, as "the Warden."

When Jones and his paratroopers were alerted during the first first week in February for the combat jump mission to Corregidor they had already been overseas two years and one month. It was December 1942 when their troopship had docked at the port of Cairns in North Queensland, Australia, after a forty-two-day voyage from California. At that time their unit was commanded by Colonel Kenneth H. Kinsler and was officially known as the 503d Parachute Infantry Regiment, with a strength of 1,958 officers and men. From the docks at Cairns the paratroopers were trucked seventeen miles inland to a deserted rural area where they constructed a large tent encampment and began a rigorous training program to prepare themselves for combat. Three miles beyond the encampment was the hamlet of Gordonvale which, because of its unpaved streets and small size, looked like it belonged on the set of a movie about the old American west. On weekends the paratroopers would either walk to Gordonvale, or catch a slow-moving train up to the more lively city of Cairns, to do what paratroopers still seem to do more than any other kind of soldier: chase after women and carouse in bars where they can get into fights with straightlegs, local civilians, and each other. Despite their rowdy off-duty behavior the paratroopers were consistently treated warmly by their tolerant Australian cousins.

Parachute jumps were made frequently during the training in Australia, resulting in the usual injuries and an occasional death. The first member of the regiment to lose his life in a training jump was Private Robert H. White, who during a maneuver conducted near Cairns landed in some high tension wires and died by electrocution. Shortly after White's death the paratroopers used machetes to clear a new drop zone just east of Gordonvale and named it White Field in his honor. The new DZ had been in use only one month when a demonstration jump by the entire regiment was scheduled for the benefit of two VIPs, General MacArthur and the commander in chief of the Australian Army, General Sir Thomas A. Blamey. Training and demonstration jumps were then (and still are) made from an altitude of 1,000 feet, which allows the jumper adequate time to activate his reserve parachute if his main chute fails to open. However, because this jump was taking place at dusk, when the visibility of the VIPs would be impaired, the jump altitude was lowered to 600 feet, where an experienced paratrooper still has time to get his reserve out.

The planes were passing over White Field in perfect formation with blossoming parachutes filling the sky when suddenly one of the paratroopers, Private Donald "Shanghai" Wilson, fell to his death with an unopened parachute. Generals MacArthur and Blamey were greatly saddened by this tragic event. The surviving paratroopers took it in stride, for each of them clearly understood when they first volunteered for parachute duty that they would often be flirting with sudden death.

Later that same night in the beer tents of the encampment the paratroopers could be heard mournfully singing "Beautiful Streamer" and "Blood on the Risers," two songs that had been especially written for the American parachute troops. "Beautiful Streamer" was a slow, soft ballad sung to the tune of "Beautiful Dreamer," then popular in a recording by Frank Sinatra. Its lyrics were the last words of a paratrooper who was falling through space with a parachute that hadn't opened yet, and who was praying hard it would. It didn't.

"Blood on the Risers" was the more popular of the two songs. It was usually sung with great gusto to the tune of the Civil War classic, "The Battle Hymn of the Republic." Its rather grisly lyrics were about a trooper whose parachute failed to open. The words to the many verses were a bit difficult to remember, especially after the paratroopers had consumed several canteen cups of lukewarm beer drawn out of wooden kegs, from the Great Northern Brewery in Cairns. But when it came to the easy-to-remember chorus, the paratroopers billowed the canvas roofs of their tents by loudly chiming in with, "Gory, gory, what a helluva way to die, he ain't gonna jump no more!"

After spending eight months in Australia wondering if they were ever going to see combat, the paratroopers were moved during the latter part of August 1943 from the Gordonvale area across the Coral Sea to a new encampment located near Port Moresby on New Guinea. By that time General MacArthur's leapfrog campaign on New Guinea was moving into high gear. The paratroopers were needed to seize an abandoned airfield on the Huon Peninsula at a place called Nadzab. This was the same airfield from which Amelia Earhart, America's most celebrated aviatrix, took off in 1935 and was never seen again. Few, if any, Japanese troops were expected to be there.

September 5 was the date set for the regiment's drop at Nadzab. Early in the morning of that day General MacArthur paid a visit to the paratroopers preparing to emplane at their departure airfields. Accompanied by his aide and a photographer, the general casually strolled along the edge of the runway, stopping occasionally to wish startled clusters of busy paratroopers well on the forthcoming drop.

At precisely 10:22 that morning the jumpmaster of the lead aircraft passing over Nadzab shouted "Go!" and stepped out the door. Four and one-half minutes later the entire regiment was on the ground. All three battalions had been dropped with pinpoint accuracy. This was the first accurate mass delivery of American paratroopers during the war. General MacArthur observed the whole show from a B-17 bomber flying high above the paratroop planes. He was thrilled at the sight of all the parachutes neatly clustered well inside the drop zone. Upon landing back at Port Moresby he remarked to General George Kenney, the Fifth Air Force commander, that the parachute drop was "the most perfect example of training and discipline" he had ever witnessed.

As predicted by American intelligence experts, there were no enemy troops at Nadzab. Yet two paratroopers were killed when their chutes failed to open and a third died of injuries suffered when he fell to earth while climbing down out of an extremely tall tree in which he had landed. Thirty-three others were injured during rough landings. Aggressive patrolling, and a separate combat mission assigned to Lieutenant Colonel John J. Tolson's 3d Battalion, did eventually produce some light contact with Japanese forces evacuating the nearby city of Lae. By September 19 the entire regiment was back in its base camp near Port Moresby. Three days later the paratroopers were stunned by the news that their regimental commander, Colonel Kinsler, had committed suicide by shooting himself for no apparent reason after having a few dinner-hour drinks with some of his officers and a subsequent evening rendezvous with an Australian nurse. Upon Kinsler's death, command of the regiment passed to Lieutenant Colonel Jones who had been serving as commander of the 2d Battalion.

With Jones as their new commander, the paratroopers were returned to Australia for a brief rest, which was followed by intensified training in jungle warfare. By June 1944, while other American paratroopers in England were still preparing for the Normandy invasion, the regiment was back in New Guinea conducting combat patrols to eliminate the few remaining Japanese units threatening the large American base at Hollandia. It was while they were engaging in small clashes around Hollandia that the paratroopers were alerted for possible action on Noemfoor Island, located 350 miles west of Hollandia in New Guinea's Geelvink Bay. Cyclone Task Force, a unit composed of 13,500 American and Australian soldiers, had orders to make an amphibious landing on Noemfoor and clear it of some 3,200 Japanese troops believed to be on the island. Brigadier General Edwin D.

Patrick, the American commander of Cyclone Task Force, was told that if things got too rough on Noemfoor for his outfit, he had only to ask for assistance and Colonel Jones and the 503d Parachute Infantry Regiment would be sent in to lend a hand.

Cyclone Task Force made an unopposed landing on Noemfoor early in the morning of July 2. As General Patrick's troops were advancing inland later that same afternoon they captured a prisoner who told his interrogator that over 3,000 Japanese reinforcements had been landed on the island one week ago. On receiving that bit of startling news Patrick fired an urgent message back to Hollandia requesting that the 503d Parachute Infantry be dropped in as soon as possible to assist in what apparently was going to be a tough fight. Colonel Jones was instructed to have one of his battalions jump on Noemfoor early the next day, July 3, and his remaining two battalions jump in on the succeeding two days.

The area selected by General Patrick's staff for the paratroopers to use as a drop zone was Kamiri airdrome, which was well within friendly lines. Built by Japanese engineer troops and slave laborers brought in from Java, Kamiri airdrome was actually nothing more than a 250- by 5,000-foot cleared area with a 100-foot-wide runway extending the full length of the clearing. The plan was for the jump aircraft to fly over the runway two abreast so that the paratroopers might land in the soft sandy areas abutting the airstrip. But when, on the morning of the first drop, General Patrick saw that a great many of his amphibious assault vehicles were still parked beside the runway, he radioed Hollandia recommending that the planes fly over in single file. He feared that many paratroopers would be injured if they landed on top of the parked vehicles.

Unfortunately for the paratroopers, Patrick's message was transmitted after they took off and it never reached them. At 10:00 A.M. sharp, the jump planes roared over the island two abreast. During the next twenty minutes a total of 739 paratroopers rained down on Kamiri airdrome. Of that number, seventy-two were severely injured during rough landings—thirty-one with compound bone fractures (tips of broken bones protruding through the skin) caused by collisions with the many amtracks, bulldozers, and other military hardware parked beside the runway.

Colonel Jones jumped from the lead aircraft. He managed to miss all the parked vehicles but crashed directly on the rock-hard coral runway, receiving a sharp blow to his head. Had Jones not been wearing a helmet, his skull undoubtedly would have been crushed. Even though the helmet saved his life, he suffered a throbbing headache that lasted for several days and caused him to wonder if his skull had been fractured. A man of iron determination, he refused to report his injury to medical authorities. Finally, after eight days, the headache left him.

Of the eighteen men who jumped on Noemfoor from Colonel Jones's plane, nine were critically injured. His radio operator, who landed right beside him, broke both legs. Major Cameron Knox, commander of the 1st Battalion, suffered a broken foot.

The following day, July 4, the 3d Battalion—now commanded by Major John Erickson—began jumping over Kamiri from the same aircraft used on the first drop. This time, however, all heavy machinery had been driven back into the jungle, far away from the runway. Most jumpers managed to make soft landings alongside the airstrip. But a great many other less fortunate troopers were forced to make bone-splintering landings on the runway. All told, Erickson's battalion suffered fifty-six severely injured jump casualties.

Colonel Jones was furious about the injuries being suffered by his men. Thus far he had lost the services of one battalion commander, three rifle company commanders, the regimental communications officer, and several squad and platoon sergeants. The regiment's casualty rate already stood at an alarming 8.89 percent. Ordinarily, this is not a bad average for jumping onto an enemy-held island. But in this case, not one of the casualties had been caused by an enemy bullet.

Rather than incur certain additional losses that another jump on the coral airstrip would entail, Colonel Jones insisted that his 2d Battalion, commanded by Lieutenant Colonel John Britton, be brought in by sea. A few days later, Britton's battalion arrived aboard a fleet of LCIs (landing craft, infantry), making an unopposed landing over the beach.

Throughout the rest of July and on into the middle of August, Jones and his paratroopers remained on Noemfoor as part of Cyclone Task Force, chasing after elusive groups of Japanese soldiers. Fighting with their usual tenacity, and refusing to be taken prisoner, the Japanese made the paratroopers pay dearly for every bit of the island they won. Combat in the jungle-covered hills generally was restricted to violent clashes between squad-size units of eleven men. Although these clashes were brief, seldom lasting more than a few minutes, there was always a lot of bloodshed. During one such encounter, Sergeant Roy E. Eubanks, a squad leader in Company D, won the regiment's first Congressional Medal of Honor. Eubanks never got to wear the medal, for he was killed in the action for which it was awarded.

MacArthur's headquarters declared Noemfoor secure on August 31. Three days before that date the 503d was pulled back to a reserve area adjacent to its costly drop zone, Kamiri airdrome. During the nearly two months it fought on Noemfoor, the regiment was credited with killing 1,000 enemy soldiers. Sixty paratroopers had been killed and another 303 wounded.

Shortly after arriving back at Kamiri airdrome, the 503d Parachute Infantry Regiment was reinforced with the addition of two new units, which raised its strength up to slightly over 3,000 officers and men. The two new units were the 462d Parachute Field Artillery Battalion, commanded by Major Arlis E. Kline, and Company C of the 161st Parachute Engineer Battalion whose commander was Captain James Byer. With the addition of these two units, the regiment had its name officially changed to the 503d Parachute Regimental Combat Team, a name it was to keep until the end of the war.

With Noemfoor fully secured, members of the combat team were kept busy conducting tactical training exercises and occasionally working as stevedores helping to unload ships bringing supplies to the island. Quite often while performing stevedore duty hungry paratroopers pilfered whole cases of canned food which were then spirited away to their campsite and shared with other members of the combat team. This illicit activity prompted angry quartermaster officers aboard the supply ships to unofficially name the paratroop outfit "Colonel Jones and His 3,000 Thieves."

The paratroopers remained on Noemfoor until mid-November, when they were shipped 1,500 miles northwest to the island of Leyte in the Philippines. After spending five boring weeks in reserve on Leyte the combat team was assigned to Rear Admiral Arthur D. Struble's Western Visayan Task Force and given the mission of making an amphibious assault on the island of Mindoro with that unit. D day for the Mindoro landings was set for December 15, one day prior to the date selected by Hitler for the beginning of the Battle of the Bulge.

The few hundred Japanese soldiers on Mindoro chose not to resist the landing of Admiral Struble's powerful task force. Instead, they withdrew into the hills, leaving behind only friendly crowds of Filipinos to greet the paratroopers as they waded ashore over Green and Blue beaches near the village of San Jose. Only eight days after landing on Mindoro American engineer battalions had built two new airfields and reconditioned a third that the Japanese had been using. Meanwhile, Colonel Jones and his paratroopers were kept employed manning a section of the beachhead defense line and sending out combat patrols in search of small parties of enemy soldiers reported to them by local civilians.

Much to the amazement of all paratroopers on Mindoro the Japanese seemed to be strenuously avoiding contact with them. On one occasion, however, a full-blown battle erupted between the patrolling members of Company B and a company-size Japanese force discovered in the village of Palauan. The skirmishing ended with Company B liberating the village at a cost of four paratroopers killed and fourteen others wounded. Twenty-six enemy dead were counted, the survivors having withdrawn into the jungle, taking their wounded with them. With the area secured the paratroopers hastened to lower a Japanese flag still flying high atop a pole in the center of town and replace it with an American flag one of their number was carrying in his pack. At that point a villager appeared clutching a flag of the Philippine

Republic that he had kept hidden ever since the Japanese came to Mindoro three years earlier. A heated debate ensued as to which flag should be raised. The issue was settled by the heavily armed paratroopers, who invoked a kind of old-fashioned American gunboat diplomacy by attaching both flags to the halyard and hoisting them to the top of the pole—with the American colors uppermost.

On February 5, a courier from General Krueger's headquarters delivered a sealed pouch containing the formal written order for the Corregidor mission to Colonel Jones as he and his troopers were enjoying a hard-earned two-week stay in a rest camp overlooking Mindoro's scenic Bugsanga River valley. The order informed Jones that a special tactical unit, dubbed Rock Force, had been assembled to retake Corregidor and that he, Jones, had been named its commander.

Looking over the list of organizations that had been placed under his temporary command, Jones saw that it comprised mainly units from the 24th Infantry "Taro Leaf" Division which was still fighting on the Bataan Peninsula. Chief among them was the reinforced 3d Battalion, 34th Infantry Regiment commanded by Lieutenant Colonel Edward M. Postlethwait, who was still suffering from wounds he sustained during his regiment's earlier combat on Leyte.

Postlethwait was thoroughly familiar with the Philippines, especially Bataan where his unit was now fighting. His first duty assignment after graduating from West Point in 1937 had been a three-year tour with the 57th Infantry (Filipino Scouts) Regiment stationed just south of Manila at Fort McKinley. During those prewar years he had taken part in numerous training maneuvers on Bataan.

Although he was now at war in the Philippines, Postlethwait had many pleasant memories of the islands. In July 1939 he had married his bride, Merce Taraseth of Bloomfield, Illinois, in the chapel at Fort McKinley. While on their honeymoon, and on many occasions thereafter, the couple traveled extensively, visiting many areas on Luzon and its neighboring islands. Several trips out to Corregidor were planned but something always came up to cause a last-minute postponement. In the summer of 1940, without ever having visited Corregidor, the Postlethwaits boarded a passenger liner taking them back stateside to a new duty assignment. Less than an hour after clearing Manila's bustling docks the big ship was passing by the Rock, shimmering in the hot noonday sun. Looking out across the blue-gray waters of the bay, Postlethwait remarked to his wife, "Look, dear, there goes Corregidor. I do hope to get reassigned here some day so that I might visit that beautiful little island." Postlethwait's wish would be granted far sooner than he suspected. His new stateside duty assignment was to Fort Jackson, South Carolina, with the newly activated 34th Infantry, which was destined to storm Corregidor during the coming world war.

Colonel Jones spent the remainder of February 5 studying aerial photos and terrain studies of Corregidor. Early the next morning—with only ten days until D day—he made a hasty reconnaissance of the Rock while seated in the Plexiglas nose section of a B-25 bomber making a low-level strike at Japanese strongholds on Bataan. When Jones returned from that flight he drew up a plan of attack that called for two of his reinforced battalions to jump onto Corregidor on D day. Postlethwait's infantrymen, meanwhile, would undertake an amphibious assault that same day to link up with the paratroopers. The third and final segment of Jones's regimental combat team would drop onto the island on D-plus-1 to assist in mopping up what remained of the enemy.

Captain Ikira Itagaki of the Imperial Japanese Navy was the enemy commander on Corregidor. For quite some time his superiors in Manila had been warning him to be on guard against an attack by parachute troops. But as a seafaring man, Itagaki was convinced that Corregidor's difficult terrain made it an impossible objective for paratroopers. He therefore concentrated his efforts on defending the Rock's likely amphibious-landing beaches. To comply with orders from his superiors, he also had the airstrip out on the tail of the island mined and covered by heavy machine guns. Once those minimal antiairborne defensive measures were taken, Itagaki resumed his wait for the inevitable amphibious attack, fully confident that his battle-hardened troops would repel it.

Colonel Jones was advised by Sixth Army intelligence officers that the Japanese had only about 600 troops defending the Rock. This estimate was woefully inaccurate. Captain Itagaki actually had slightly more than 5,000 troops at his disposal, most of whom were tough Japanese Imperial Marines who were spoiling for a fight.

To achieve tactical surprise, and at the same time gain immediate access to the highest terrain on Corregidor, Jones and his paratroopers were slated to jump directly on top of the enemy's strongest positions, using two miniature drop zones up on Topside. One of the DZs was the old parade ground, 325 by 250 yards, fronting Mile-long Barracks. The other was the nine-hole golf course, 350 by 185 yards. The combined square footage of those two DZs constitutes the smallest area into which paratroopers of any nation were required to jump during World War II or since that time.

Neither of the selected drop zones had been used for its original purpose during the last three years. Both were heavily pockmarked with bomb craters and shell holes. And both were littered with large chunks of concrete, rocks, twisted tin roofing, and all sorts of smaller debris that had been blasted asunder first during the Japanese siege and more recently by American bombers. In addition to those glaring hazards, the southern edges of both DZs were bordered by precipitous cliffs that dropped off to boulder-strewn beaches some 500 feet below.

From prewar weather records, it was learned that prevailing easterly winds of up to twenty-five miles per hour blew across Corregidor at this time of year. Colonel Jones knew that routine training jumps were canceled when the wind speed was clocked at only fifteen miles per hour. But this certainly was no training jump and risks had to be taken. Unless the jumpmasters aboard each plane selected the correct exit points many of the troopers would be carried over the cliffs to land in the shark-infested waters of Manila Bay. Because of the numerous jump hazards on and adjacent to the DZs, Colonel Jones estimated that his jump casualties alone on D day would amount to 50 percent of his command.

Although Sixth Army intelligence underestimated Japanese

strength on Corregidor, their studies of the island's varied terrain were flawless. With the aid of existing maps and interviews with soldiers who had served on Corregidor, the intelligence experts constructed a large mockup of the entire island. As soon as it was completed they presented it to Colonel Jones to use in planning the drops and briefing his unit commanders on the ground tactical plan.

News of the impending combat jump was kept secret from the paratroopers themselves until February 8, when Jones personally issued the attack order to his battalion commanders in a large canvas tent that served as the regimental war room. Using a wooden pencil to point at the terrain model as he spoke, Jones directed that the initial parachute assault force be composed of Lieutenant Colonel John Erickson's 3d Battalion, plus staff officers and radio operators from the RCT headquarters, Company C, 161st Airborne Engineer Battalion, and Battery D, 462d Parachute Field Artillery Battalion.

With this force, Erickson was to jump at 8:30 A.M. on D day to secure both DZs for use that afternoon by the second parachute assault wave. He was also to occupy firing positions looking down on Bottomside's sandy beaches.

Occupation of the heights overlooking Bottomside was critical. At 10:30 A.M. on D day, Postlethwait's infantry battalion was to storm ashore on Bottomside. Since they were sailing from the tip of the Bataan Peninsula, the obvious place for Postlethwait's troops to go ashore would be on Corregidor's closest (northern) coastline just as the Japanese had done when they stormed the Rock. But to surprise the Japanese defenders and take advantage of all the confusion being created by the paratroopers, Postlethwait's battalion would sail from Bataan, round Corregidor's monsterlike headlands, and land over the sands of Black Beach on the south side of the island. Postlethwait's D-day mission was to occupy Malinta Hill and block all enemy forces east of that location from going to the aid of their comrades up on Topside.

A second drop would take place on Topside on D day. This parachute assault wave would be led by Major Lawson B. Caskey, the commander of the 2d Battalion. Along with his own battalion, Caskey would bring in more headquarters personnel, the regiment's Service Company, and Battery B of the 462d Parachute Field Artillery. Once on the ground, Caskey's battalion was to assist Erickson's in clearing Topside of enemy troops.

On D-plus-1, Jones planned to conduct a third drop on Topside. This final drop would consist of the 503d's 1st Battalion and Battery A of the 462d Artillery. It would be led by the 1st Battalion commander, Major Robert "Pug" Woods.

Jump aircraft for all three drops would be provided by Colonel John Lackey's 317th Troop Carrier Group. Because of Corregidor's small size and prevailing ground winds, Lackey knew that it was going to be most difficult for his pilots to accurately drop the paratroopers into their tiny drop zones. There was zero allowance for pilot error on this mission. If things didn't go exactly as planned, the paratroopers would be blown over the edges of the cliffs and possibly drown in the sea.

Final plans for the drop called for Lackey's planes to approach Corregidor from the south, two abreast, in long columns at an altitude of only 500 feet above Topside. All aircraft flying in the lefthand column would drop their paratroopers on the old parade ground while those on the right would make their drops on the golf course.

Each aircraft would be over its drop zone for six seconds. During that brief period a "stick" of eight paratroopers would jump from each plane. Other paratroopers aboard the planes would have to wait for successive passes over the island before making their jumps. To avoid midair collisions during the succeeding passes, the left and right columns would fly counterrotating orbits that would take them out over the bay and then back over their DZs. It was determined that each paratrooper would drift about 250 feet westward during the twenty-five seconds it would take for him to make his descent. Provided there were no human errors, or sudden wind gusts, all would go well, according to the Army Air Corps advisors.

During the few remaining days until D day, all of the paratroop company commanders were given the rare opportunity of making an aerial reconnaissance of Corregidor as passengers in bombers bypassing the Rock enroute to targets in northern Luzon. This was the first and only time during World War II that any paratroop company commander was able to actually see his objective before jumping on it. Meanwhile, back on Mindoro, small groups of paratroopers were taken into the regimental war room to receive detailed briefings on their responsibilities during the impending mission.

On February 14, U.S. Navy Destroyer Division 46, commanded by Captain R.W. Cavanaugh, arrived at its assigned battle station a few miles west of Corregidor. The mission of this naval task force was to provide protection to minesweepers clearing the approaches to Manila Bay, and to commence bombardment of the Rock in preparation for the airborne assault that was to take place in just two days. Throughout the morning hours of their first day on station, the ships of Destroyer Division 46 blazed away at Corregidor without drawing return fire. Crews aboard the ships were just beginning to develop a carefree attitude about the lack of enemy resistance to their presence when, shortly before noon, a smoke-billowing marker round fired by a Japanese gun on Corregidor exploded harmlessly astern of the *U.S.S. Fletcher*.

That the enemy round had missed hitting the *Fletcher* came as no surprise to her crew. Thus far in the war this destroyer had led a remarkably charmed life despite the fact that a great many things about her were associated with the "unlucky" number thirteen. As the *Fletcher*'s crew members were fond of telling strangers, their ship's bow number of 445 added up to thirteen, and her complement of officers numbered thirteen. During earlier fighting in the South Pacific, the *Fletcher* took part in the epic four-day Battle of Guadalcanal. That brutal slugfest reached its climax on Friday, November 13, 1942. On that day, the *Fletcher* was one of thirteen ships trading shots at close quarters with the Japanese fleet. Although eight of her sister ships and many hundreds of American sailors, including two rear admirals, were lost that day, the *Fletcher* managed to shoot her way through the maelstrom and emerge without so much as a chip in her paint. Since that battle the *Fletcher*'s string of good luck had remained unbroken through a great many wild encounters with Japanese warships and kamikaze planes that tried to sink her. But now that string was about to be broken.

A Promise Kept

The first shot fired at the *Fletcher* off Corregidor was quickly followed by two more which, although they also exploded harmlessly to the destroyer's port and starboard flanks, served to establish her exact position for the Japanese gunners trying to range in on her. Having bracketed their target, the Japanese fired an armor-piercing shell that struck the *Fletcher*'s bow just forward of her number one gun turret. The exploding shell sent out a blast of white-hot shrapnel that penetrated the turret's thin skin, knocked the gun out of action, killed eight gun-crew members, and wounded four others. That was not the end of the shell's destructive path. Its tungsten core pierced the *Fletcher*'s deck, penetrating down to the forward magazine (ammunition storage area) where it ignited a fierce blaze that threatened to blow the ship apart.

The only survivor of the blast that destroyed number one turret was Storekeeper Third Class Keith E. Snyder, who was serving as the gun's aimer. The entire left side of Snyder's body, from his scalp to his toes, was perforated by shrapnel. With blood oozing from the numerous jagged tears in his body, Snyder managed to pick himself up and stumble out of the smoke-filled turret and slump down on the deck, where he took stock of his condition. It was then he discovered, much to his horror, that all of the flesh and muscle between his left wrist and elbow had been blown away, leaving only two exposed and badly broken bones in approximately their correct positions. Surprisingly, his left hand "looked good as new."

Fortunately for Snyder, his shipmates quickly carried him to a first aid station that had been temporarily established directly under the booming gun barrel of turret number two. There a pharmacist's mate worked feverishly to prevent him from bleeding to death. As the last of his many wounds was being bandaged a doctor came on the scene and sedated him so heavily that he began to lose consciousness despite the roar of gunfire all about him.

Meanwhile, a damage control party at turret number one was frantically trying to beat down the blaze spreading up to the main deck from the forward magazine. Suddenly a lone sailor, Watertender Second Class Elmer Charles Bigelow, elbowed his way through the party clutching a fire extinguisher under each arm. Refusing to waste precious time putting on rescue breathing equipment, Bigelow descended an iron ladder leading into the inferno raging below deck. Within a few minutes after he disappeared from view the tongues of flame and thick cloud of acrid smoke that had been gushing up from the ship's bowels abruptly died out. The heroic twenty-four-year-old Bigelow had single-handedly quelled the blaze and saved his ship from certain destruction. When he emerged from below deck a few minutes later, Bigelow was still clutching the two fire extinguishers, now empty, and was wearing a broad smile across his boyish face.

The *Fletcher* was not the only American vessel to be damaged by the deadeyed enemy gunners on Corregidor. Moments after she had been hit a wooden-hulled minesweeper, the *YMS 48*, took a first-round hit that set her ablaze and caused heavy casualties. When this occurred a second destroyer, the *U.S.S. Hopewell*, closed on the stricken minesweeper at flank speed to take on survivors. The Japanese had the proper range now, and they quickly scored three hits on the well-intentioned ship. With several small fires burning out of control along her starboard side, the *Hopewell* was ordered to withdraw from the battle area. A fourth shell struck her while she was retiring, knocking the main battery out of operation and cutting communications and control circuits forward. It was only through the herculean efforts of her damage and control parties that the *Hopewell* managed to remain afloat and live to fight another day. Her losses during this encounter were seven killed and twelve wounded.

Upon the *Hopewell*'s withdrawal from the battle scene, the mission of rescuing survivors of the still-burning minesweeper passed to the *Fletcher*, which by now was back in action thanks to Watertender Second Class Bigelow. With her remaining guns firing on Corregidor, the wounded *Fletcher* steamed over to the minesweeper where her crewmen pulled numerous dazed survivors from the water. Then, on orders from Captain Cavanaugh, the division commander, the *Fletcher* turned her guns on the abandoned hulk of the YMS 48, which had burned to the waterline, and sank her so she would not become a navigational hazard for oncoming vessels.

A Promise Kept

Because of the numerous battle casualties the *Fletcher* and *Hopewell* had aboard, and the damage each of those ships had sustained, Captain Cavanaugh ordered them to steam north to Subic Bay where floating emergency medical and repair facilities had been established a few days earlier. There several teams of repair specialists methodically worked throughout the night so as to have both ships ready to return to their Corregidor battle stations in the morning. Meanwhile, in a quiet cove located near the repair facilities, teams of navy surgeons worked into the night in a makeshift hospital that had been constructed on the tank deck of an LST (landing ship, tank). There was nothing the doctors could do to save the mutilated arm of Storekeeper Snyder who had been so badly wounded aboard the *Fletcher*. While white flashes from torches of the welders patching up Snyder's nearby ship illuminated their floating hospital, a surgical team amputated his arm at the elbow.

Later that same night aboard the *Fletcher*, Watertender Bigelow was just coming off watch when he struck up a conversation with his boss, Chief Machinist Mate Millard "Pappy" Blevins. Although he had kept it to himself, young Bigelow had been experiencing great pain in his chest and dizzy spells ever since quelling the magazine fire earlier that morning. As the two men were discussing the combat they had been through and the deaths of their fellow crewmen, Bigelow said to his boss, "Chief Blevins, if I should ever die aboard this ship please don't let them bury me at sea." Though puzzled by the apparently healthy sailor's request, Blevins gave him a reassuring pat on the shoulder saying, "Don't worry about that happening, Bigelow, we're going to take good care of you." The next morning, Bigelow was found dead in his bunk. In compliance with his request, Bigelow's body was transferred ashore for burial. His death marked the thirteenth battle casualty suffered by the *Fletcher*. Six months after his death, Bigelow was posthumously awarded the Congressional Medal of Honor, his nation's highest decoration for gallantry above and beyond the call of duty.

4
GERONIMO!

Reveille came early on D day for the first lift of para-troopers scheduled to jump on Corregidor. At 4:30 A.M. they were standing at attention in the predawn darkness of Mindoro listening to squad and platoon sergeants bellowing out their "All present or accounted for!" personnel status reports. From the reveille formations the troopers made their ways to dimly lit chow tents where they were given two choices for breakfast: coffee and a heaping spoonful of scrambled dehydrated eggs, or coffee and two pancakes with syrup. Nearly everyone opted for pancakes rather than the pungent dehydrated eggs, which even the most talented army cooks were seldom able to make palatable.

Having packed their equipment and drawn basic loads of ammunition, hand grenades, and canned K-rations the night before, the troopers had little to do after breakfast but wait for the arrival of truck convoys that would transport them to Elmore and Hill airfields, each of which was located about a half-hour's ride from the combat team's base camp. The convoys arrived right on schedule and by 6:00 A.M. had delivered the first lift and all of its equipment to the main gates of the departure airfields, where a fleet of fifty-eight dew-covered airplanes sat quietly glistening in the golden rays of the rising sun. All of the waiting aircraft were Douglas C-47 "Skytrain" models, which had only one jump door and could accommodate up to twenty-four jumpers.

The staff officers responsible for planning this operation had left no stone unturned looking for ways to make the first lift's loading and departure work smoothly. They even arranged to have the hood of each truck in the convoys marked with a chalked number that corresponded with the number chalked on the nose of its designated aircraft. On entering at the airfield gates, the trucks halted momentarily to pick up ground guides who hopped on the running board beside the drivers and directed them to the correct aircraft. There the paratroopers disembarked to begin loading heavy weapons and equipment bundles on the planes and chuting up for a combat jump.

Had it not been for the cooperation and generosity of the Eleventh Airborne Division's commanding general, Major General Joe Swing, D day for the Corregidor drop would have had to be postponed for at least one week and possibly longer. During the planning phase of this mission it was discovered that the 503d Parachute RCT simply did not have enough serviceable parachutes on hand to drop all its troops on the Rock. When this problem became known to General Swing he directed his division supply officer to send 1,500 packed chutes over to Mindoro addressed to Lieutenant Elden C. Campbell, leader of the 503d's Parachute Maintenance Platoon.

Much like medieval knights who required the assistance of another person while donning heavy body armor and mounting the horse they would ride into a jousting match, the Corregidor-bound paratroopers had to rely on a buddy for aid in putting on their combat gear and boarding the airplane that would transport them into battle. It was a relatively easy task for the parachute riflemen to get ready for a combat jump. All they had to do was stand in neat rows beside their aircraft and help one another strap on the many small tools of their trade. But for the parachute artillerymen the procedure was far more difficult. They were required to carry into combat essentially the same personal fighting tools and equipment as the riflemen. But before they could even begin the process of getting themselves ready for combat they first had to perform the backbreaking job of fastening their heavy crew-served weapons and equipment containers to exterior bomb racks located under the wings and bellies of their airplanes.

The standard artillery piece then used by parachute artillerymen was the Pack 75, a 75mm howitzer weighing 1,268 pounds. Although far smaller and shorter ranged than the 105mm howitzer used to support regular infantry divisions, the Pack 75 still packed quite a punch. First developed in the 1930s for use by mountain troops, this minihowitzer was hastily borrowed in 1942 for service by the newly activated parachute troops because it could be disassembled for transport on the backs of sturdy mule teams. Its relatively short range of 9,475 yards mattered little to the parachute artillerymen, who knew that their targets would seldom be far away from where they landed behind enemy lines, and who were looking for a weapon that could be dropped from an airplane. Experimentation proved that an entire 108-man battery along with its complement of four Pack 75s, a basic load of ammunition, defensive light machine guns, and survey equipment could be dropped by nine C-47 airplanes.

All but a few items of the battery's hardware were fixed under the wings and bellies of the airplanes in padded containers that resembled coffins, and to which were affixed standard Air Force cargo chutes. When the battery flew over its drop zone, the pilots dropped their "coffin bombs" and the troops jumped right along with them. Once on the ground, the artillerymen gathered up the many scattered parts of their howitzers, put them together, and started shooting. During daylight, it took nearly a half-hour to get a single Pack 75 into action. At night, the same procedure took a full hour, or until the sun came up to reveal the whereabouts of lost "coffins." This was indeed a crude method of operation, but it worked. And it was the way parachute artillery arrived on the battlefields of World War II.

Oddly enough, ten of the men strapping on parachutes that morning were nonparatrooper specialists from navy, air force, and other army units. All had volunteered to jump into combat with the 503d Parachute Regimental Combat Team even though they had never parachuted before. Included in that little group of volunteers were members of JASCO (Joint Assault Signal Company) and SAP (Support Aircraft Party) teams that would operate a sophisticated radio communications network linking Colonel Jones's headquarters on Corregidor with the many naval and air units providing fire support to Rock Force throughout the operation. Also a part of that group was Combat Photo Team Q, a four-man detachment of army photographers headed by Lieutenant Dick D. Williams, who would record for posterity the dramatic events that were about to take place on Corregidor. Thanks to the courageous actions of Combat Photo Team Q, the Corregidor jumps and subsequent ground fighting on that island still rank as the best and most thoroughly filmed operation in which American parachute troops have participated.

The final member of that small group of inexperienced jumpers was Sergeant Harry M. Akune, a translator-interrogator from Sixth Army Headquarters who had entered military service in a most unusual way. Harry Akune was a Japanese-American. His father had been born in Japan and was twice wounded while serving as a combat infantryman in the Japanese Army during the Russo-Japanese War of 1904–1905. When Harry was only thirteen years old his mother died, leaving his father with five young sons to raise. Shortly thereafter, Harry's father returned to Japan, taking his five sons with him. Harry and his brother, Ken, subsequently returned to California where they had been born, settling in Los Angeles. When war broke out between Japan and the United States, Harry and his brother, along with 116,000 other Japanese-Americans living on the West Coast, were compelled by a U.S. government edict to abandon their businesses, houses, and personal belongings and be incarcerated in what were euphemistically termed "relocation camps" but were actually American versions of German concentration camps, complete with barbed wire fences and armed guards.

The same edict that ordered them confined also declared the Japanese-Americans unfit for military service. However, in December 1942—a full year after the bombing of Pearl Harbor—the military service restriction clause was withdrawn and U.S. Army recruiters began appearing at the camps scattered throughout California, Utah, Colorado, Wyoming, Arizona, and Arkansas. Harry and his brother enlisted, trading in their drab confinement camp clothing for new U.S. Army uniforms. After basic training, Harry's brother was assigned to the legendary all-Japanese–American 442d Infantry Regiment that later covered itself with glory while fighting German troops in Europe. Harry was schooled as an interrogator-translator and shipped to the Pacific Theater of Operations. There he rapidly rose up to the rank of sergeant and saw his first combat with the 33d Infantry Division before volunteering to jump on Corregidor.

In addition to his unfamiliarity with parachuting, Harry Akune was faced with another serious problem. The man who was to be his boss during this operation, Captain Francis X. Donovan, the 503d's Intelligence Officer, had already made it quite obvious to Harry that he was an unwelcome addition to his intelligence team. Earlier that morning while the first lift was still back at the base camp waiting for the trucks to arrive Harry had laid his helmet, rifle, and the rest of his equipment on the hood of Captain Donovan's jeep, explaining before he did so that he had to leave temporarily to answer the call of nature. When Harry returned a few minutes later he discovered that Donovan had left for the airport with the jeep and all of his belongings. Perplexed by what had happened, Harry hitched a ride on one of the trucks when they arrived, finally catching up with Donovan after frantically searching over half the airfield looking for him. Still out of breath when he found Donovan putting on his parachute, and not seeing his jeep anywhere about, Harry saluted and inquired, "Sir, where is my weapon and equipment that I left on your jeep?" Without looking up from what he was doing, the captain coolly replied, "Sorry, I have no idea where it is." Then, after watching Harry conduct a fruitless search of the immediate area, Donovan spoke to him again: "Sergeant Akune, it's getting late; I suggest you start chuting up." There being nothing else he could do, Harry did as the captain said. When he boarded his jump plane a short while later, Harry was still minus a weapon and all of his equipment.

The order to start engines was received by air crews at both airfields while the last of the heavily loaded paratroopers were completing their boarding operations. With puffs of white smoke and loud coughing noises, the powerful engines of the C-47s began sparking to life. Blasts of wind generated by the churning propellers soon created minor dust storms that intensified as the planes began jockeying into takeoff positions. Each of the airplanes shook with vibrations as the pilots kept the brakes on and revved up the engines to a deafening roar. Having already made several jumps, the experienced paratroopers were accustomed to the awful noise and trembling of the planes. But to the inexperienced nonjumpers who were a part of this first lift, it was a frightening experience.

After what seemed like an eternity, pilots of the lead ships at each airfield released their brakes. One by one they began rolling forward, their propellers furiously biting into the wind. Thundering down the runways in single file, the heavily loaded aircraft smoothly lifted into the cool morning air, gradually forming an enormous circle above Mindoro. There they shifted into standard V attack formations and headed north for Corregidor. The time was 7:15 A.M.

Throughout the past several days, the U.S. Army Air Corps and Navy had been pounding Corregidor with the heaviest and most extensive preinvasion bombardment to which any area of comparable size (less than one square mile) had been subjected anywhere during the war. The Fifth Air Force alone had dropped a staggering 3,128 tons of bombs, blowing away nearly all of the vegetation that had overrun the island during the nearly three years of Japanese occupation and, in the process, littering Topside's drop zones A and B with numerous chunks of concrete and splintered trees. The climax of the ferocious bombardment came on D day while the paratroopers were still eating their breakfasts. Fourteen U.S. Navy destroyers and eight cruisers began plastering the Rock with continuous salvos from their big guns. Overhead thirty-six Liberator aircraft began saturation bombing of Topside using 500-pound fragmentation bombs, which scattered even more debris across the drop zones. Although these preparatory bombardments were extraordinarily intense, they caused few casualties among the Japanese defenders who were well protected deep inside dozens of huge caves and bunkers on the Rock.

None of the fireworks taking place on Corregidor was yet visible to Colonel Jones, the commander of Rock Force, who was seated in back of the two pilots flying the armada's lead plane. With Colonel John H. Lackey, commander of the 317th Troop Carrier Group, as its chief pilot this was the control aircraft for the whole show. Jones and Lackey had worked out a plan for the control aircraft to circle above Corregidor while the drops were being made. Jones would direct the jumping operations by means of a voice radio hookup with all pilots and jumpmasters. To insure accuracy during the drops, a distinct "go point"—an unmistakable terrain feature to be used by jumpmasters as a reference point from which the probable extent of wind drift during descent was estimated—had been selected for each drop zone. Battery Wheeler was the go point for the parade ground DZ, while the ruins of a lone concrete building served the same purpose for the golf course DZ. All jumpmasters had been instructed to count six seconds after passing over the go point before allowing their sticks to jump. Jones would adjust the count up or down based upon his observations of the jumpers as they landed on each DZ.

As he had explained to his staff officers and battalion commanders, Jones planned to conduct the battle in four phases. Phase one would be the initial parachute landings on Topside; phase two the amphibious assault on Bottomside's Black Beach by infantrymen coming from the Bataan Peninsula; phase three the destruction of enemy forces on Topside; and phase four the destruction of enemy forces east of Malinta Hill. Since intelligence officers at Sixth Army had stated that there were only about 600 Japanese troops on Corregidor, Jones expected the battle to be fierce but of short duration.

There were exactly 1,000 paratroopers in this first lift. Included in that count were the executive officers (second in command) of all the companies that would be arriving with the second lift. It was the duty of those executive officers to familiarize themselves with Topside's terrain so that when their units jumped in they would be able to quickly guide them to their designated sectors within the airhead. Because the first lift would be jumping into the middle of the enemy camp, practically all its members were armed with automatic weapons and double issues of ammunition and hand grenades.

For their part, the paratroopers seated aboard the jump planes trailing behind Colonel Jones were full of confidence in their ability to seize control of the Rock. Virtually all of these men were veterans of the regiment's earlier combat missions and therefore knew what to expect from the enemy when they landed on Corregidor. Numerous briefings conducted around the miniature terrain model of the island during the past few days had provided each man with detailed information about the battle plan and what was required of him. Every detail had been thoroughly planned out. All that remained now was to jump and fight.

Unlike all the other men who were seated around him loaded for bear, Sergeant Harry Akune still had no weapon, no helmet, or other combat equipment. With less than a half-hour remaining until jump time, he approached Captain Donovan who was armed with a carbine and a pistol. Over the roar of the engines Harry shouted to Donovan, "Sir, I see that you have two weapons . . . could I borrow one of them?" Cupping his hands to his mouth, Donovan shouted back, "Not, now, Sergeant Akune. But you come see me after the jump and I'll let you have whichever one I'm not using at that time."

Harry could not believe his ears, but his eyes told him the captain had meant what he just said. So he backed away from Donovan and returned to his seat. A few minutes later a nearby paratrooper who had overheard Harry speaking with Donovan loaned him a Thompson submachine gun and two clips of ammunition.

At a point thirty miles out from Corregidor the flying armada assumed a new shape, with the jump planes forming into two separate columns. The left column was headed for the parade ground drop zone. It was composed of the 3d Battalion Headquarters Company, Company H, members of the regimental staff, and some artillery and engineer troops. The right column was bound for the golf course drop zone and was carrying Companies G and I, plus other artillerymen and engineers. The two columns were fast closing in on the Rock when a flight of thirty-one A-20s zoomed past them to hose down the two DZs with .50-caliber machine gun fire.

A bare sixty seconds before jump time, all of the American preparatory gunfire falling on Corregidor was shifted from Topside to Malinta Hill and other targets out on the tail of the island, leaving much of Topside covered by a blanket of churning dust. The dust was of great concern to Lieutenant Colonel Erickson, the 3d Battalion commander, who was leaning out the door of the lead aircraft in the left column looking for some sign of Battery Wheeler. Fortunately, a strong gust of ground wind suddenly blew across Topside with only ten seconds remaining to jump time, revealing the whereabouts of both go points and most of Topside's other terrain features. As his aircraft passed over Battery Wheeler, Erickson slowly counted to six and leaped out the door followed by Captain Joseph M. Conway, the commander of Company H, then by Technical Sergeant Arthur O. Smithback, the battalion's mail orderly, and the remainder of his stick. While jumping from their planes many of the men yelled "Geronimo!"—the war cry of America's World War II paratroopers. Simultaneously with Erickson's exit, the other column of jump planes began dropping its troops over the golf course. The time was 8:33 A.M. Rock Force had arrived three minutes late over Corregidor.

The first thing noticed by the initial sticks of jumpers descending on the parade ground and golf course DZs was the great velocity of the wind. Only moments ago it had helped them by blowing away the blanket of dust concealing the go points. But now it was pushing them toward the southern extremities of both drop zones and the edges of the cliffs that fell sharply away to shark-infested waters some 500 feet below. Disaster was slimly averted when the jumpers pulled sharply on their front risers, spilling practically all of the air from their canopies, thus enabling them to come to earth only a few feet away from the edges of the perilous cliffs.

Seeing this from his vantage point aboard the orbiting control aircraft, Jones immediately ordered the jumping altitude lowered to 400 feet so as to shorten the time of descent. Then he instructed all jumpmasters to count ten seconds after passing the go points instead of the original six seconds to compensate for the excessive wind drift. His instructions were followed to the letter, resulting in improved landing patterns for most, but not all, succeeding jumpers.

First Sergeant Malcolm E. Crosier of Company G was in one of the first few planeloads to jump in the vicinity of the golf course DZ. Crosier knew that his stick had been dropped north of the DZ and, with his first earthward glance, could see that the wind was carrying him straight into a wooded area that had just been hit by the American bombers. Before the bombardment this section of Topside had contained dozens of tall trees. But the bombs had knocked practically all of them down, leaving dozens of shredded stumps bristling with splinters the size of pencils.

By using several good moves acquired during his three years of parachuting experience Crosier managed to avoid total disaster, touching down between two large menacing stumps that seemed to be reaching out to snare him. However, as he was going through the customary PLF (parachute landing fall) maneuver—which evenly distributes the landing shock throughout the body and usually prevents serious injury to the jumper—Crosier's right leg became impaled on a third stump. Looking up at his leg, Crosier was horrified to see one enormous splinter sticking clear through the calf muscle and a second one deeply imbedded in his thigh. With no medics in the immediate vicinity, Crosier gritted his teeth and did what he had to do. Raising himself up on his uninjured leg, he grabbed the other one with both hands and yanked it off the stump. When the excruciating pain began to subside a few minutes later he released his vicelike grip on the injured leg, wiped his blood-covered hands off on his trouser legs, and calmly bandaged the wounds. Then he hobbled off in the direction of the golf course to begin rounding up his troops who were "scattered all over creation."

Only a short distance away from where First Sergeant Crosier had landed, Private First Class Dominico Muzio, a member of the regiment's mortar platoon, escaped serious injury when he thumped down in the middle of several burning logs. Muzio actually fell on one of the logs while making his PLF but managed to roll on to the ground before the flames could harm him. Quickly freeing himself from the parachute's harness, Muzio headed off in the direction of a billowing yellow parachute that marked the spot where the padded bundle containing his squad's 81mm mortar had landed. While moving uphill to where the mortar lay, he glanced down at the waters surrounding the island. There he saw three U.S. Navy PT boats darting in toward the shoreline to rescue a few unfortunate jumpers who had landed in the bay.

Among the stranded paratroopers floundering in the bay trying to remain afloat and remove his equipment at the same time was Private First Class Amazon B. Impson, Jr., a Choctaw Indian from Finley, Oklahoma. Amazon and his younger brother Jack, were both members of Battery A, 462d Parachute Artillery Battalion. Because they had been born only eleven months apart, and were inseparable when in combat, Amazon and Jack were known to everyone in the outfit as the Impson twins. Just as soon as he shed his weighty ammunition belt, Amazon inflated his life preserver and began looking about for his brother who had jumped right behind him. Almost on cue, Jack splashed down beside him. When he bobbed to the surface, Amazon couldn't resist chiding him, "Now this is really getting ridiculous, Jack. You're going to have to stop following me every single place I go!"

The Impsons were helping a third paratrooper stay afloat when rescued by the crew of PT 376. Skippered by Lieutenant John A. Mapp, the *Spirit of 76* was one of twelve such boats that had been stationed in the vicinity of the Rock's drop zones with orders to rescue any paratrooper who landed in the water.

Because the defending Japanese on Topside had been forced to remain underground throughout the fierce preparatory bombardment that ended only a minute before the first drop, the first several sticks of jumpers were able to land, assemble, and occupy their assigned positions without being fired upon. This grace period was shortlived, however. It ended when a Japanese marine officer in one of the bunkers near the parade ground became suspicious about the fact that the continuous drumbeat of American gunfire had been shifted elsewhere and that he could now distinctly hear the steady drone of aircraft engines directly overhead. His suspicion grew stronger when he heard foreign voices not far from his bunker. That caused him to draw his pistol and step outside to investigate. On seeing the Americans landing almost on top of his position the officer ran back to the bunker's entrance frantically screaming, "Paratroopers! Paratroopers!" The battle was on.

With small and scattered groups of panic-stricken Japanese marines taking pot shots at them, the paratroopers continued raining down on Topside's two drop zones. Owing to their panic, the Japanese were unable to achieve much accuracy with their rifle volleys. However, as the jump aircraft continued flying circular patterns only 400 feet above each DZ some of the enemy marksmen began scoring hits.

The regiment's Roman Catholic chaplain, Lieutenant John J. Powers, was standing hooked up, ready to jump, when the copilot of his aircraft was shot dead. The aircraft continued on, passing directly over the Battery Wheeler go point. Father Powers' parachute had just popped open when a Japanese bullet tore through the thigh of his left leg. Less than a minute later the wind caught his parachute and drove him into the outer wall of Battery Wheeler with such force that four ribs were broken and he was knocked unconscious.

Fate was interdenominational that day, dealing an almost identical hand to the regiment's protestant chaplain, Lieutenant Robert E. Herb, who jumped from another aircraft only minutes later. Glancing earthward for a place to land, Chaplain Herb spotted three Japanese marines shooting at him. In an attempt to avoid their bullets and get to earth as quickly as possible, Herb grabbed both of his front risers, pulling them sharply downward to his chest. That maneuver increased his rate of descent, but it also put him on a collision course with an unseen twenty-foot tree trunk standing slightly downhill from Battery Wheeler. With his eyes still glued on the three enemy marines who were trying to kill him, Herb never saw the tree trunk until a split second before crashing into it, too late for evasive action. The force of that sudden stop was so great that it broke his left leg at four separate points, smashed both kneecaps, and knocked him un-concious.

When he awoke a few minutes later, the chaplain discovered that he had fallen into a shell hole where he was protected from small arms fire and that part of his parachute was fluttering atop the tree trunk. The three Japanese who had been unable to score a hit during his descent were still blazing away at his parachute, slowly cutting it to ribbons. He was still staring up at the parachute when two medics crawled into the hole with him, dragging a bloodstained and bullet-riddled wooden door they had been using as a stretcher. One of the medics gave Herb a shot of morphine, explaining as he did so that he and his partner were going to place him on the door and carry him to the regimental aid station located in Mile-long Barracks. While a squad of nearby paratroopers went about the task of silencing the enemy riflemen shooting at Herb's parachute, the medics got on with the painful job of lifting him onto the makeshift stretcher.

The airplane carrying paratroop Lieutenant William E. Blake and the regiment's demolition platoon was approaching the Rock for the first pass when it was forced to drop out of the tightly knit flying formation after getting hit by a Japanese bullet that set its left engine on fire. With the aircraft gradually losing altitude and sheets of flame blocking its jump door, the pilot cut off the flaming engine's fuel supply, hoping the fire would blow itself out. Then he instructed the crew chief to go back into the troop compart-ment and tell Lieutenant Blake that he was going to bypass Corregidor and head for the Bataan Peninsula to make a crash landing with everyone still aboard the aircraft.

In the troop compartment, Lieutenant Blake and his men had decided that they were ready to jump through the flames and take their chances with the sharks in the sea rather than do nothing until the plane eventually exploded. Several troopers were angrily shouting, "Let's get out of this son of a bitch!" when the crew chief ran up to Blake, telling him of the pilot's plan to make an emergency crash landing.

Blake was angered by the pilot's decision, which offered little chance for survival, and went forward to tell him so. While the two men were talking the fire blew itself out. Seeing the Bataan

Peninsula in the distance, Blake inquired, "Can we reach there on just one engine?" "Yes," said the pilot, "but only if you have your men lighten our load by throwing all their equipment overboard."

Blake turned to reenter the troop compartment, telling the pilot as he did so, "There's no way I'm going to let you crash-land this plane with my men and me aboard it. As soon as you get us over land we're going to jump before you go and kill yourself and your crew in a crash landing." With that, Blake returned to his men, ordering them to throw into the sea everything that wasn't nailed down.

Still gradually losing altitude, Blake's aircraft passed over the Bataan Peninsula where he and his men safely jumped near the town of Castillejos. Moments after landing they were approached by several Filipino guerrillas who offered to guide them northward to San Marcelino Airfield, which was occupied by American forces. Meanwhile, the pilot of the stricken aircraft, having gotten rid of his entire payload, managed to keep it airborne long enough to make a smooth landing at the airfield.

Despite all the anticipated injuries and mishaps taking place on Topside's drop zones, the paratroopers had achieved complete surprise over the enemy. Colonel Jones was thoroughly pleased by the current state of affairs for he knew that in an assault of this nature the crucial element of surprise often gives the attack force commander what amounts to the strength of an additional 1,000 men. Just the mere sight of descending paratroopers creates pandemonium among the defending forces and neutralizes their plans for repelling an attack by troops using conventional land assault methods.

Taking full advantage of the existing situation, the paratroopers rapidly coalesced into small fighting units and aggressively attacked individual snipers and other enemy positions on and around the drop zones. The swiftness of these small-scale attacks being made while other jumpers were still in the air so unnerved the defenders that they were forced to withdraw to better fighting positions.

Several small clusters of Japanese troops who were caught moving across the DZs when the jumps began put up a gallant defense. But they were quickly overwhelmed by the superior firepower of the heavily armed paratroopers. Other than at those isolated points of resistance, the Japanese were unable to make a concerted effort to oppose the devastating attack that had been suddenly thrust upon them from the sky—the last place they expected the Americans to come from.

Because Captain Itagaki had refused to believe that the Rock could be attacked by paratroopers, there were few Japanese marines and sailors up on Topside when the attack began. Instead, the main Japanese defenses were located down along the shoreline, concealed in elaborate bunker networks blocking approaches leading inland to James, Cheney, and Ramsey ravines, all of which provided excellent routes up to Topside. If the Americans had attacked the Rock as Itagaki expected they would—that is by an amphibious assault followed by a climb up to Topside, using the ravines to reach the high ground—the attack most certainly would have been exceedingly costly.

Ironically, one of the first defenders to die in the attack was Captain Itagaki himself, the unbeliever. For the past two days, Itagaki had been receiving reports from clandestine Japanese radio stations operating on Battaan informing him that the Americans were assembling landing craft in the vicinity of Mariveles, a small fishing village located near the southern tip of the peninsula. At 8:30 on the morning of D day, Itagaki left his command bunker on Topside and began hurrying with his aide and a squad of marine security guards to an observation post overlooking the Bataan Peninsula to see for himself just what the Americans were up to. Itagaki was so desperately concerned about the threat of an amphibious attack on his island fortress that he failed to hear the leading paratroop airplanes that were then closing in behind him from the south. Suddenly, Itagaki's attention was rudely diverted as a platoon of misdropped paratroopers began landing all about him and his party. The Japanese fired first, killing two of the Americans. But the remainder of the American platoon was able to quickly assemble behind a small knoll and launch a vigorous attack, killing Itagaki, all of his security guards, and wounding his aide. Thus, only minutes after the attack on Corregidor began, its commander was dead and the isolated defending

Geronimo!

Japanese forces were left to fight the battle minus their chief tactician.

By this time, two sticks had already jumped from the command aircraft and Colonel Jones was satisfied that his boys were being accurately dropped. It was time for him to get on the ground and take charge of things. On the aircraft's third pass over the parade ground DZ he led his orderly and a few other paratroopers out the door at slightly under 400 feet and was painfully injured upon landing. Like so many of his men limping across the DZs, the colonel had one of his legs skewered by a king-sized wooden splinter. Although it "hurt like hell" to do so, Jones pulled the splinter from his leg, then went to help his orderly who had suffered a broken ankle while landing nearby.

After tending to his orderly, Jones moved across the parade ground and established his headquarters in the ruins of Mile-long Barracks. Several sections of that gargantuan structure had been destroyed by both Japanese and American guns, but there were still plenty of structurally safe rooms left to accommodate the regimental headquarters and staff, the engineer company, plus the headquarters of the 462d Parachute Field Artillery Battalion.

Mile-long Barracks was also the home of the medical company. By 9:30 A.M. the medics had set up shop in several rooms on the ground floor and had their hands full treating dozens of men who had been injured while making rough landings. Only those men who had broken legs or severe wounds were kept at the aid station for further treatment. All of the other walking wounded simply had their wounds bandaged up and then reported back to their units to resume full duty.

Also by 9:30, the regimental communications officer, Captain Charles R. Rambo, had established radio contact between the RCT Command Post (CP) on the ground floor of Mile-long Barracks and Lieutenant Colonel Erickson's 3d Battalion CP located in the basement of the old Spanish Lighthouse out on the edge of the golf course DZ. Once Captain Rambo completed setting up his local radio network he went on to establish a shortwave radio link with the rear base staff officers back on Mindoro, informing them that all was going well on the Rock.

59

The newest residents of Mile-long Barracks were just beginning to make themselves at home when one of the last paratroopers to jump over the golf course DZ suffered a streamer—an unopened, snarled parachute. His bad luck was compounded when he landed right in the middle of Topside's empty concrete swimming pool.

Elsewhere, Sergeant Harry Akune, the hapless Japanese-American who had volunteered to jump with Rock Force, was suspended beneath his parachute, coming in hard and fast on a collision course with a jagged tree stump. He gave a quick jerk on his risers which enabled him to miss the stump, but caused him to land on the downhill side of Battery Wheeler. Staggering to his feet a moment later, Akune was pleased to discover that he had broken no bones and was all in one piece. So he unbuckled his parachute harness, shouldered his weapon, and began climbing uphill to locate the other men with whom he had jumped.

Akune was some twenty feet from the crest of the hill when he looked up and saw three paratroopers aiming their rifles down at him. Fear gripped Akune when he remembered that the only thing American-looking about himself was the weapon he was carrying. Surely, he thought, the paratroopers had mistaken him for an enemy soldier and were getting ready to kill him. And he was right.

Just in the nick of time, a fourth paratrooper, Sergeant Richard Harley, came on the scene. Most fortunately for Akune, Harley had previously met him on Mindoro and recognized him at once. Sensing what was about to happen, Harley shouted at the men, ordering them not to open fire. Akune heaved a sigh of relief and after profusely thanking Harley for saving his life continued on his way.

Japanese bullets were still zinging across Topside when, at 9:40 A.M., two paratroopers, Technical Sergeant Frank Arrigo and Private First Class Clyde L. Bates, both of Headquarters Company, began climbing a thirty-foot wooden telephone pole that was still standing in front of Mile-long Barracks. When Bates reached the top he pulled from his jacket a bedsheet-size American flag that he had jumped with and fastened it to the pole with several strands of communications wire. Old Glory was greeted with a round of cheers ringing in from all across Topside. This was the first American flag to fly over the Rock since May 6, 1942. The paratroopers intended to keep her flying, day and night, until the battle ended.

A bare five minutes after Old Glory was unfurled, the last paratrooper of the first lift made a bone-crushing landing amid Topside's rubble and broken trees. Casualties during the phase one drop had run higher than Colonel Jones had expected. Roughly 25 percent of his force had either been injured during rough landings or killed in skirmishes with the defenders.

Those casualties notwithstanding, phase one of the assualt upon Corregidor had been a resounding success. By 10:00 A.M. Rock Force had completed all of its initial tactical missions and had driven most of the Japanese off Topside.

To make certain that both of Topside's drop zones remained secure for the second lift drops, Lieutenant Colonel Erickson ordered his three rifle company commanders to slightly enlarge the airhead by pushing out just far enough to block routes leading into the jump fields from Morrison Hill, Battery Chicago, and the old aboveground hospital buildings. This slight expansion of the airhead line resulted in more light skirmishing during which several Japanese marines were driven from their defensive positions and killed. Inside the perimeter, paratroop artillerymen and engineers fought as infantrymen, flushing snipers out of the upper floors of Mile-long Barracks, the movie theater, and the post headquarters buildings.

When his leading patrols reached the outer edges of Topside, Lieutenant Colonel Erickson sent word to them to place two .50-caliber machine guns in firing positions overlooking Bottomside's Black Beach where assault boats loaded with American infantrymen were preparing to come ashore.

Phase two of the operation was about to begin.

5
THE INFANTRYMEN HIT
BLACK BEACH

While the paratroopers were jumping on Topside, Lieutenant Colonel Postlethwait's 3d Battlion, 34th Infantry Regiment was sailing through choppy seas for Bottomside's Black Beach from its embarkation point at Mariveles on the Bataan Peninsula. The port of Mariveles held special significance for these infantrymen. All of them knew that it marked the spot where the infamous Death March had begun for the vanquished Battling Bastards of Bataan, and that it was also the place from which the Japanese had put out in small boats to make their costly, though successful, night attack on Corregidor.

Clear skies and a bright sun gave the seagoing infantrymen an unobstructed view of the dramatic events taking place out on the Rock. On seeing an occasional jumper land in the sea and hearing the sounds of gunfire echoing down from Topside, one infantryman remarked to his buddy, "Those crazy paratroopers can keep their jump pay. . . . Uncle Sam would have to pay me a hell of a lot more than an extra fifty bucks a month to do what those guys are doing out there."

A flotilla consisting of twenty-five LCMs (landing craft, medium) from the 592d Engineer Boat and Shore Regiment was transporting Postlethwait and his troops to Corregidor. Each of those flat-bottomed vessels could carry sixty soldiers or a medium tank, and could land its cargo directly on the beach. The LCMs were deployed in a battle formation made up of five waves of five craft each. Five destroyers formed a protective wedge directly in front of the leading assault wave, all with their five-inch guns trained on the Rock, ready to blast any enemy gun that dared to open fire.

Postlethwait was commanding much more than an ordinary infantry battalion. For this mission his unit's firepower and size had been beefed up considerably with the addition of a fourth rifle company, (Company A, 34th Infantry), five Sherman tanks from the 603d Tank Company, a platoon of antitank gunners, another platoon of combat medics, and a mobile surgical hospital.

Just before embarking at Mariveles earlier that morning, Postlethwait had announced to his assembled staff and company commanders, "Gentlemen, our mission during this operation is to cut the Rock in half by taking Malinta Hill at all costs and staying there until we have killed all the Japanese or they have killed all of us. Once we get ashore there will be no place to go but forward. So let's not waste any time when we hit the beach. Good luck."

Postlethwait's plan called for the five assault waves to land on Black Beach at fifteen-minute intervals. The first wave was composed of Company K and two of the five Sherman tanks that had been allotted for this operation. Upon hitting the beach, Company K was to fight its way inland a distance of 200 yards, then wheel to the right and attack the left half of Malinta Hill. During its climb to the 300-foot summit, Company K would be supported by .50-caliber machine gun fire provided by the paratroopers on Topside and the tanks, which were to remain down on Bottomside as mobile pillboxes. Postlethwait himself would accompany the first wave ashore so as to gain an immediate assessment of the situation within the beachhead. His command post was to be located at the base of Malinta Hill where the shoreline road passes around its southern end. From that location he would direct the actions of the succeeding waves as they came ashore.

Company L and two more of the Shermans would land in the second wave. Leaving the tanks on Bottomside, the men of Company L were to dash inland a distance of 100 yards, then turn to the right and join Company K by attacking the right half of the hill.

Hard on the heels of those first two waves would come a third consisting of Company I and the last tank. Company I had the job of attacking all the way across Bottomside and securing the North Dock area.

Company M, the battalion's heavy weapons company, would come ashore in the fourth wave. This unit had orders to rapidly set up its 4.2-inch mortars right in the center of Bottomside, amid the ruins of what had once been the thriving town of San Jose. There they were to commence firing as soon as possible directly over the heads of the Company K and L troops attacking Malinta Hill on preselected targets located out on the tail of the island.

The fifth and final wave was the 1st Battalion's Company A, which had been loaned to Postlethwait for this operation. Company A had the relatively easy task of moving inland from the beach to the center of Bottomside. There it was to establish defensive positions around Company M's mortars and also prevent the Japanese from using Malinta Tunnel's west portal.

Like the paratroopers of Rock Force, Postlethwait's infantrymen were a rough and ready bunch, veterans of considerable hard combat with Japanese forces. Also like the paratroopers, these infantrymen were fully confident of their ability to carry out the job they were being sent to do on the Rock. Their regiment, the 34th Infantry, had a proud heritage dating back to World War I when it fought with great distinction in France against Germany's finest troops. In this war, the regiment had seen its first combat in April 1944 during MacArthur's decisive advance into western New Guinea. There Postlethwait and his men took part in the bitter fighting to capture Hollandia's Cyclops Airfield from which the 503d Parachute Infantry later took off to make its combat jump on Noemfoor Island. Upon completion of mop-up operations in and around Hollandia, the 34th Infantry was given a brief rest and then sent to make an amphibious assault landing on Biak Island in New Guinea's Geelvink Bay. That landing was bitterly contested by the Japanese, but after only two days of heavy fighting the Americans were successful in capturing Soridao and Boroke Airfields.

When things settled down on Biak, the infantrymen were returned to New Guinea. They subsequently embarked on a 1,500-mile voyage northward to participate in the first battle for the long-awaited liberation of the Philippines. On D day—October 20, 1944—Postlethwait led his battalion ashore in the first wave to land over Red Beach on Leyte's east coast where General MacArthur made his emotion-packed announcement: "People of the Philippines, I have returned!"

From Red Beach the 34th Infantry pushed inland against heavy resistance, establishing a Southwest Pacific combat record of seventy-eight days of unrelieved fighting. Their drive took place in alternating torrential downpours and blast furnace temperatures and did not end until they had advanced through thirty miles of dense jungle terrain to the Ormac sector on Leyte's west coast.

During that drive across Leyte the 34th Infantry met and destroyed Japan's crack 1st Infantry Division, the conquerors of Manchuria. With Leyte secured the bearded and mud-caked infantrymen were given a well-deserved period of rest and rehabilitation after which they were dispatched on yet another amphibious assault operation. This time the objective was located on Luzon's west coast, just above the Subic Bay area. Operating as a combat team attached to the 38th Infantry Division, the 34th Infantry made an unopposed landing at San Miguel on January 29, 1945, marching fourteen miles inland that same day to the northern part of the Bataan Peninsula. The next day, however, the Japanese brought Postlethwait's battalion to an abrupt halt with intense artillery and mortar fire at a place called Zig Zag Pass. Unable to penetrate the Japanese defenses in northern Bataan, the commanding general of the 38th Division wisely made use of the American superiority at sea by sending one of his own regiments, and Postlethwait's reinforced battalion, on a fifty-mile amphibious end run all the way down to Marvieles at the southern tip of the peninsula. The Mariveles landing had taken place on February 15—only one day prior to the planned assault on Corregidor—against light opposition. Postlethwait and his men were kept in reserve aboard ship during the actual attack on Mariveles. When things quieted down in the beachhead later that day, they were ordered ashore to make final preparations for the assault on the Rock.

From his vantage point aboard the leading LCM rounding Corregidor's great bulbous headlands, Lieutenant Colonel Postlethwait could see the destroyers *Picking, Wickes,* and *Young* lying only 500 yards out from Black Beach methodically shelling Malinta Hill. Each destroyer fired single shots until it ranged in on a selected cave entrance or cliff overhang that might contain a gun emplacement. Once the correct range was determined, the destroyer would cut loose with thunderous salvos, causing landslides that covered the target with tons of rock and dirt.

Despite the terrible pounding they were taking, the defending Japanese occasionally managed to get off some counter fire using three-inch field pieces cleverly concealed in small caves located about halfway up the eastern slopes of Topside. Most of the Japanese shells fell short of the destroyers, but one of them scored a direct hit on the *YMS 46,* one of three minesweepers clearing the approaches to Black Beach. The shell exploded midship, killing three crewmen and wounding four others. Undeterred by this incident, the three sweepers kept inching in toward the beach with their 20mm guns and .50 calibers blazing, clearly demonstrating the claim of their crews that they could both minesweep and fight at the same time.

Their task complete, the sweeps turned away from the beach for the relative safety of the open sea. They were replaced on station by four rocket firing LCI(R)s (landing craft infantry, [rocket]) which moved in to administer a drenching bombardment on just about every square foot of Bottomside. In between the time she was firing her third and fourth salvos, LCI (R) 338 was struck four times by enemy fire that killed several crewmen. But the stout little craft continued firing until her rocket magazines were emptied. Then she turned about and raked the beach with her .50-caliber machine guns while withdrawing to make way for the first wave of LCMs heading in for the beach.

The LCMs began receiving indiscriminately aimed fire from a lone machine gun nest located somewhere up inside of Topside's thickly jungled Ramsey Ravine. Three LCMs took hits but none of the infantrymen crouching low on the steel decks was injured.

Pausing only long enough to reload, the enemy gunner fired a second long burst. This time he zeroed in on Postlethwait's LCM, killing the coxswain and wounding three infantrymen. It was not until Navy gunners aboard the LCMs sent a hail of .50-caliber bullets into Ramsey Ravine that the unseen Japanese gun ceased firing.

At 10:28 A.M, two minutes ahead of schedule, the LCMs crunched their bows into the sands of Black Beach. Wildly shouting infantrymen rushed ashore firing rifles and machine guns in all directions. But they quickly discovered there was no need for either the yelling or shooting. The beachhead line was undefended. Not a single Japanese was there to oppose their noisy arrival on the Rock.

The only visible trace of the enemy's presence on Black Beach was a belt of land mines that had been planted some thirty feet in from the water's edge. Thanks to the heavy preassault bombardment by the U.S. Navy, all of the grapefruit-size mines were now clearly visible to the soldiers who gingerly stepped over and around them. Continuing inland, the infantrymen passed through the ruins of San Jose and then made their scheduled right turn, forming a new assault line facing Malinta Hill's western slopes. A whistle blast sounded by Captain Frank D. Centenni, the commander of Company K, sent the troops to the base of the hill where they began climbing on all fours like a herd of mountain goats. Again, there was no enemy opposition and although it was a difficult climb, the summit was reached without incident. Captain Centenni had difficulty believing his good fortune. Turning to his First Sergeant, he exclaimed between deep breaths, "We made it . . . thank God we made it. . . . And best of all we didn't lose a man getting up here!"

Centenni had no sooner spoken than there was an explosion down at the shoreline. One of the tanks still creeping ashore had just run over a concealed heavy mine which blew off one of its treads. Although its crew escaped injury, the tank would be out of action for at least the next several hours while the damaged tread was repaired. Moments later another tank struck a mine and was also put out of action. The disabling of those two tanks did not impede the advance of Company L, which landed unopposed in the second wave and began scaling the southern half of Malinta Hill.

The third and fourth waves also made unopposed landings. But as troops of the fifth wave were pouring ashore they were taken under fire by the same machine gun that had fired at the first wave as it was approaching the beach. Because the Japanese were firing from a cave located just beneath the paratrooper's .50-caliber positions on Topside, the infantrymen had the unique and nerve-wracking experience of being both supported and attacked by machine gun fire coming from the same direction.

Japanese mortar shells also began falling on the beach, causing more casualties and confusion. A jeep and the antitank gun it was towing took direct hits. The jeep driver survived the mortar blast but was machine-gunned while diving for cover. Another mortar shell killed two staff officers as they were running toward the battalion headquarters at the base of Malinta Hill.

More men kept coming ashore, all of them madly shooting at real and suspected Japanese gun emplacements. Sergeant Donald Wood, a squad leader in Company L, spotted a second enemy machine gun nest in the vicinity of San Jose Point. An old machine gunner himself, Wood crouched low in the sand until he heard the Japanese pause to quickly reload. Then he rose up and dashed forward, hurling a grenade that knocked the gun and its crew out of action.

Down at the shoreline, Sergeant Gerald Rostello of Company M had his right leg torn open by shrapnel from a mine. Nevertheless he continued moving through the knee-deep surf, dragging other more seriously wounded members of his platoon up onto dry ground so that they would not drown. When he had pulled the last wounded man ashore, Rostello limped back into the water and climbed into the cab of an ammunition truck that was still aboard an LCM. The truck's engine was running, so Rostello floored the gas pedal and guided the bucking vehicle through surf and sand to safety behind a pile of broken concrete slabs, expertly missing several exposed mines in the process.

Elsewhere on the fireswept beach, Lieutenant William Skobolewsky was going about his self-appointed task of marking out a safe path through the minefield for the battalion's other trucks and jeeps waiting to come ashore. With bullets striking all around him, Skobolewsky crawled forward gently sticking his bayonet into the sand, probing for the feel of metal. Each time the lieutenant found a mine he would quickly dig it out of the sand with his hands and then gently lay it off to one side of the path.

Two civilian war correspondents, Richard G. Harris of the United Press, and Homer Bigart of the Chicago Herald Tribune, had landed with the last assault wave. Both of them became caught in a crossfire situation the instant they hit the beach. With Japanese and American bullets cracking over his head, Bigart nervously glanced around from where he was lying in the surf, looking for a safe place to hide. Much to his horror, the newsman discovered he was only a few feet away from a truck filled with ammunition and other explosives. That caused him to throw caution to the wind and dash fifty yards inland to what he thought was going to be a position of safety beside one of the disabled American tanks. Huffing and puffing, Bigart flopped down beside the tank. The first thing he saw there was one of the tank crewmen topple over dead after getting hit by a stream of machine gun bullets that tore into his back and came out his chest.

Bigart was still staring wide-eyed at the dead man when a mortar shell exploded only twenty feet from him, killing another member of the tank crew. Terrified, the newsman sprinted to a nearby bomb crater. From there he watched in awe as a combat medic, Private First Class Harold Asman, repeatedly dashed about through the hail of bullets and exploding shells administering first aid to seriously wounded soldiers.

Gradually, the enemy fire slackened and then came to a halt. Bigart then walked over to the courageous medic, who was kneeling in the sand bandaging a man's arm, and said to him, "Son, you ought to be given a medal for your heroics. . . . You could have gotten yourself killed while running around out here." Without looking up from what he was doing, the young medic replied, "No big deal, sir, I was just doing what I'm getting paid to do."

Now that his troops were ashore and the enemy guns had been silenced for the time being, Lieutenant Colonel Postlethwait radioed Rock Force headquarters in Mile-long Barracks that all of his assigned objectives had been reached and that he was preparing to initiate mop-up operations. Overhearing Postleth-wait sending his optimistic battle report, Corporal Robert F. Todd, the battalion bugler, pulled a neatly folded American flag from his pack. Not seeing anything that he might use as a pole, the bugler climbed some twenty feet up Malinta Hill where he carefully draped the flag over a large boulder for all to see.

Meanwhile, up on top of Malinta Hill the infantrymen of Companies K and L were thoroughly pleased with themselves for having seized the difficult objective so quickly and easily. But as they knew from past battle experiences, it was far too early for celebrating. Before them lay the task of fanning out and establishing strong defensive positions from which they could meet and repel the expected counterattack. Captain Centenni, the commander of Company K, began deploying his troops across the northern half of the summit. The commander of Company L, Lieutenant Lewis F. Stearns, did likewise with his men across the other half of the hill.

The 3d Platoon of Company K was just beginning to redeploy across the crest of Malinta Hill when its point man came upon the entrance to a cave. Not taking any chances, the point leveled his Thompson submachine gun and fired a short burst into the cave. Still holding his Thompson at the ready, the point man walked up to the entrance and peeked inside. All he could see was the rusted remains of a huge searchlight that had once been a part of the Rock's prewar American defense system. Believing the cave to be empty, the point started walking away from it when, out of the corner of his eye, he caught sight of something moving near the left side of the searchlight. Pretending not to notice, he took one more step forward. Then he spun around and emptied his weapon into the cave, killing two Japanese sailors who had been doing their best to hide behind the searchlight.

The platoon moved on, its members dropping hand grenades down the numerous large ventilation shafts protruding like mush-rooms from the top of the hill. The grenade explosions sounded far away, causing the infantrymen to wonder what, if any, damage they were doing down below.

To make certain that his half of the hill was blocked off, Captain

Corregidor . . . the "ole hard Rock." This view looks to the west, toward the South China Sea. For four centuries prior to the outbreak of World War II this island fortress had been manned by artillerymen. . . . first Spanish, later American, whose duty it was to guard the entrance to strategic Manila Bay. This aerial view shows the rugged terrain that had to be overcome by Rock Force. *(U.S. Army)*

Corregidor circa 1938, showing Topside's parklike grounds. At left, the headquarters of Major General George F. Moore, who commanded Corregidor's Fort Mills and all other defense works located in Manila Bay. The flagpole at center of photo had formerly been the main mast of a Spanish ship sunk in Manila Bay during the Spanish-American War of 1898. At right, the home of General Moore and his family. *(National Archives)*

Topside as it looked in 1939. The large building in background was known as Mile Long Barracks. At 1,520 feet it was as long as New York's Empire State Building is tall, and the longest military barracks in the world. The island's motion picture theater, Cine Corregidor, is at center. The buildings in foreground, homes of senior grade officers, were razed in 1960 to make room for Corregidor's World War II Memorial and museum. *(Frederick Roth, III)*

Topside's Cine Corregidor, or motion picture theater, circa 1939. During the February 1945 battle for Corregidor's liberation, this theater was used as a morgue by an American graves registration unit. *(National Archives)*

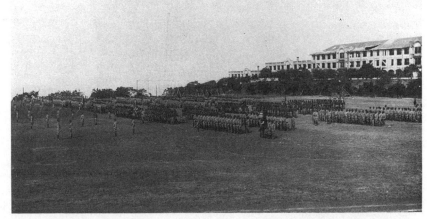

American and Filipino troops of Corregidor's garrison during a military ceremony on Topside's parade ground in the summer of 1939. Mile Long Barracks is in the background. At the time of the February 1945 parachute assault by American forces, this parade ground served as Drop Zone A and was littered with large chunks of concrete and other objects that had been blasted asunder during the Japanese siege of 1941–42 and by the American preassault bombardment. *(Frederick Roth, III)*

Middleside's troop barracks, June 1940. At center, a trolley car can be seen heading up to Topside. *(Howard Cary)*

Bottomside, Corregidor's low lying waist section, located between Middleside and the west face of Malinta Hill. The road at left leads up to Middleside and Topside. Immediately to the right is Malinta Hill with its extensive tunnel network. This 1982 photo shows Corregidor's reconstructed South Dock; North Dock is barely visible in the upper right hand corner. It was from North Dock that General MacArthur escaped Corregidor on March 11, 1942; it was also the point of his triumphant return on March 2, 1945. On the day Rock Force landed on Corregidor, the South Dock section of Bottomside was codenamed Black Beach. Troops of the 34th Infantry Regiment made their amphibious assault landing over this beach and then fought their way to the top of Malinta Hill where they established blocking positions to prevent Japanese troops on the tail of the island from moving to reinforce Topside, where the paratroopers had landed. *(National Archives)*

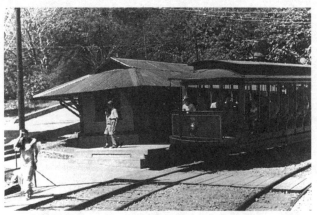

During the early 1930s, American engineers installed over 13 miles of trolley track on Corregidor to carry heavy military hardware and passengers to the island's higher elevations. This stop was located on Bottomside. After capturing the island in 1942 the Japanese dismantled the wreckage of the trolley system and shipped it to Japan, where scrap metal was in great demand. *(National Archives)*

Malinta Hill's Lateral No. 12, April 24, 1942. U.S. Army finance personnel conduct business as usual during the Japanese siege of Corregidor. While Malinta Hill's tunnels were impervious to shellfire, they were extremely short on living space. Corregidor fell to Japanese troops 12 days after this photo was taken. (*U.S. Army*)

Topside, May 6, 1942. A sword-bearing Japanese officer supervises lowering of the American flag on the day of Corregidor's capture. (*National Archives*)

Mindoro, February 14, 1945. Using a terrain model of Corregidor provided by Sixth Army Headquarters, Rock Force commander Colonel George M. Jones (hand extended) issues the attack order to battalion commanders and staff officers of the 503rd Parachute Regimental Combat Team. From left to right: Maj. Arlis B. Kline, commander of the 462nd Parachute Artillery Battalion; Lt. Lester H. LeVine, the regimental S-1 Adjutant (with face partially obscured); Unknown officer in background; Col. Jones; Maj. Ernest C. Clark, the Regimental S-3 Plans Officer; Capt. Francis X. Donovon, the Regimental S-2 Intelligence Officer; Lt. Col. John L. Erickson, 3rd Battalion Commander; Maj. Lawson B. Caskey, 2nd Battalion Commander; and Lt. William J. Benardo, a nonparatrooper communications officer from Sixth Army Headquarters who volunteered to jump with Rock Force. (*U.S. Army*)

The U.S.S. *Fletcher*, one of several destroyers that provided gunfire support to Rock Force. (*U.S. Navy*)

Engineering gang of the U.S.S. *Fletcher*, South Pacific, 1944. While bombarding Corregidor two days prior to D Day, *Fletcher* took a direct hit from a Japanese shell fired from Corregidor. That one enemy shell knocked out Turret No. 1 (shown here), killing eight sailors inside it and igniting a fire in the ship's forward ammunition storage area. The blaze was extinguished by Watertender Elmer C. Bigelow who is shown standing at extreme right of photo, directly in front of turret's open door. Sitting (left to right): Flc Joe E. Howell, Flc Beverly F. Tigard, F2c Jack D. Henderson, F2c Harry H. Solan, Flc Howard R. Allison, WT3c William J. Gurtner, Flc Leonard L. Wall. Kneeling: WT1c Robert Lazzaro, MM2c William G. Heim, MM1c James D. Rouse, WT2c Reed S. Stone, WT1c Elbert J. Grater, MM2c Daniel E. Montgomery. Standing, front row: MM2c Robert J. Vichouser, MM2c John M. Draper, MM2c James F. Setter, MM1c Fredrick G. Ward, CMM George Zimmerman, Flc Edwin A. Payne, Flc Robert E. Boyd, MM2c John W. Allard, WT1c Elmer C. Bigelow. Standing, back row: WT2c Woodrow W. Bevans, Flc Lancelot C. Brown, Jr., MM3c Carl Anderson, CMM John M. Krug, CWT Joseph W. Bell, MM2c Frank Andrew, Jr., and F2c William Kenooz. (*James F. Setter*)

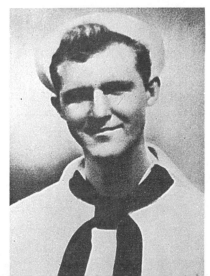

Watertender Second Class Elmer C. Bigelow, the heroic sailor who singlehandedly saved his ship from destruction. Bigelow died from injuries sustained during that action and was posthumously awarded the Congressional Medal of Honor. (*Courtesy Mr. Verna Perry*)

With a lit cigar clenched tightly in his teeth and a Thompson submachine gun strapped to his right side, First Sergeant Albert J. Baldwin of Company F, 503rd Parachute Regimental Combat Team prepares to lead a stick of paratroopers out the door of this crowded C-47 that is only minutes away from Corregidor. Baldwin and his men were part of D Day's second lift, which began jumping at 12:40 PM. (U.S. Army)

Lieutenant Harry M. Akune, Tokyo, Japan, November 1945. When he volunteered to jump on Corregidor with Rock Force this Japanese-American was a translator-interrogator sergeant assigned to Sixth Army Headquarters and had never before made a parachute jump. Moments after landing on Corregidor he was nearly killed by a fellow American who mistook him for an enemy soldier. (Harry M. Akune)

D Day, February 16, 1945. This painting depicts paratroopers of Rock Force being dropped on Corregidor's Topside. In the foreground, PT boats can be seen racing to rescue those who landed in the water. Some 20 paratroopers made water landings; all were rescued. Other paratroopers who missed Topside's drop zones and landed on the low ground next to the shoreline were also rescued. Navy lieutenants Raymond Shafer (who later became governor of Pennsylvania) and Charles Adams paddled ashore in rubber life rafts from PT 373 and, while under sniper fire, returned 17 stranded paratroopers to their boat. *(U.S. Navy)*

This is how the paratroopers looked from the decks of U.S. Navy destroyers delivering suppressive fires on Bottomside and Malinta Hill while the drops were being made up on Topside. *(U.S. Navy)*

Private First Class Ammizon B. Impson, Jr. (right), and his brother, Private First Class Jack N. Impson. These two Choctaw Indian paratroopers from Finley, Oklahoma jumped over Corregidor's Drop Zone B (golf course) in the first lift on D Day with Battery D, 462nd Parachute Artillery Battalion. A strong gust caught their parachutes, blowing them past DZ B and down the 500-foot cliffs into the shark infested waters of Manila Bay. They had been in the water only a few minutes when rescued by a PT boat that returned them to shore. Jack was subsequently seriously wounded during the final phase of ground fighting on Corregidor. (*Robert C. Impson*)

Paratroopers of the first lift seen landing near Topside's swimming pool. (*U.S. Army*)

This exceedingly rare photo was taken by a paratrooper in the first assault echelon as he jumped out over Topside's Drop Zone B (the golf course) which was bordered on the north by ruins of senior officers' housing and on the south and east by 500-foot cliffs that fell away to the shoreline. At lower left corner is a paratrooper whose chute has not yet blossomed open. This photo illustrates the extremely low altitude (about 300 feet here) at which many of the Corregidor jumps were made. *(Henry Daneau)*

The view from Topside, looking east toward the tail of the island. Portions of Bottomside's Black Beach can be seen at right center of photo. Malinta Hill is at left center. (*U.S. Army*)

Rescued paratroopers crowd the deck of PT 375 as she patrols close in to Corregidor's shoreline on D Day, looking for more stranded jumpers. (*U.S. Navy*)

Here come the infantrymen! This aerial photo was taken at 10:35 AM on D Day, just as assault boats that had landed the first wave of troops from the 34th Infantry Regiment were pulling away from Black Beach. Boats of the second wave can be seen at right, making their runs into the beachhead. The large circular white area is where a Japanese mine just exploded. Abandoned parachutes litter Drop Zone A (parade field) seen at lower left corner of photo, and Drop Zone B (golf course) at right center. Topside's Mile Long Barracks, its adjacent motion picture theater, and officers quarters are clearly visible. (*U.S. Air Force*)

With his helmet pierced by a Japanese bullet and blood running down the side of his face, Technical Sergeant Thomas J. Barnes of Battery A, 462nd Parachute Artillery Battalion scans Drop Zone B (the golf course) looking for the enemy soldier who shot him. Sgt. Barnes was one of the first paratroopers to jump on Corregidor. His M1A1 .30 caliber carbine with its folding metal stock was issued only to paratroopers. Its weight, including the metal magazine holding 15 cartridges, was only 5.75 pounds. *(U.S. Army)*

Artillerymen of the 462nd Parachute Field Artillery Battalion under fire on Topside's Drop Zone A (parade field). The 75mm howitzer shown here was known as the "Pack 75" and had a range of 9,475 yards. It weighed 1,268 pounds and had to be broken down and packed in several padded containers which were dropped like bombs from the wings and bellies of the same airplanes their guncrews jumped from. Once on the ground, parachute artillerymen needed roughly a half hour to round up the various parts of their howitzers and get them into action. *(U.S. Army)*

Topside's Drop Zone B as it looked one week after D Day, looking to the north. The Bataan peninsula is visible in the background. Prior to World War II, Drop Zone B had been a nine-hole golf course. But by the time the drop was made in February 1945, the well-kept fairways and manicured putting greens had been replaced by raw dirt and 20-foot shell craters. *(U.S. Army)*

U.S. Navy LST's loaded with paratroopers of the 1st Battalion, 503rd Parachute Regimental Combat Team, arrive at Bottomside's Black Beach late in the afternoon of D-plus-1 (February 17, 1945). The 1st Battalion had been scheduled to jump on D Day, but Colonel Jones cancelled their drop to avoid additional jump casualties on Topside's debris littered fields. *(U.S. Army)*

Japanese suicide boats shown at entrances to caves in which they were stored on Corregidor. These 18-foot plywood boats were powered by a Japanese version of a 6-cylinder Chevrolet engine. Each boat carried upwards of 500 pounds of explosives. A coxswain standing in the stern guided the boats during their crashing attacks against American ships. Suicide boats first appeared in January 1945 during the American landings in Lingayan Gulf north of Manila. *(U.S. Army)*

Topside's old Spanish lighthouse served as the headquarters of Lt. Col. John Erickson, commander of the 3rd Battalion, 503rd Parachute Regimental Combat Team. *(U.S. Army)*

This is one of the two 12-inch disappearing guns of Battery Crockett. It could fire a 1,000 pound shell a distance of eight miles and was mounted on a carriage that was raised mechanically for firing. The energy generated by the gun's recoil after each shot automatically lowered it into this pit, where it could be safely reloaded and remain concealed until raised for the next firing. The walls of this concrete pit were 20 feet thick. Cabello Island can be seen to the east. *(U.S. Army)*

Crew of PT 376 which rescued American paratroopers who landed in the water. Left to right: Bradley (alone at left front), Krupa, Unknown, Doyle (wearing white hat and T-shirt), Overby, Lt. Knapp, Collins, Kasowski, Soft, Daniels, Panamin, Hankins, and Sebert. (*Norman H. Smith*)

Toward the end of the fighting on Corregidor several Japanese defenders attempted to reach the Bataan peninsula using rafts thrown together with whatever was handy. Most were picked up by patrolling PT boats. This photo, taken aboard PT 376, shows an American sailor guarding prisoners. (*Norman H. Smith*)

Paratroop Private Lloyd G. McCarter, the one-man gang who received the Congressional Medal of Honor for the role he played in stopping a Japanese banzai attack on Topside. (*Courtesy Lou Varrone*)

Paratroopers of Rock Force shown attacking Japanese troops holed up in one of the hundreds of caves located along the coastline of Corregidor. (*U.S. Army*)

Major Robert H. Woods, youthful commander of the 1st Battalion, 503rd Parachute Regimental Combat Team. He was killed February 24, 1945, along with several members of his staff, during the final phase of ground fighting. (*R. M. Atkins*)

February 26, 1945, near Corregidor's Monkey Point. Early morning sea mist surrounds "Murder Inc.," a 68,500-pound Sherman tank, as it inches forward in support of paratroopers clearing the tail of the island. Moments after this photo was taken, the tank commander shown here fired his 75mm gun into a cave reportedly containing only enemy soldiers. However, the cave actually contained several tons of ammunition which exploded, killing 52 nearby Americans and wounding another 144. Force of the blast was so great that it sent the tank rolling end over end some 50 yards where it came to rest upside down. Only one of the tank's 5-man crew survived. He was rescued through a hole cut in the tank's hull with an acetylene torch borrowed from a U.S. Navy destroyer. (*Dominico Muzio*)

General MacArthur (left center) shown early in the morning of March 2, 1945 as he was boarding PT 373 in Manila for his triumphant return to Corregidor. *(James D. White)*

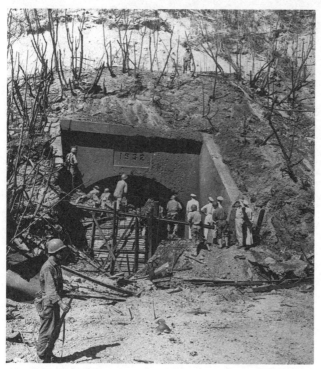

March 2, 1945. Paratroopers guard General MacArthur and members of his staff as they peer into the east entrance of Malinta Tunnel during a brief inspection tour of the Rock prior to the flag raising ceremony held on Topside. *(U.S. Army)*

Topside, March 2, 1945. With General MacArthur and the troops of Rock Force proudly saluting her, Old Glory is raised to the top of same flagpole from which she was lowered by Japanese troops on May 6, 1942. The ruins of Mile Long Barracks are visible in the background. *(U.S. Army)*

Topside, February 16, 1979. Exactly 34 years to the day after their historic jump on Corregidor veteran paratroopers of the 503rd Parachute Regimental Combat Team and their wives returned to the Rock for the dedications of this monument honoring all who served with Rock Force. The monument was designed by former paratrooper Harry J. Drews, who lost a leg within 100 yards of this spot near the ruins of Mile Long Barracks. The wartime commander of Rock Force, General George M. Jones, is at exact center, wearing a baseball cap. Just to the right of this monument are the ruins of Cine Corregidor. *(CSM Le Roy F. Tolson)*

Shown at the 1974 reunion of the U.S.S. *Fletcher*'s crew are Mrs. Verna (Bigelow) Perry, mother of Watertender First Class Elmer C. Bigelow who died saving his ship, and former crewmember Keith E. Snyder who lost his left arm during the battle for Corregidor's liberation. *(CMM Millard Blevins)*

Rock Force Commander George M. Jones in 1958, after his promotion to brigadier general. (*U.S. Army*)

Members of Company E, 503rd Parachute Infantry Regiment pose in front of Mile Long Barracks with a Japanese flag captured during the fighting on Topside. Standing (left to right): Lt. Donald E. Abbott (executive officer), Sgt. William L. Dobbs, T-5 George A. Chiuses, T-5 Robert L. Brown, Cpl. Curtis R. Carroll, 1st Sgt. A. E. Vance, Cpl. Charles W. Smith and Capt. Hudson C. Hill (company commander). Kneeling: Capt. Samuel Smith (former company commander), P.F.C. Kenneth J. Holder, Lt. Lewis B. Crawford, Lt. Roscoe Corder, P.F.C. John Osborne, and P.F.C. Murray Shifter. P.F.C. Holder was killed in action on Negros island one month after this photo was taken. (*Donald E. Abbott*)

Mindoro, February 15, 1945. Private First Class Dominico
B. Muzio shown with the parachutes and combat equipment
he will be wearing the next day during the airborne attack
on Corregidor. Note that he is holding a 30-caliber folding
stock carbine, a specialized weapon issued only to paratroopers during World War II. Unlike all other paratroop organizations whose members jumped with their weapons either
packed in padded containers or strapped to their bodies,
the 503rd Parachute Infantry troopers always jumped into
battle holding their rifles so that they would be prepared to
fight during descent and immediately upon landing. *(Dominico B. Muzio)*

Rear Admiral John D. Bulkeley, U.S.N. A 1933 graduate of the U.S. Naval Academy, Bulkeley fought in the Philippine rearguard actions of 1941–42 when he was a lieutenant in command of a motor torpedo boat squadron. On the night of March 11, 1942, he evacuated General MacArthur and family from Corregidor. In subsequent World War II battles he continued to demonstrate the value of PT boats throughout the Pacific and in Europe where, as a lieutenant commander, he participated in the Normandy and southern France invasions. Following the war he was elevated to flag officer rank. *(U.S. Navy)*

Always on the alert for enemy snipers, two members of the 3rd Battalion, 34th Infantry Regiment stand guard as a demolition team seals the entrance of a cave occupied by Japanese marines who refused to come out and surrender. *(U.S. Army)*

Protected by their "floating artillery" (the U.S. Navy destroyer shown just off shore in this photo), a paratroop combat patrol departs Topside in search of Japanese troops located in caves down along Corregidor's shoreline. (*U.S. Army*)

A Pack 75 howitzer gun crew from the 462nd Parachute Field Artillery Battalion utilizes point blank fire to destroy enemy troops holed up in a cave at the base of Malinta Hill. *(U.S. Army)*

February 16, 1945. Escorted by U.S. Navy destroyers, the small fleet of landing craft carrying the 3rd Battalion, 34th Infantry Regiment rounds the western tip of Corregidor on the final leg of its approach to Bottomside's Black Beach. *(U.S. Navy)*

Middleside, February 22, 1945. A paratroop rifle squad crawls through bombed out ruins while enroute to attack an enemy stronghold. *(U.S. Army)*

This aerial view of Topside was taken by a U.S. Air Corps photo reconnaissance airplane only two days prior to the airborne assault on Corregidor. At lower center is Officer's Row. Mile Long Barracks can be seen at center, and Middleside Barracks is at upper right. Topside's prewar hospital is to the left of Middleside Barracks. Barely visible under the cloud at right center is the empty swimming pool beside the Officer's Club. (*U.S. Air Corps*)

In this preassault aerial view of Corregidor's Bottomside sector Malinta Hill can be seen at left side of photo. North Dock's facilities are at lower center. Lorca Dock (where General MacArthur both departed and returned) can be seen protruding at left, and the square shaped Mine Dock is at center. Engineer Dock is at the extreme right of the North Dock area. In the background can be seen the "L" shaped South Dock area and Black Beach where the 34th Infantry came ashore on D Day to storm Malinta Hill. Roads leading up to Topside can be seen at right side of this photo. (*U.S. Air Corps*)

Centenni dispatched two rifle squads to the extreme left flank of his company's position with orders to occupy a pair of knolls that overlooked the north shore road. On the larger of those two knolls the riflemen found the twisted metal remains of a cable hoist. Because the hoisting apparatus closely resembled a football goal post the men nicknamed this promontory "Goal Post Ridge." The other one they dubbed "Little Knob."

While positions were being secured atop Malinta Hill, platoons from companies A, I, and M were busy establishing blocking positions at various points down on Bottomside. The men of Company A discovered that their job of preventing the Japanese from using the west portal of Malinta Tunnel had been made quite easy by the U.S. Navy. Tons of rock and sand blasted loose by destroyer gunfire was covering practically all of the huge opening through which trucks once passed while traveling through the tunnel. All that now remained was a slit so small that it could accommodate only foot traffic. Leaving nothing to chance, however, the weapons platoon leader of Company A zeroed in three machine guns and two bazookas on that one small opening.

Now that the island had been effectively cut in two, an eerie silence fell across Bottomside. The only sounds to be heard were occasional bursts of rifle and machine gun fire from paratroopers skirmishing with Japanese holdouts on Topside, and the chugging engines of LCMs trying to keep their snouts anchored in the sand while the last of the battalion's supplies were being carried ashore. When the unloading operations were completed, stretcher-bearers gently carried the wounded aboard one of the LCMs that had been hurriedly transformed into a floating ambulance. Then, with equal care, the covered bodies of thirteen dead infantrymen were carried aboard a second LCM.

Engines roared and chains clanked as the heavy steel ramps of the LCMs slowly began closing like the jaws of giant sea oysters. When the last ramp slammed shut, the LCMs backed away from the shoreline one at a time, taking their precious cargoes out of harm's way.

It was now high noon on Corregidor. A blazing hot tropical sun beat down on the American paratroopers and infantrymen still laboring to get fully organized in their new surroundings. Meanwhile, far out over the South China Sea a flight of airplanes bringing the second lift of paratroopers to the Rock was just beginning to divide itself into two parallel columns, one bound for drop zone A, the other for drop zone B.

The second lift was running twenty-five minutes behind schedule due to a dust storm that had prevented an on-time departure from Mindoro.

6
SECOND LIFT RECEIVES A
WARM WELCOME

Just after noon on D day, an angry Colonel Jones limped into the crowded confines of his headquarters for another update on the tactical situation. A messenger had just informed him that the second lift would be arriving twenty-five minutes later than the plan called for.

Jones was greeted by Major Ernest C. Clark, the regimental S-3 (operations) officer, who immediately cleared a path to the newspaper-size situation map hanging on a bullet-scarred wall. The map was marked with a series of blue and red symbols. Blue showed the precise locations of all the Rock Force units; red marked places on the island where enemy forces had been encountered. Jones became mildly concerned when he noticed that the number of red symbols had increased since he last visited the War Room only a half-hour ago. However, Jones was confident that he was holding the upper tactical hand on the Rock. He now had one battalion of paratroopers deployed in a snug perimeter around Topside's drop zones; a battalion of infantrymen strung across Bottomside and along the top of Malinta Hill; and a second battalion of paratroopers due to arrive within the hour from Mindoro. With that much firepower at his disposal, thought Jones, he should easily be able to defeat the expected counterattack. But he was becoming increasingly suspicious that the Rock just might be infested with more than the 600 Japanese estimated to be there by Sixth Army intelligence.

His suspicions were well founded. There were actually a little over 5,000 Imperial Marines and other Japanese combat troops remaining on Corregidor. Two thousand were still down along the shoreline base of Topside where they had been caught flat-footed by the surprise parachute assault. The remaining 3,000 constituted a reserve force that was safely dispersed throughout the many tunnels under Malinta Hill.

Unfortunately for the Japanese, their numerical superiority was considerably offset by a number of factors. The most serious was that they had already lost possession of Topside, the one piece of terrain that was indispensable to the defense of the island. Nearly as serious was the vicelike grip the Americans had already thrown across Bottomside and Malinta Hill, effectively cutting the island in two. Added to those difficulties was the death of their commanding officer, Captain Itagaki, in the opening minutes of the airborne attack, and the loss of all interisland communications systems, which had been knocked out of order by the ferocious preassault bombardments.

Under far less severe circumstances three years earlier, America's General Wainwright—unwilling to sacrifice his long-suffering troops—surrendered Corregidor to Colonel Gempachi Sato, commander of the Japanese amphibious force that stormed the Rock in the middle of the night. But even with their defenses shattered, their commander dead, and certain death staring them in the face, the Japanese refused to admit defeat. Virtually every last one of Corregidor's current defenders was imbued with Bushido, the sacred code of Japan's feudal samurai class.

The word *Bushido* was coined during Japan's Tokugawa Shogunate of the 1600s. It originally meant "the way of the samurai" and encouraged all who believed in it to practice the samurai warrior's virtues of honor, willpower, and great personal courage in battle. By the time World War II began, Japan's military leaders had transformed Bushido into nearly a state religion that made young men extremely proud to serve in the armed forces. Its emphasis on honor above life also made them willing to die for their emperor, either by getting killed in combat or by committing suicide on the field of battle to avoid the unpardonable sin of being taken prisoner. To do so would mean their names would be enshrined forever in Tokyo's Yasukuni-jinja, the shrine that honors all soldiers fallen in battle since the Meiji Restoration, and they would mystically become one of the demigods who hovered over Japan as an invincible spirit army.

Dying for the emperor was expected of every Japanese serviceman from private to general officer rank during World War II. All of them were taught to believe that if ever they happened to be lying seriously wounded when a tactical withdrawal of their unit became necessary in combat, they would either be shot by one of their own medics, or provided with some kind of weapon to finish themselves off.

A review of World War II combat statistics shows that the Japanese fighting troops of all ranks lived, and died, according to the tenets of Bushido. In nearly all of the Pacific campaigns, fewer than 5 percent ever allowed themselves to be taken alive. On the rare occasions when prisoners were taken it was usually because they were so badly disabled that they were unable to kill themselves, or were unconscious when found.

To the American fighting man Bushido and all it stood for was an unfathomable mystery. None could comprehend how the Japanese could be inspired to fight so courageously for their emperor yet made to believe that committing suicide would help their nation's cause.

All of this should make it easier to understand the incredible savage events that occurred as the members of Rock Force went about the grim task of taking Corregidor away from the Japanese.

In the absence of orders from their dead combat leader, Captain Itagaki, many of the Imperial Marines occupying defensive positions down along the shoreline base of Topside took it upon themselves to start climbing up through Cheney, James, and Ramsey ravines to attack the paratroopers who had landed on the high ground. The first batch of climbers reached Topside's outer edges at 12:40 P.M., just in time to be awestruck by the simultaneous arrival of the behind-schedule second lift.

This tardy incoming lift was composed of the regiment's 2d Battalion, (companies D, E, and F), its Service Company and remaining headquarters personnel, plus Battery B, 462d Parachute Field Artillery. Knowing that the first lift had jumped some four hours before them, and presumably had Topside under its control, many paratroopers aboard the approaching airplanes felt this was going to be little more than a routine training jump.

The second lift's ranking officer was the affable Lieutenant Colonel John J. "Smiling Jack" Tolson III, former commander of the regiment's 3d Battalion and now assigned to General Krueger's Sixth Army Headquarters G-3 (plans and operations) section. It was he who originally prevailed on Krueger to utilize paratroopers to recapture the Rock. Tolson had been borrowed from Sixth Army by Colonel Jones and was serving as regimental executive officer for this mission.

Standing in the leading aircraft's open jump door was Major Lawson B. Caskey, the 2d Battalion's thirty-three-year-old commanding officer. Caskey had enlisted in the army as a private in 1934. By the fall of 1940 he had advanced to the rank of master sergeant—no mean achievement in the peacetime army—and was a member of the 29th Infantry at Fort Benning, Georgia, where the experimental Parachute Test Platoon was then conducting its initial jump trials. Obtaining a commission the following year, he joined the paratroops, experiencing a meteoric rise up through the officer ranks.

Just under six feet tall, deeply tanned, and slight of build with closely cut blond hair and ice-blue eyes, Caskey looked more like a tennis pro than the stern military disciplinarian that he was. He is best remembered by those who served in his battalion for his coolness under fire and for becoming greatly irritated by anyone who used foul language in his presence. On one memorable occasion while the regiment was in Australia, Caskey sat eating his dinner in the battalion officers mess when he happened to overhear a captain at a nearby table punctuating his table talk with considerable profanity. In a voice just loud enough for all in the mess to hear, Caskey chastised the captain saying, "Look here, mister, I don't care to listen to that kind of language!" Then, pointing in the direction of the latrine (men's room), he added, "Now if you must continue talking like that, I suggest you go do it out there where I can't hear you."

After a few seconds of awkward silence the red-faced captain apologized for his ungentlemanly conduct. "You're excused" said Caskey. With that the captain and everyone else resumed eating their dinners, discreetly pretending that nothing unusual had happened. That was the last time anyone in Caskey's battalion used profanity within earshot of him.

When Caskey's C-47 streaked across Corregidor he bolted from it, guiding his entire stick to the exact spot where it was supposed to land. Light enemy rifle fire greeted his stick and all the other incoming late arrivals.

Private Allen J. Whitney of Company F had been told during the repetitious tactical briefings conducted on Mindoro in preparation for this jump that his entire platoon would be dropped over the golf course drop zone and would be landing in the immediate vincinity of a large empty swimming pool, which would be the platoon's assembly point. All jumpers were to start looking for the pool right after their chutes popped open.

Within seconds after stepping out of his aircraft during its first pass over the golf course, Whitney became unable to see the swimming pool or anything else below him. His parachute's extremely hard opening shock had pulled all of the ammunition wrapped around the upper half of his body, plus his reserve chute, firmly against his chin, thus locking his head in an upward position. A clumsily executed backward landing knocked the wind out of Whitney and wrenched his left knee so badly he thought the leg was broken. He was still writhing in pain, clutching his leg, and wondering how he was going to make his way to the swimming pool, when a medic appeared from out of nowhere and collapsed his billowing chute. While giving the leg a few painful diagnostic squeezes the medic remarked, "Things could have been a lot worse for you, pal. You almost landed in that pool over there." Raising himself up on one elbow, Whitney saw the pool for the first time. It was not quite ten feet away from where he was lying.

The medic helped Whitney to his feet, assured him the leg was not broken, and then pointed him in the direction of the regimental aid station in Mile-long Barracks. The aid station was filled to capacity with men suffering from battle wounds and jump injuries far more serious than his own. Many of the busy medics were themselves walking wounded cases. One of them told Whitney, "Sorry, but unless you've got a bullet in you, or some other kind of visible wound, I'm going to have to ask you to leave." Without a word of protest, Whitney limped out of the aid station. While making his way back to his unit, he noticed that the volume of enemy rifle fire coming from the outer regions of Topside seemed to be getting heavier.

There were only a few tall trees still standing beside the golf course DZ. Twenty-two-year-old Private First Class Delby A. Huff, a Browning automatic rifleman also assigned to Company F, had the misfortune to land in one of them. He came to a halt with his chute caught in the top of the tree and the soles of his jump boots still some six inches off the ground. To the other jumpers who had landed around him, Huff appeared to be standing fully upright and in control of his situation. So while he was busy tugging at his parachute, trying to shake it loose, his companions ran off to the assembly area leaving him still hanging above Corregidor.

After much difficulty, Huff reached a knife in his right trouser pocket and cut himself free of the harness. When he caught up with his fellow squad members a few minutes later they were preparing to attack a sniper who had been harassing them. A few of his buddies turned to him asking, "What the hell took you so long to get here?" To which Huff replied, "Never mind, you guys, it's a long story."

Because of the extremely low altitude at which the drops were again being made—between 300 and 400 feet—the paratroopers were on the ground a bare twenty seconds after jumping from their aircraft. The low altitude of the C-47 jump planes and their reduced airspeed of only 110 miles per hour combined to make them very easy targets for the defending Japanese.

One of the first aircraft in this lift to be hit by groundfire was loaded with members of Company F's 1st Platoon. Twenty-two-year-old Lieutenant William T. Calhoun of DeLeon, Texas, was the officer in charge of this platoon and was serving as its jumpmaster. Even at his young age, Calhoun was a paratrooper of considerable experience. He had served two years as an enlisted man in the 101st Airborne Division before obtaining a commission through Fort Benning's Officer Candidate School and joining the 503d in January 1944. Calhoun was no stranger to combat, either. During the closing days of the regiment's mission on Noemfoor Island he had taken a Japanese sniper's 7.6mm rifle bullet in his right hip and was hospitalized for three weeks before being able to rejoin his platoon.

As Calhoun's aircraft was approaching the Rock on the first of three passes it would make over the golf course DZ he was kneeling in the open door, looking for the first glimpse of land and the go point which was to appear under the left wing. Beside him stood Platoon Sergeant Philip Todd, ready to lead the first eight-man stick out the door at Calhoun's command. The aircraft's speed was gradually being reduced when Todd tapped Calhoun on the shoulder and pointed to several cruisers and destroyers below them. "Won't be long now" shouted Calhoun. A few more seconds ticked by and then Todd yelled, "There it is, sir, Corregidor!"

Craning his neck to look under the wing, Calhoun saw a bare cliff rising up out of the water. Next came the outer edges of Topside with hundreds of the first lift's collapsed parachutes scattered across it. Both Todd and Calhoun began hearing the familiar cracking noise of rifle fire but thought it must be coming from firefights taking place down on the drop zones. Suddenly they were both surprised by a loud BLAM! as a Japanese bullet tore through the middle of the airplane's floor and passed out through the roof without harming anyone. With that, Sergeant Todd looked at his platoon leader and grinned, glad that he was about to leave their flying bulls-eye.

Calhoun counted off six seconds after passing the go point and then shoved a parachute bundle of 60mm mortar ammunition out the door. He counted two more seconds before slapping Todd on the thigh and yelling, "Go!" The plane circled out, coming back fifteen minutes later on the second run. This time Calhoun shoved out another bundle of mortar ammo prior to signaling Staff Sergeant Chris W. Johnson and his stick out the door. Again Japanese bullets cracked by the plane but none found their mark this time. Calhoun led the third stick out on the final pass. He landed in large bomb crater, striking its rocky side so hard that he splintered the stock of his rifle. The sudden stop knocked the wind out of him and bruised the left side of his rib cage. Several days would pass before he was able to breath without feeling pain throughout his chest.

Company F's 2d Platoon was jumpmastered by Lieutenant Edward T. Flash of Cleveland, Ohio. As his aircraft was making its first pass several bullets tore through the floor, all of them striking a member of the first stick who was already standing hooked up ready to jump. Flash quickly unhooked the man as two paratroopers from the second stick rushed forward to administer first aid so that Flash could return to the open door and his jumpmaster duties.

On the second pass, Flash's aircraft was again holed by rifle fire, and aluminum splinters were sent flying throughout the length of the cabin. A standing jumper received several cuts but when Flash started to reach up and unhook him the man pleaded, "Sir, I'm okay. This is a history-making jump and I want to be in on it. Please, you gotta let me jump!" Although the man was bleeding from several minor cuts, Flash nodded his consent and returned to the jump door. Less than a minute later the injured man shouted, "Thank you, sir!" as he shuffled past Flash while on his way out the door.

Captain Hudson C. Hill, the commanding officer of Company E, was a veteran of the regiment's earlier combat jump on Noemfoor Island. On that jump he had broken his right wrist in a collision with an American truck parked on the drop zone. When his chute blossomed over Corregidor's parade ground DZ he quickly glanced earthward, searching for a rubble-free spot in which he might safely land. All he could see, however, were the ruins of several three-story concrete buildings toward which the wind was blowing him on a collision course.

Hill was still trying to steer himself into a grassy area he had just sighted beyond the buildings when a gust of wind caught his chute and slammed him down upon a shattered rooftop. There he slid to a stop beside a large bomb hole that extended all the way down to the building's first floor. The sudden stop both dazed Hill and collapsed his parachute, which slithered into the bomb hole like a snake entering its nest. He was just reaching out for a protruding roof timber on which he planned to steady himself while getting up when he lost what little balance he had and toppled into the hole, landing on the first floor with a loud thud and breaking off seven teeth at the gumline.

Although badly injured, Hill soon discovered that he was actually a very lucky man. Looking out at the clearing in which he had tried to land he saw the bodies of six paratroopers who had just been gunned down while he was unstrapping his parachute inside the building. All of them had jumped from his airplane.

As the drops continued a squad of Japanese Imperial Marines assembled along the western edge of the parade ground DZ where they began shooting at the airplanes and the descending paratroopers. As each Japanese emptied his rifle he would run under a paratroopers who was preparing to land and spear him on his bayonet.

Into this melee fell Sergeant Edward Gulsvick, already bleeding from two bullet holes in his right leg. Gulsvick landed with an empty submachinegun in his hands. Despite his painful wounds he quickly bounced upright and slapped a fresh twenty-round magazine of .45-caliber slugs into his weapon. Then, with his billowing parachute nearly pulling him over, he loosed a blast of fire that killed the entire enemy squad. That accomplished, Gulsvick climbed out of his harness and began administering first aid to a paratrooper who had just been bayoneted but was still alive. While doing so, Gulsvick was shot and killed by a sniper.

Elsewhere over that same drop zone, Sergeant Gertus Jones, a section chief in Battery B, 462d Parachute Artillery, saw during his descent that he was heading for the rooftop of a three-story building. By giving a sharp jerk on his risers he managed to miss the roof but still ran into trouble when he struck the building's rear wall between the second and third floors, crushing his aluminum canteen on a window ledge.

Other than a sore hip and a pair of bruised kneecaps, Sergeant Jones was in fair condition as he lay in the backyard waiting for his head to stop spinning from the effects of the collision. When his eyes came back into focus he unstrapped his parachute harness, picked up his carbine, and walked around to the front of the building where the rest of his stick and the battery's guns had been dropped. On rounding the corner of the building he discovered the body of Private First Class James Manning, who had been killed during his descent. Leaving Manning where he lay, Jones doubletimed out onto the DZ to help his men who were already starting to assemble a Pack 75 howitzer.

The wisdom of dropping artillery in with the parachute assault echelons was proven, quite effectively, by an incident that occurred while the second lift was still in the process of jumping on the Rock. It involved a Pack 75 gun crew that was called upon to come to the rescue of Captain Hill, the commander of Company E. At the time the call for help went out, Hill was still inside the building where he had fallen about twenty minutes previously and knocked out several of his teeth. Several other paratroopers had joined Hill in the building but no one could leave it as the Japanese had a pair of machine guns zeroed in on its front and back sides.

Peeking out through broken windows on the building's third floor, one of the paratroopers discovered that the enemy machine guns were firing from pillboxes located only a few hundred feet from the house. He yelled that information down to Captain Hill who grabbed his PRC 536 radio and made contact with Lieutenant Donald Abbott, his executive officer who had earlier jumped with the first lift. This was the first contact the two officers had since the Hill's arrival. Lieutenant Abbott proceeded to give his boss an update on the company's situation, telling him that sixty men had already arrived in the assembly area. Abbott also stated that a whole six-man stick of Company E men had jumped too soon and drifted over the cliff south of Battery Crocket.

Cutting in, Hill informed Abbott of his predicament, instructing him to round up a Pack 75 crew and have them knock out the troublesome pillboxes. Soon the welcome sound of artillery shells could be heard crashing against the pillboxes and the machine-gun fire came to a halt.

Hill and his companions then dashed out of the building and began carrying wounded paratroopers up to Mile-long Barracks. All told they carried eleven men to the regimental aid station.

Then they returned to the front yard of the house where they retrieved the bodies of nine other men. They did not bother going back to collect the twenty enemy dead in that same area.

U.S. Navy PT boats again played a major role in rescuing misdropped paratroopers. Seldom was a jumper in the water more than a few minutes before he was pulled aboard one of the dozen boats still aggressively patrolling less than 100 yards off the beach.

Not all misdropped paratroopers ended up in the water. Seven of them managed to land on a small grassy plateau situated near Geary Point, some 250 feet below and to the east of Topside's golf course DZ. They banded together and climbed down to the water's edge where they were eventually spotted by the crew of PT 376. Unable to get right up to the shore, the boat crew launched two inflatable life rafts and, with Japanese bullets plunking all about them, ferried all seven of the grateful paratroopers out to the boat. The rescued men were fed a sandwich before being deposited on Black Beach where they reported for duty with Lieutenant Colonel Postlethwait's outfit until the road leading up to Topside could be opened.

This was Corporal Peter J. Komer's third combat jump. He had been with the 503d Parachute Infantry Regiment since it was first formed and, at age thirty, was one of its oldest members. On his two previous combat jump missions (Nadzab and Noemfoor Island), Komer served as a rifleman in Company A. Just recently, he had been transferred to Service Company and made chief assistant to the much-respected Howard Templeman, a civilian American Red Cross field director assigned to the regiment. Templeman was also jumping today but from a different aircraft.

Komer jumped over the edge of the parade ground DZ on the aircraft's second pass just as a strong gust of wind was blowing across Topside. He felt the wind grab control of his chute and thought for sure that it was going to drive him over the edge of the DZ and down into the sea. His luck held, however, and he managed to land in a shellhole only ten yards from the edge of the cliff.

As twenty-two-year-old Private First Class Perry E. Bandt of

Phillipsburg, Kansas, descended over the parade ground DZ he became worried about all the extra weight he was carrying and what effect it was going to have on him when he landed. Bandt had good reason to worry. He was an assistant machinegunner— the man who feeds ammunition into the gun as it is being fired. As such he was required to jump with a supply of 500 rounds of belted .30-caliber ammunition tightly wrapped around his body and a carbine strapped to his left leg. Bandt and the other assistant machinegunners in the regiment would occasionally joke about the loads they jumped with, saying they felt like the sailor who, during abandon-ship drills, had to jump overboard with the ship's anchor chained to him. But now that he could see the rubble-strewn DZ rushing up to meet him Bandt was not in a laughing mood.

Although he did his best to avoid it, Bandt collided with a large chunk of concrete as he landed. Striking the obstacle with his left side, he heard a loud cracking noise and felt a sharp pain knife into his leg. When his head stopped spinning, he was relieved to see that there were no protruding bones nor any sign of blood. Proceeding to unstrap his carbine, Bandt discovered the source of the loud cracking noise. The carbine's wooden stock was broken in half.

Captain Emmett R. Spicer, the 462d Parachute Field Artillery Battalion's doctor, was well known for his considerable skill as a combat surgeon and for being a stickler when it came to filling out paperwork associated with his job. Spicer jumped with this lift and immediately reported to the regimental aid station to let them know he was aboard. He then started back to his own aid station, stopping along the way to treat a paratrooper who had lost an eye to a tree stump upon landing. Before sending the injured trooper on to the aid station, Dr. Spicer filled out the required battle casualty tag and tied it to a pocket flap on the man's jacket.

Dr. Spicer continued moving toward his battalion aid station, stopping several times to treat other wounded troopers. Even though his helmet and armband bore the unmistakable international Red Cross markings, he was shot through the chest by an Imperial Marine while trying to reach a severely wounded man.

Having seen this type of wound many times before, Spicer knew that he did not have long to live. Yet, incredibly, he propped himself up sufficiently to fill out his own battle casualty tag. Calmly, and with great care, he printed his name, rank, serial number on the tag. In the block marked "Diagnosis" he carefully printed: "GSW (gunshot wound), perforation left chest. Severe."

A patrol found the doctor's properly tagged body a few hours after his death. Beside him lay his open first aid kit, an empty morphine syrette, and the remains of his last cigarette. Captain Spicer was posthumously awarded a Silver Star Medal for having saved the lives of many men that day.

By 1:45 P.M. all of the second lift's paratroopers had jumped over the Rock and the airplanes were on the way back to Mindoro, many of them containing bullet holes. The lift commander, Lieutenant Colonel Tolson, jumped with one of the last sticks, breaking his left ankle upon landing.

So far a total of 2,050 members of the 503d Parachute Regimental Combat Team had been delivered to Corregidor from Mindoro. Of that number three died when their parachutes failed to open. Fifty others had been shot and killed while still in midair. Eight more died from injuries sustained when they landed on the outer edges of Topside and their half-inflated parachutes pulled them over the edge of the cliffs for a 500-foot fall to the rocky shore below. Crashes into partially destroyed buildings and the other immovable objects littering the DZs resulted in six more deaths. Another 210 troopers were lying in the various unit aid stations with an assortment of serious wounds and jump injuries that ranged from concussions to severe compound fractures. Over and above those numbers, another twenty-five men were listed as missing in action.

That was the discouraging casualty count for only the first two lifts. And as bad as they were, those figures did not include the few hundred other paratroopers who had been turned away from the overcrowded aid stations suffering from lesser injuries such as sprains, cuts, and bruises.

The number of deaths and jump injuries incurred by the first two lifts so disturbed Colonel Jones that he began discussing with his staff the advisability of canceling the first Battalion's drop, scheduled to begin at 8:30 the next morning. As the regimental staff was meeting in the War Room to discuss that and other matters, Major Caskey's newly arrived 2d Battalion took over from Lieutenant Colonel Erickson's 3d Battalion the job of providing security around the southern half of Topside, the two drop zones, and Mile-long Barracks. Caskey established his command post on the first floor of Mile-long Barracks while his three rifle companies began taking over many of the positions that had been dug by Erickson's men.

One section of Topside being organized for defense by Major Caskey's battalion was Senior Officer's Row, a long line of two-story houses along the southeastern edge of the parade ground. Senior Officer's Row had been built during the 1920s and was so named because it was the area in which Corregidor's field grade officers and their families resided. A broad street ran along the front of the houses and there were still enough trees standing to make it shady in spots. The street extended southeast for 200 yards where it passed to the rear of Battery Boston, a small living-room-sized antiaircraft emplacement, and then continued on for another 100 yards, passing behind Battery Wheeler, which had been serving as the go point for jumpmasters aiming for the parade ground DZ. Battery Wheeler was by far the larger of the two fortifications. Constructed on the site of a former Spanish gun platform, it consisted of massive reinforced concrete walls measuring 150 yards across its front, was nearly 50 yards deep, and had several belowground chambers. During the course of the next few days it would alternately be defended by Japanese and American troops and the scene of much hard fighting.

In his attack order issued on Mindoro before the jump, Major Caskey had assigned the defense of Senior Officer's Row and the clearing of Batteries Boston and Wheeler to Lieutenant William T. Bailey, the commanding officer of Company F. Immediately following the drop, Bailey assembled his company and proceeded to Senior Officer's Row, encountering little opposition along the route.

Well before the jump, Bailey had studied aerial photographs of Corregidor and selected Building 28-D, the westernmost house on Senior Officer's Row, to be his company command post.

He was met there by Captain L.S. Brown, the 2d Battalion S-3 officer. Brown informed Bailey that he had just been out to Battery Wheeler and found it to be unoccupied by the enemy. However, the antiaircraft guns located in Battery Boston were still being held by two squads of Japanese who had recently been seen firing on the jump planes.

Because the enemy force defending the antiaircraft battery was so small, Lieutenant Bailey decided to send only the 1st Platoon, commanded by Lieutenant Calhoun, for the mission. Bailey's order to Calhoun was, "Clean out Battery Boston as quickly as you can, then go search Battery Wheeler for any Nips that might be hiding out in it."

Calhoun was still smarting from the rib injuries sustained during his rough landing less than an hour ago. And, one of the three rifle squads that constituted his platoon was nowhere to be found. In fact, it was still aboard an airplane being jumpmastered by Company F's topkick, First Sergeant Albert J. Baldwin. While making its second pass over the DZ its left engine was put out of commission by ground fire. Not wanting to risk a third pass, during which his one remaining good engine might also get shot out, the pilot received permission to leave the formation and return to Mindoro with the jumpmaster and the last stick of jumpers still aboard. Calhoun was also minus the services of Sergeant John Wright and Privates First Class Roland H. Reynolds and Philip R. Smith, all of whom had been badly injured during their rough landings.

Even though shorthanded and partially disabled himself, Calhoun began maneuvering toward Battery Boston with two scouts, Private Lloyd G. McCarter and Private First Class Richard A. Lampman preceding the main body of the platoon by some thirty yards. Both scouts were handpicked for the dangerous task of being the first to engage the enemy. Private McCarter was already something of a legend in Company F for his reckless heroics in past battles, for having repeatedly gone AWOL (absent without leave, a court-martial offense), and for brawling with anyone foolish enough to take him on when the regiment had been resting in Australia and New Guinea.

Using suppressive fire from his own bazooka teams and Private

First Class Henry McCory's 60mm mortar squad, Lieutenant Calhoun rapidly advanced the platoon across the open expanse of shelltorn ground leading to Battery Boston. The Japanese defiantly returned fire but were quickly overrun by the two scouts, Lampman and McCarter. Lampman killed seven of the enemy by firing his Browning automatic rifle from the hip as he was dashing forward. McCarter killed eight more with short bursts from his Thompson submachine gun.

During the advance, Calhoun saw that his platoon's right flank was dangerously exposed to Battery Wheeler's high south parapet. Even though he had been told by Captain Brown that Battery Wheeler was void of enemy troops, Calhoun felt very uneasy about his flank being wide open. He sent his first squad, consisting of Sergeant William Freihoff and three men, Privates Glen E. Handlon, Delby A. Huff, and Albert F. Thomas, to investigate Battery Wheeler.

The squad was just approaching the rear of Battery Wheeler when it was surprised by a sudden burst of 6.5 Nambu light machine gun fire from a concrete tower above the north parapet. Private Handlon was killed instantly. Freihoff and Huff dashed to the battery's back wall where they descended a flight of stairs in a single bound and ran into a large room filled with American artillery shells and gunpowder canisters that had been sitting there since Corregidor fell to the Japanese. Private Thomas remained outside where he had hastily taken cover behind a mound when Handlon was killed only ten feet in front of him.

Recognizing that he and Huff were now trapped inside the battery, Sergeant Freihoff yelled out to Thomas to go and tell Lieutenant Calhoun what had happened. Calhoun and the rest of the platoon arrived a short while later and took up firing positions in a large crater only fifty yards in back of the battery. A bazooka team started banging away at the tower where the Nambu was located but its rockets exploded harmlessly against the battery's thick concrete walls. Meanwhile, Private Thomas and Sergeant Todd were looking over the crest of the crater trying to get an exact fix on the Nambu, when a single shot rang out. Thomas raised up, turned around, and fell face down into the crater, dead with a bullet through his head.

Lieutenant Calhoun was frantically trying to think of some way to rescue the trapped men. Putting Sergeant Todd temporarily in charge of the platoon, Calhoun double-timed back to Building 28-D and returned in a short while with a burly paratrooper carrying a flamethrower.

Convinced that he now had the ultimate close-combat weapon and that his trapped men would be freed in only a few more minutes, Calhoun smiled as the flamethrower operator aimed his deadly weapon at the tower and squeezed its trigger. To the dismay of everyone, nothing happened. Evidently damaged during the drop, the flamethrower failed to function.

Calhoun next had Private First Class Earl J. Soucy fire a white phosphorous rifle grenade into the open area between the tower and the battery's back wall. The plan was that when the grenade exploded and released its white-hot fragments and cloud of smoke, Freihoff and Huff were to run out to freedom. The grenade landed right where it was supposed to but did not explode. Again, something had gone seriously wrong.

The situation was finally brought to a successful conclusion when Private McCarter and Sergeant Phillips charged the tower, throwing hand grenades behind it and shooting at its firing ports. Amid all that confusion, Freihoff and Huff made good their escape. Calhoun was so happy to see them that he "could have kissed them."

While Lieutenant Calhoun was rescuing the two men trapped in Battery Wheeler, Lieutenant Colonel Erickson and his 3d Battalion paratroopers had been busy driving the Japanese off Topside's northern half and setting up blocking positions along the edge of the bluff where heavily wooded ravines led up from the seashore. Keeping his headquarters in the Spanish lighthouse, Erickson dispatched Company G eastward down the slopes toward Middleside to set up night positions across the head of Ramsey Ravine, one of the best routes leading up to Topside. In that new location Company G was only 250 yards from the closest elements of Lieutenant Colonel Postlethwait's infantry battalion deployed across Bottomside. Company H, meanwhile, was sent 300 yards north to occupy the gutted aboveground hospital in the center of Topside plus Morrison

Hill, which dominates the entire northeast section of Topside and routes leading out of James Ravine. Company I had the task of blocking the head of Ramsey Ravine with two platoons and keeping its other platoon within the battalion's original defensive perimeter as a ready reserve force.

There was some additional light skirmishing during these moves, resulting in fifty-five more paratroopers wounded and slightly more than that number of Japanese killed.

In the meantime, the question of additional drops had been settled. Colonel Jones felt that since the first two phases of the operation had been a success, opposition had been lighter than expected, and the Japanese were obviously disorganized, there was no need to risk further jump casualties. Accordingly, he sent a radio message to Major General Charles P. Hall's XI Corps Headquarters (under which Rock Force was now operating), requesting that the jump scheduled for the following morning by Major Robert H. Woods' 1st Battalion be canceled. The request was approved. An alternate plan for delivering the third lift to Corregidor was drawn up. The paratroopers would be flown from Mindoro to Luzon's San Marcelino Airfield and then trucked to the Subic Bay area to board LCMs for the short voyage to the Rock.

With the sun beginning to set, Colonel Jones consolidated his tactical position shrewdly. He ordered the paratroop companies occupying Topside's Morrison Hill and hospital buildings to pull back inside the original defensive perimeter and dig in for the night alongside the newly arrived companies of the 2d Battalion. Still lacking the battalion that was back on Mindoro, and expecting some sort of counterattack after dark, Jones wanted the Japanese to run into a buzzsaw of firepower if they made their move against his positions on Topside.

As they took up their new positions the paratroopers started rooting around Topside, searching through the buildings just held by the Japanese.

While rummaging through the second floor of Mile-long Barracks, Corporal Peter J. Komer found a room filled with bolts of fine Japanese silk. Some had bullet holes through them, but most were still like new. Komer helped himself to two bolts, one green and one pink. Some twenty years later, the pink bolt would be used to make a wedding dress for Komer's daughter.

Continuing down the hallway, Komer met several paratroopers who had just discovered a room containing over thirty cases of sake, sherry, whiskey, and beer. Already encumbered with the two bolts of silk, Komer only managed to lug away one case of sherry and a dozen bottles of beer. At the suggestion of his boss, Red Cross field director Howard Templeman, Komer delivered the case of sherry to the regimental aid station for distribution among the mob of wounded men and overworked medics.

Over on Senior Officers Row, the men of Company F began searching the homes, finding evidence that most of them had been used by the Japanese as administrative offices and living quarters. In one dining room they found a table still set with chopsticks and large bowls of cooked rice and vegetables, a meal interrupted by the first lift's arrival. Many other ground floor rooms were arranged with American military filing cabinets and wooden desks loaded with various Japanese documents that no one could read.

Colonel Jones's orderly did not let his broken ankle stop him from souvenir hunting. With a friend, he found and delivered a case of Japanese Suntory whiskey to the colonel's quarters adjacent to the War Room.

When nobody was looking, other paratroopers cut umbrella-size souvenir swatches of camouflage nylon from damaged parachutes and stuffed them in their packs. They had to do this secretly for though it was permissible to take almost any other kind of souvenir, cutting a parachute—even a damaged one— was destruction of government property, a court-martial offense. One of those swatches was presented to the author during the writing of this book.

The afternoon had passed quietly for Lieutenant Colonel Postlethwait's reinforced battalion. Hardly more than a few rifle shots had been fired across his piece of the Rock since the LCMs pulled away from Black Beach. It was a totally new and uncomfortable experience for these combat infantrymen to be held back in defensive positions while the enemy was known to be close at hand. But like it or not, their mission was to dig in and stay put until further orders were received from the Rock Force commander.

Postlethwait's troops knew that the Japanese preferred to do their fighting at night. So while there was still some daylight remaining the three companies of infantrymen strung across Bottomside's sandy region worked to improve the foxholes and machine-gun emplacements they had dug.

The battalion's other two companies were busy stringing telephone lines between their positions atop Malinta Hill and on down to Malinta Point by way of Goal Post Ridge and Little Knob. Field telephones were double-checked to insure communication between all platoons and the central switchboard at battalion headquarters. Few soldiers on the hill were able to do much digging because of the extremely rocky soil. In place of the protective foxholes that they usually dug every night while in combat, the troops collected hundreds of loose stone fragments and constructed low walls around their individual fighting positions.

The one and only advantage the infantrymen atop Malinta Hill had over their companions down on Bottomside was a panoramic view of the Rock's scenery. They could overlook the entire eastern half of the island, which stretched out before them like a living topographical map.

During the 1930s American construction crews had built an observation post on Malinta Hill, Base End Station B-23. It was dug into solid rock and had a two-foot-thick slab of reinforced concrete for a roof. Every soldier ever stationed on Corregidor knew the location of B-23 since it was from there that numerous live firing exercises were directed against floating targets simulating enemy vessels that had penetrated to positions located east of the Rock. When Postlethwait's troops found B-23 still in serviceable condition they recommissioned it as an observation post, stationing teams of 81mm mortar and artillery forward observers there around the clock.

As darkness fell across Corregidor on this first day of the recapture operation the assault phase closed with the paratroopers holding a tight perimeter on Topside, the infantrymen holding

Bottomside and Malinta Hill, and everyone holding his breath: Rumor had it that the Rock was prepared for destruction with concealed demolition charges of great power which could be detonated either electrically or by radio remote control by the Japanese.

7
BIG TROUBLE ON
MALINTA HILL

Now that a thick blanket of darkness had enveloped the Philippines on this first day of the most difficult small-scale parachute assault in history, Corregidor grew strangely quite and peaceful. With millions of stars twinkling overhead in the coal black sky and refreshingly cool breezes blowing in off the South China Sea, the tired infantrymen and paratroopers of Rock Force sat waiting for the Japanese to begin their customary night probing attacks.

As the evening wore on, several paratroopers manning Topside's outer perimeter defensive line began reporting that they could hear noises to their front. They could discern the sounds of feet moving and the rustling of bushes, both strong indicators that the Japanese were up to something.

What the paratroopers could not see was that ever since the onset of darkness Japanese Marines, alone and in three-man groups, had been stealthily emerging from the dozens of caves, bunkers, and American-built artillery batteries that honeycombed the Rock. For the time being at least, the Japanese were limiting themselves to intelligence-gathering activities to determine the precise locations and strength of the American positions.

Employing their standard night reconnaissance methods, several Japanese patrols around Topside's rim advanced to within

100 yards of the American forces' perimeter. Then from covered positions they fired several rifle shots in rapid succession, trying to provoke return fire that would disclose the defenders' positions. But that tactic did not work because the paratroopers were under strict orders not to open fire unless they could see the enemy face to face.

Next, the Japanese tried moving in closer, throwing hand grenades and waiting for the telltale flashes of American return fire. When that also failed to produce the desired response several lone Imperial Marines were sent crawling forward with orders to infiltrate the perimeter, cause several casualties among the Americans, and return with a report of what they had seen and done.

Owing to the darkness and their familiarity with the locations of Topside's many subterranean passageways, several infiltrators managed to slip through the American lines undetected. Two of them made it all the way to the western end of Mile-long Barracks. At 9:00 P.M., they started running along the outside wall of the barracks, tossing grenades into ground-floor rooms which they believed to be full of sleeping Americans but were actually vacant. The two intruders managed to throw only a half-dozen grenades before they approached a recessed stairway where a paratrooper was standing guard at the entrance to the 2d Battalion command post. Keeping his cool, the paratrooper ducked back into the doorway until the Japanese passed directly in front of him. Then he shot them to ribbons with a full twenty-round burst from his Thompson submachine gun.

The noise of the grenade explosions, shrapnel ricocheting around inside Mile-long Barracks, and the roar of the sentry's submachine gun caused considerable excitement. Colonel Jones immediately placed all Topside units on full battle alert, which raised the lethal potential of the situation to the maximum. The 503d Parachute Infantry had a long-standing policy prohibiting night movement within friendly lines, a carryover from the regiment's jungle fighting days. Once it became dark, no one was to stray from his assigned position, not even to answer the call of nature. To do so was to risk getting shot by a fellow squad member. All troopers were instructed to consider any movement at night as hostile and to fire without warning. This shoot-first, ask-questions-later policy was rigidly enforced. Occasionally it resulted in a friend mistakenly shooting a friend who forgot to stay put after dark. When that happened no apologies were given nor expected.

For the next full hour every man within the Topside perimeter peered into the darkness with his finger on the trigger of his weapon. During this period of increased vigilance the paratroopers received valuable assistance from the two U.S. Navy destroyers that were kept on station around the clock. At irregular intervals the destroyers fired star shells (parachute flares). Bursting high above Topside, each shell turned night into day for slightly more than one minute. The brilliantly burning flares and full battle alert combined to bring a temporary end to all enemy movement. At 10:00 P.M. the alert was lowered to 25 percent. Soon thereafter the exhausted paratroopers began drifting off to sleep with only one in four of their number standing guard.

Things had just quieted down all across Topside when the paratroopers in Company F's third platoon began hearing someone walking in back of them. Just before darkness, all members of this platoon had been pulled back from exposed positions along the edge of the bluff; they now occupied the battered buildings on Senior Officers Row. The troopers were split up in pairs in the many rooms of the houses. With nothing but concrete floors to sleep on, they made themselves as comfortable as possible on mattresses made of parachutes gathered from the nearby parade field drop zone.

Each time these troopers heard a noise they wanted to open fire on it. But since their company was situated along the outer edge of the defensive perimeter, they had orders not to shoot unless the Japanese tried to enter their building. As a result of that restriction, the troopers had done nothing about the noises other than to report them and keep a sharp lookout with loaded weapons cradled in their arms or laying at their sides when not on guard duty.

At a little after 10:30 P.M. Lieutenant Edward T. Flash, the 3d Platoon leader, looked up from the floor on which he was lying and saw a Japanese standing in the doorway. With great care, the wide-eyed Flash began reaching for the carbine at his side. His hand had just touched the carbine's wooden stock when his roommate, Staff Sergeant Charles H. Hoyt, startled him by firing a blast from a Thompson submachine gun directly over the top of his head. The muzzle blast singed Flash's hair and scalp. Hoyt's burst struck the Japanese in the chest, sending him tumbling down the front steps and into the front yard where he lay gasping and moaning as his life ebbed away.

This incident put all paratroopers back on full battle alert. But the alert lasted only a half-hour, after which the majority of troopers were permitted to again begin drifting off to an uneasy sleep.

Tranquillity still prevailed at midnight when the duty officer at Rock Force headquarters made the following entry in the unit battle diary: "All quiet on Corregidor. Enemy seems to have had enough trouble for this night."

The ink from that entry was not yet dry when the silence was shattered by Japanese machine guns, hand grenades, and mortar shells. This time, the disturbance occurred on top of Malinta Hill and at the outposts on Goal Post Ridge and Little Knob.

Postlethwait's infantrymen were under attack by a reinforced company of Imperial Marines who had emerged from the eastern portal of Malinta Tunnel and advanced undetected along the north shore road to Goal Post Ridge and Little Knob. There they ran into the riflemen from Company K who were manning those outposts, blocking the most direct routes leading to Bottomside.

Although the shoreline road was narrow, the Japanese managed to attack with two platoons abreast. On approaching the outposts they were met by a fusillade of rifle fire that brought them to a temporary halt. The Japanese quickly regrouped and lunged again at Goal Post Ridge and Little Knob. This time they overran both outposts, causing heavy casualties among the Americans.

Meanwhile, on top of Malinta Hill Captain Frank Centenni, commanding officer of Company K, had been frantically cranking the company's field telephone for the last several minutes, trying to make contact with the two outposts. His efforts were useless because the land lines had been cut.

Centenni was still crouched over the telephone set trying to get through to his outposts when a sergeant tapped him on the back saying, "Captain, someone's climbing up the hill."

Several of Centenni's riflemen aimed downhill, taking up trigger slack as they waited to see if the approaching unidentified figure was friend or foe.

The crunching footsteps and heavy breathing grew louder, causing one of the riflemen to demand, "Halt! Who goes there?"

An angry familiar voice replied, "Hold your damned fire!" Climbing up from Little Knob was Private Rivers P. Bourque of Delacambre, Louisiana. Over his right shoulder he carried a buddy whose legs were mangled. Every few feet, he stopped to help a third man whose face and hands were covered with blood.

As his wounded companions were being carried off to the company aid station, Bourque told Centenni how the Japanese had twice attacked his squad, killing or wounding everyone but himself and Private First Class James L. Cassise. Bourque went on to say that Cassise had crawled through the darkness, rescued the outpost's two most seriously wounded survivors, and dragged them to a hiding place behind a huge boulder. Cassise, said Bourque, had volunteered to remain behind with the wounded and was still down there among the Japanese.

Less than five minutes after Bourque finished telling his horror story, two unwounded men from the Goal Post Ridge outpost reached the top of Malinta Hill. They reported that the enemy had killed six of their eleven men. And, just as had happened over on Little Knob, two of the wounded were left behind under the care of a third man, Private Clarence Baumea. By an odd coincidence, both Baumea and Cassise were from the state of Michigan.

Captain Centenni agonized over what to do about his men stranded out on the outposts. He briefly considered mounting a rescue operation to get them out. But his orders were to hold Malinta Hill no matter what happened. There would be no rescue operation. Not now anyway.

Scarcely had Centenni reached that difficult decision when the night erupted in fury and death. Another contingent of Imperial Marines had slipped out of Malinta Tunnel and were now laboring up the steep northwest side of the hill straight toward Company K's positions. Although a courageous undertaking, the attack itself was doomed to failure because the Japanese had to charge up nearly vertical slopes against Centenni's troops.

On Topside, where most of the paratroopers had just just been awakened, everyone grabbed their weapon and sat up. The distant explosions and wild screams of the Imperial Marines caused one paratroop sergeant to remark, "Oh oh, we got big trouble on Malinta Hill."

Captain Centenni's troops held their fire until the Japanese were practically on top of them. The first assault wave had closed to within ten feet when the men of Company K loosed a blast of rifle fire that cut through the enemy ranks like a giant knife. Bodies of those Japanese just killed toppled backward, knocking tangled clusters of attackers all the way back down to the bottom of the hill.

Even though stunned by the unexpected ferocity of the American defense the Imperial Marines kept charging up the hill. By the light of exploding star shells the Americans could see the attackers' faces under helmet rims as they advanced with a rifle in one hand, a grenade in the other. At times the two sides engaged each other in hand-to-hand combat, using everything from bare knuckles to bayonets.

The hillside seethed with Japanese, all loudly shouting as they tried to seize control of the summit. Their frenzied high-pitched yells hurt the ears of the Americans almost as much the blasts from incoming mortar rounds.

Nineteen-year-old Private Adolph Neamend of Bethlehem, Pennsylvania, emptied an eight-round clip of M-1 bullets into the belly of a howling foe. Seconds later, another Japanese tossed a hand grenade, hitting Private Raymond Crenshaw in the chest with it. Having been a star shortstop on his high school baseball team in Clinton, Oklahoma, Crenshaw instantly fielded the still sputtering grenade, throwing it down the hill where it exploded among the attackers.

Japanese mortar shells were landing with alarming accuracy on the flanks of Company K. One of them hit on top of the first platoon's machine gun squad, killing the entire crew and destroying the gun. Another shellburst killed nine and wounded three of Centenni's men who were in the process of moving to reinforce the second platoon's sector.

As they always manage to do, no matter how great the peril, American medics scurried through the firing, tending to the wounded. Most of the injured riflemen were able to continue fighting once their wounds were bound up. But some needed surgery if they were to survive and fight another day. The delicate job of carrying seriously wounded cases downhill to the battalion aid station was the responsibility of Medical Sergeant Willard Harp of Durhamville, New York, and six corpsmen who acted as litter bearers. In a remarkable display of courage and physical stamina, this band of medics safely delivered a dozen badly wounded soldiers to the battalion surgeon. The surgeon was able to save all but one of them.

The skirmishing lasted for an hour and a half. The Japanese inflicted considerable injury on Company K but failed to gain control of the hill. Finally realizing that they were not going to carry the hill, the Japanese made a phased withdrawal back to Malinta Tunnel, taking most of their wounded and dead comrades with them. The remainder of the night passed with both sides tending to their wounds.

Heavy fighting had still been in progress atop Malinta Hill when the Japanese sent two rifle companies skirting around its base to launch a coordinated attack on Postlethwait's other companies deployed across Bottomside. At a little after 3:00 A.M., a deafening blast shook the ground being defended by Company A. Japanese engineer troops had placed explosives in a cliff opposite the company with the intention of burying the Americans alive under tons of earth and rock. But far too much TNT had been used. Instead of a landslide crushing Company A, an enormous chunk of the cliff flew clear over the heads of the troops, landing harmlessly in the waters of Manila Bay.

Thick clouds of dust and smoke were still swirling about when the shaken men of Company A heard splashes in the surf just off San Jose Point. The soldiers fired into the surf and heard screams. They kept on shooting until the screaming stopped and, at first light, discovered the bodies of twenty-three Imperial Marines washed up on Black Beach. Each had a waterproof TNT satchel strapped to his belly; they had apparently intended to slip ashore and sacrifice themselves as human bombs among the American positions on Bottomside.

During the time that the kamikaze swimmers had been approaching Black Beach, some thirty Imperial Marines filed out of a large cave in the side of Malinta Hill and proceeded to a trolley underpass where they reformed to launch an attack on Black Beach. Staff Sergeant Eugene M. Plantdon of Milford, New Hampshire, and Private First Class Robert K. Taylor, of Long Island, New York, were standing guard directly above the underpass. They could see the enemy lining up for the assault and could hear their sergeants excitedly whispering last-minute instructions. Suddenly, the two Americans heard shouts of "Banzai!" and saw the Imperial Marines take off running across a two-hundred-yard expanse of rocky soil leading to Black Beach.

Plantdon and Taylor opened fire, hitting the enemy force on its left rear flank. Seconds later, the unmistakable heavy sound of American machine guns erupted from the direction of the beach. The Japanese officer leading the charge staggered backward a few steps before falling mortally wounded on his samurai sword. His men took cover in two large bomb craters where they began discussing what to do about the deadly crossfire they were caught in. There they remained, leaderless and in a state of confusion, as the Americans bombarded them with hand grenades, eventually killing or wounding all. Six wounded Imperial Marines managed to crawl from the craters and infiltrate to within fifty yards of San Jose Point. There they were discovered and killed.

At first light, Captain Centenni and his men looked down from their positions on Malinta Hill and counted thirty-six dead Imperial Marines. Heavy trails of blood showed where many others had been carried away. Another twenty-seven severely wounded Japanese lay sprawled across the eastern face of the hill. Hordes of large green flies and other insects swarmed over their gaping wounds, causing such tortured cries that the Americans killed them to end their agony, but the smell of their bodies soon became worse than the groaning had been.

Still greatly concerned about his men marooned at the outposts, Captain Centenni dispatched an eight-man patrol to see if there were any survivors of the prolonged Japanese attack. The patrol members slid down the hillside and moved through the dead bodies, reaching Little Knob without incident. There they found one man still alive. The others had died during the night.

The patrol pushed on toward Goal Post Ridge but soon walked into an ambush. Four patrol members died in a hail of machine gun bullets. The others managed to break contact and retreat back up to Malinta Hill.

Outraged because some of his men were still down there, helpless and at the mercy of the enemy, Captain Centenni mustered another patrol. Knowing that he was critically short of manpower, Centenni decided to lead it himself.

The patrol went down the slope and proceeded undisturbed to the point where the first patrol met disaster. They passed through that area without drawing fire and headed for Goal Post Ridge, still some fifty yards away. Moments later all hell broke loose as the Japanese sprung another well-concealed ambush.

Captain Centenni fell dead in his tracks. Meanwhile his men dropped to the ground and returned fire, killing four Japanese. In a brisk firefight the patrol managed to back out of the ambush site and safely withdraw to Malinta Hill. While withdrawing the patrol members tried to take the body of their captain, but the enemy kept his remains covered by rifle fire, forcing them to depart empty-handed.

With Centenni dead, command of Company K passed to his executive officer, twenty-four-year-old Lieutenant Henry G. "Hank" Kitnik of Broughton, Pennsylvania. The first thing Kitnik did was to ask the platoon leaders for head counts. When the figures were tallied, Kitnik discovered that of the nearly 200 healthy men who had stormed ashore the previous day, he was now commanding ninety-three effectives, many of whom were walking wounded.

Lieutenant Colonel Postlethwait was justifiably proud of the good fight his battalion had fought throughout the night as it crushed every attempt the enemy made to seize Malinta Hill and force a breakthrough to Bottomside and beyond. At 7:00 that morning—February 17, D day-plus-1—Postlethwait started making the rounds of his battalion to personally extend congratulations to each company commander for a job well done.

Elsewhere on the Rock, Colonel Jones and his paratroopers were beginning phase three of the reconquest: the destruction of enemy forces on Topside.

8
CLEARING TOPSIDE

The morning of February 17 had dawned rather quietly for the two battalions of paratroopers manning Topside's tightly knit perimeter. Despite having been awakened several times throughout the night by prowling Japanese, and by the noisy battle on Malinta Hill, most of the paratroopers were reasonably well rested.

As soon as daylight provided a clear view of Topside's littered landscape, squad-size paratrooper patrols made security sweeps along the outer edges of the perimeter to make certain no more enemy soldiers were still lurking about. No contact was made during the sweeps, which ranged an average of 100 yards out from the perimeter. However, several patrol members reported seeing spent Japanese rifle shell casings, footprints, and blood trails, all of which were clear indications that the perimeter had been thoroughly reconnoitered during the night.

It took only a half-hour to complete the sweeps and for the patrols to reenter the perimeter. There, troopers clustered around small campfires to heat the canned K-ration breakfasts they had carried in on the jump. Elsewhere within the perimeter troopers were busy oiling rifles and machine guns in preparation for the day's planned action, which called for gradually enlarging the perimeter and eliminating small pockets of enemy resistance along the way.

Clearing Topside

To make a smooth transition into the clearing operations, Colonel Jones had divided Topside into two battle zones of equal size. Lieutenant Colonel John Erickson's 3d Battalion drew the northern zone of action, and Major Lawson Caskey's 2d Battalion got the mission of clearing the southern zone. Jones gave each of his battalion commanders a combat order that was clear-cut and easy to understand: "Kill all the enemy in your respective zones." Still completely unaware of the enemy's true battle strength, all of the paratroopers—from Colonel Jones to the lowest ranking private—confidently expected to have the Rock tidied up in another day or two at most.

At precisely 7:30 A.M. Captain Joseph M. Conway's Company H from Lieutenant Colonel Erickson's battalion launched an attack north of the perimeter. The objective was Morrison Hill, Topside's dominant terrain feature, which had initially been taken the previous day and then abandoned at dusk when the paratroopers pulled back into their defensive perimeter for the night. The persistent Japanese had reoccupied the hill almost as soon as the paratroopers abandoned it. However, the Imperial Marines made the tactical error of reestablishing themselves in hastily constructed fighting positions that proved easy to knock out. By 10:00 A.M. Morrison Hill once more belonged to Rock Force. The cost was two slightly wounded paratroopers. Thirty-seven Japanese were killed.

While Captain Conway's men were storming Morrison Hill, the 3d Battalion's Company I, commanded by Captain Lyle M. Murphy, was clearing an area extending from the lighthouse eastward toward Breakwater Point. Because of the rugged nature of the bomb-blasted terrain in this area, Captain Murphy deployed his company in platoon-size patrols during the advance.

Murphy and his men made it all the way to the profusely cratered quarter of Topside that used to be the golf course without firing a shot. As they were passing the ruins of what had been the pro shop, the company's lead scout heard a distant voice shouting in English. The shouting came from his immediate front, about 200 feet down a slope leading to the shoreline. Fearing a Japanese trick, the scout aimed his Thompson submachine gun in that direction and yelled, "Come on out in the open where I can see you!"

At that, a lone paratrooper, Private First Class John F. Romero, emerged from a clump of bushes. As soon as Romero had established eye to eye contact with the scout he nodded in the direction of the bushes and was joined by seven other troopers, five of whom were wearing badly stained bandages.

It took several minutes for them to make their way up the hill to link up with the scout who rushed down to help, and with Captain Murphy who had come forward to see what was holding up his unit's advance. Romero explained that yesterday's strong winds had carried him and the others well past their drop zone, forcing them to land at various points far down the steep slope leading to Bottomside. After joining together on the slope, they had begun fighting their way on up toward Topside. Still well short of their goal at the onset of darkness, they took cover in the bushes and spent the night caring for the wounded and watching heavily armed Japanese patrols pass within a few feet of them.

Other than welcoming the paratroopers back into the regiment, there was little else Captain Murphy could do for them. After one of his company medics tended to their wounds, the captain showed them a trail leading back to the perimeter and then got his company moving forward once again.

Up to this point, Murphy and his troopers had experienced no contact with the enemy while clearing their zone of action. But just minutes after Private Romero and his buddies had left the situation changed—several Japanese riflemen began taking pot shots at the Americans from a series of caves carved into the hillside.

Murphy's troopers reacted violently, pouring rifle and machine-gun fire into the cave openings closest to them. While maneuvering to within hand-grenade range of the caves the Americans used a battle drill that had proven successful on other islands where they had been forced to dig out diehard Japanese soldiers refusing to surrender. The battle drill was an uncomplicated procedure that used brute force and took maximum advantage of the superior firepower usually available to the American force.

It began with stationing a few men armed with submachine guns and rifles at points covering the approaches to a Japanese position. While they provided suppressive fire, a squad-size assault team would work forward to the designated cave entrance and toss in a few hand grenades. If the enemy continued to resist, a flamethrower team would be called forward. To avoid backflash from incessant winds, and to assure the deepest penetration possible, flamethrower operators had learned to project unignited fuel deep within the enemy's lair and then set it ablaze with a white phosphorous grenade or tracer bullets. If the surviving Japanese still could not be induced to come out and surrender, engineer demolition teams moved in and blew the entrances shut with TNT.

Using this very effective method of operation, by noon Murphy's men had managed to advance all the way to an area directly above Breakwater Point and about halfway down the slope leading to Bottomside. During the advance, they had sealed eleven caves at a cost of no casualties.

Things did not go quite so smoothly along the southern half of Topside, which had been defended throughout the night by Major Lawson Caskey's 2d Battalion. There the day began with a most unusual—almost humorous—combat action.

Unknown to Colonel Jones and all members of Rock Force, the defending Japanese had two fully operable American civilian automobiles hidden away on Corregidor. One of the captive vehicles was General MacArthur's personal staff car, a long, black 1935 Cadillac limousine, which had been ferried to the Rock by U.S. Army Transportation Corps troops during the hectic 1941 evacuation of Manila. Upon its arrival on the island, the staff car had been driven into one of Malinta Hill's arched laterals for safekeeping until the expected American relief expedition arrived to expel the invading Japanese. But that, as we have seen, did not happen. Consequently, MacArthur's car eventually fell into the hands of Colonel Sato's troops when they captured the Rock. Due to the extreme shortage of gasoline throughout the Philippines during the war years, the victorious Japanese occupation troops did not return MacArthur's car to Manila for public exhibition as a war trophy. Instead, they left it out on the Rock, parked in the same lateral where its American driver had left it back in 1941. On only a few rare occasions since that time had MacArthur's gas-guzzling limousine been used to transport high-ranking Japanese Army and Navy staff officers who visited the Rock, inspecting its defenses as the American forces began closing in on the Philippines.

The second American vehicle hidden away on Corregidor was a sporty, bright red, 1938 Ford roadster, complete with rumble seat. In prewar days the roadster had belonged to a coast artillery officer quartered on Topside. When the heavy Bataan-based Japanese siege guns began bombarding the Rock early in 1942, the car's owner drove it into one of Topside's vacant underground ammunition bunkers, apparently planning on retrieving it when the crisis had passed.

Like MacArthur's dust-covered staff car, the smart-looking roadster was in perfect running condition. Because its small engine was so fuel efficient, the Japanese had been using it to transport lesser-rank visiting officers about the island. The well-protected bunker serving as its hideaway was positioned right beside a long winding road leading down to Bottomside's dock facilities.

In the 2d Battalion's Company F area, Lieutenant Edward Flash and his platoon of paratroopers were huddled around campfires eating breakfast when a sentinel on watch at the perimeter startled them by suddenly shouting, "Hey you guys, come look at this. You won't believe your eyes!"

Running out to the sentinel's post, the Americans were astonished to see the Ford roadster rolling downhill with three Japanese marines sitting inside it, three more crammed into the rumble seat, and several others running along behind trying to jump on board. Since this was the first American automobile the paratroopers had seen in nearly two years—and a bright red one at that—they were mesmerized.

Nearly a full minute passed before this bizarre scene was brought to a violent end when a paratrooper fired a long burst of

.50-caliber machine gun bullets into the side of the roadster, causing it to crash beside the road and burst into flames. The survivors and those who were running after the car were quickly gunned down by other paratroopers, who had by then recovered their wits.

Shortly after this incident, Lieutenant Flash and his men were dispatched by their company commander, Lieutenant William T. Bailey, on a mission to locate wounded and dead paratroopers still listed as missing in action. The search area was located northeast of Battery Wheeler where a set of railway tracks passed in front of several large concrete warehouses. Upon entering that area Flash's men discovered a cluster of three dead paratroopers lying on the tracks. All three were still wearing their parachutes, clear evidence that they had been killed before reaching the ground.

Medics accompanying the platoon had just finished removing the parachutes from each of the dead men when Staff Sergeant Charles H. Hoyt was hit and knocked to the ground by a sniper's bullet. Several hours earlier, Hoyt had mortally wounded a Japanese marine who had sneaked into the building in which he lay sleeping. But now Hoyt himself lay seriously injured with a Japanese bullet in his chest. A fusillade of shots fired by Flash's men silenced the sniper, thus permitting the medics and a few of the platoon's riflemen to withdraw from that area carrying Sergeant Hoyt and the three dead men. Despite the best efforts of a team of surgeons, Sergeant Hoyt died shortly after being delivered to the regimental aid station in Mile-long Barracks.

Meanwhile, Flash and his remaining platoon members continued through the warehouse area in search of additional missing paratroopers. Having been previously exposed to how very clever the Japanese were at setting deadly booby traps, Flash's men exercised extreme caution when opening the heavy steel door leading into each warehouse. They fastened a steel wire to the door handle, stood well off to one side, then slowly pulled the door fully open. This time-consuming precaution proved unnecessary, however, for the only items found in the warehouses were a few old, badly damaged U.S. Army radios.

On leaving the warehouse area, Flash heard an anguished cry

for help coming from near a railroad track located just below his platoon's position. For a brief moment, he thought this might be an enemy ruse designed to lure him and his men into an ambush. But a second, more pitiful cry convinced him that it could only be coming from a badly injured paratrooper.

Flash and three of his men, Privates First Class Angelos "Greek" Kambakumis, Anthony D. Lopez, and Robert R. O'Connell, took off running downhill. At the railroad tracks they came upon a grisly sight. There, in a gully beside the tracks, lay a horribly wounded paratrooper whose body had been ripped open by shell fragments. Dozens of large green flies swarmed over the sausagelike intestines protruding from gaping holes in the man's abdomen and back. Flash shooed the buzzing insects off the unsightly wounds, then covered them with antiseptic powder and bandages from first aid packets. Then he and his men gently placed the moaning trooper on a slightly twisted bedspring that they pressed into service as a litter.

The rescue party slowly raised the litter and began the strenuous uphill return trip to the warehouse area. Each member of the party carefully chose each step in an effort to provide a smooth ride for the severely wounded trooper.

The rescuers had gotten only halfway up the hill when a sniper took them under fire. The first two enemy bullets passed harmlessly over their heads, but the third bullet struck Flash, wounding him in the left forearm. Although the wound "stung like hell," it did not prevent Flash from continuing to carry his corner of the bedspring.

Next to get hit was Lopez, who sustained a slight leg wound but, like Flash, was able to continue supporting his share of the load.

Knowing that both safety and medical attention awaited them at the top of the slope, the harassed party doggedly continued on, using their own bodies to shield their passenger from additional wounds. When they were only ten feet from the summit, a sniper's bullet passed through Private Kambakumis's midsection without killing him, then richocheted off the steel bedspring and buried itself in O'Connell's left hip.

Kambakumis and O'Connell fell to the ground clutching their

wounds; the wounded litter patient landed beside them with a sickening thud.

At this point, several riflemen from the remainder of Flash's platoon, which had been providing covering fire throughout the recovery effort, rushed forward, scooped up all the wounded, and carried them to safety.

Believing his arm wound to be only minor, Flash decided to remain with his platoon while the other members of the rescue party accompanied the barely living rescued trooper to the regimental aid station. Within the next few hours, however, Flash would also be forced to seek medical attention as the pain in his arm intensified and he became aware that while he could make a fist with his left hand he could not spread his fingers apart. At the aid station, he would be given the bad news that the sniper's bullet had fractured a bone in his arm and severed a radial nerve. Considerable surgery would be required to restore his arm and hand to partial use.

Seizing and clearing Topside's largest fortifications—Batteries Geary and Wheeler—presented Rock Force with a number of serious problems. As the attacking paratroopers had discovered the previous day, the exterior walls and roofs of these American-built fortresses were virtually impervious to aerial bombs, artillery, and even the heaviest naval gunfire. The aboveground interiors contained numerous chambers and separate firing bays for each of the battery's two enormous guns, which faced the open sea. As part of their defensive preparations of the past few months, the Japanese had wisely subdivided the aboveground chambers into reinforced fighting positions so that a hand grenade or satchel charge thrown into one gun port or ventilation shaft would not necessarily neutralize all neighboring chambers. The underground interior of each battery contained a huge double-walled gunpowder magazine plus a number of tunnels leading to fire direction centers, storerooms, and gun crew living quarters.

Gaining entrance to these fortifications would be most difficult for the attacking paratroopers because there were only two means of access. One was the subterranean passageways linking each battery with its adjacent ammunition storage bunkers. The other was a series of aboveground bank-vaultlike steel doors located at the rear of each battery.

On this morning of February 17, Lieutenant William T. Bailey's Company F of Caskey's battalion was given the task of securing Battery Wheeler. Since his company had operated around this same battery the day before, and had encountered only moderate resistance, Bailey believed it to be occupied by just a handful of enemy troops. Accordingly, he sent only his 3d Platoon, commanded by Lieutenant William G. Campbell, to do the job.

Campbell himself was quite new in the regiment, having joined it less than a month earlier as a new graduate of the Army Parachute School at Fort Benning, Georgia. Campbell's lack of battle experience was a source of concern not only to his company commander but his fellow officers as well. On a number of occasions prior to the jump on the Rock, they had given him a crash course in such combat techniques as always keeping his platoon on the alert for surprise attacks, and not sticking his head up in the same place twice when reconning the enemy's positions. Japanese riflemen, cautioned Campbell's friends, were very patient individuals. Whenever they saw an American head come up out of a foxhole they would usually hold their fire, zero in on that spot, and wait for the head to reappear. Then, blam!—right between the horns.

At 9:30 A.M., Campbell moved his platoon from its night defensive positions along Senior Officers Row to the large earthen mound behind Battery Wheeler. Leaving his men protected behind the mound to make final preparations for the attack, Campbell, accompanied by Platoon Sergeant Joseph S. Shropshire, entered a nearby underground bunker which had a large rectangular opening in its top. Climbing on to a concrete table positioned beneath the opening, Campbell raised his head above ground and scanned the rear of the battery with his binoculars. After methodically looking the area over for a few minutes he ducked back inside long enough to tell Shropshire that the battery appeared to be unoccupied. Then, following a few minutes's pause during which Shropshire left briefly to get the men ready to move out, Campbell raised back up for a second look and was instantly killed by a single bullet through his head.

Leaving the dead lieutenant where he had fallen on the table, Sergeant Shropshire exited the bunker and ordered his men to fix bayonets. Seconds later, behind a cloud of smoke generated by their white phosphorous grenades, the platoon charged toward Battery Wheeler.

Meanwhile, back up on Senior Officers Row, Company F's first Platoon leader, Lieutenant Calhoun, had a ringside view of the assault being made against the battery. From his vantage point in a second-floor window of Building 28-D, Calhoun spotted six soldiers running across the battery's broad, flat roof. Believing these men to be members of the attacking 3d Platoon, he cheered out loud as they started up a staircase leading to the number two gun port. But then his heart sank as he watched a stream of tracer bullets suddenly tear into the men, tumbling five of them down the stairs.

Calhoun was "sick, just sick" over what he had witnessed. Only a few minutes later, however, he was "immensely relieved" when word filtered back to Building 28-D that the five men who had just been shot while climbing the stairs were Japanese. A machine gunner from the 3d Platoon was responsible for their deaths.

The attacking 3d Platoon managed to get only halfway to its objective before being pinned to the ground by a pair of Japanese machine guns. Platoon Sergeant Shropshire used every maneuver in the book trying to silence the enemy guns and continue his advance, but none worked.

With the enemy fire growing stronger by the minute, Shropshire had several of his men throw additional white phosphorous grenades toward the battery. Then he ordered a general withdrawal under the concealment of the grenade's billowing clouds of smoke.

Angered by Sergeant Shropshire's unauthorized withdrawal to the attack's starting point, company commander Bailey sent Lieutenant Calhoun to take charge of the platoon and get it moving forward again. About a half-hour later, Calhoun was still in the process of reorganizing the men for a second go at the battery when Lieutenant James P. Gifford and his entire 1st Platoon from Company D arrived on the scene.

Gifford informed Calhoun that he and his men had been sent by Lieutenant Joseph A. Turinski, the commanding officer of Company D, to take over the job of seizing Battery Wheeler. Given the difficult situation he had been thrust into only a short while prior to Gifford's arrival, Calhoun received this news with mixed emotions. Then he began spreading his troops along the top of the embankment where they could deliver supporting fire during the renewed attack by Gifford's platoon.

On a loud, "Follow me!" starting signal shouted by Lieutenant Gifford, the Company D men leapt to their feet and began the assault.

Japanese machine gunners, who had been lying in wait for the attack to resume, sprang into action. Their initial adjustment burst struck short of the mark, kicking up dirt in front of the paratroopers who continued to advance using the infantry's standard fire and maneuver drill.

Private Paul A. Hughart was advancing through the smoke screen when he glanced to his right and saw Sergeant Amleto Pucci get hit and fall beside a large shell hole. Taking a few quick sidesteps to where Pucci lay motionless on his back, Hughart looked down and grimaced. There, in the front of Pucci's helmet, was a neat round bullet hole.

Hughart slid into the shell hole to reload his rifle and was joined a few seconds later by two other men, Sergeant Nelson M. Stowe and Corporal James Nagy.

"Where's Pucci?" inquired Stowe.

"That's him lying right out there," replied Hughart. "He's dead; just got a bullet through the head."

Stowe and Nagy crawled out to where Pucci lay and pulled him into the shell hole. All three men were kneeling and looking at the bullet hole drilled squarely in the front of the "dead" man's helmet when he moaned and opened his eyes. The enemy bullet had pierced the helmet at an extremely sharp angle, caromed around its curved interior, and gone out the back, knocking Pucci unconscious in the process. Except for a throbbing headache,

114

and the badly damaged helmet, Sergeant Pucci was none the worse for his brush with death.

Supported by the tremendous volume of small arms fire coming from the Company F troopers deployed along the embankment behind them, Gifford's platoon reached the battery's rear wall. Unable to gain entrance through its locked steel doors, and anxious to continue the momentum of their attack, Gifford's men scrambled up a flight of concrete stairs leading to the roof. On the roof, they encountered wave after wave of Japanese who rushed out to meet them brandishing everything from bayonets to bare knuckles. A fierce free-for-all ensued at extremely close quarters. When the smoke and dust cleared some fifteen minutes later, Battery Wheeler was once again in American hands. Spread across the battery's rooftop were the dead bodies of sixty-three Imperial Marines. The paratroopers of Companies D and F had also suffered a significant number of casualties: six killed and fourteen wounded.

Artillery, "the greatest killer on the battlefield," as instructors in the U.S. Army's Artillery School at Fort Sill, Oklahoma, are fond of saying, played a key role during the clearing of Topside. Time and time again on this high ground, and on many other parts of the Rock, the gunners of the 462d Parachute Field Artillery Battalion would be called upon to bail their paratroop infantry brethren out of extremely difficult tactical situations. And on each occasion their help was requested, the courageous artillerymen proved that what the instructors were saying back at Fort Sill was really true.

During all of their earlier campaigns with Colonel Jones's combat team, the artillerymen of the 462d had utilized their Pack 75 howitzers in the conventional manner. That meant firing shells over the heads of the paratroop infantry onto enemy positions to "soften them up" and make it easier for the infantry to overrun them. On Corregidor's small battlefields, however, the artillerymen had to revert to an old combat firing technique that had not been used by the U.S. Army since Civil War days and would not be used again after World War II until the Vietnam War. This old technique was called direct fire: The artillerymen lowered their howitzer barrels to the horizontal, pointed them straight at the target, and then yanked the lanyard, usually scoring a first-round hit. For obvious reasons, the artillerymen had to be in the front lines, right alongside the infantry, when using direct fire.

About midmorning on the seventeenth, a platoon from Captain Hudson Hill's Company E trapped a large force of Imperial Marines in a concrete bunker that had only one doorway and one window. Positioned midway between Battery Wheeler and Mile-long Barracks, the bunker overlooked all foot traffic routes connecting those two locations.

Even though they did not have a flamethrower team or demolition men available to assist them, the Company E paratroopers tried rushing the bunker by themselves. However, they were almost immediately beaten back by a tremendous volume of rifle and machine gun bullets spewing forth from the doorway and window. Seeing that he could not neutralize the bunker with the light infantry weapons available to him, the paratroop platoon leader requested artillery support.

Not quite fifteen minutes later, Captain Henry W. "Hoot" Gibson, the commanding officer of the 462d's Battery B, arrived on the scene with several of his men and two Pack 75s. While the paratroop infantrymen took cover and kept a steady drumbeat of rifle fire on the bunker, Gibson's men dragged their howitzers to the top of a small exposed knoll overlooking the bunker.

The range from the howitzer to the bunker was a mere 200 yards. With Japanese bullets cracking over the heads of both gun crews and himself, Gibson directed one gunner to lay in on the bunker's door and the other gunner to lay in on its window. Then he had each piece shoot one HE (high-explosive) round. These initial rounds hit left of their targets, but the next few were right on the money, smashing both the doorway and window. Seeing this, Gibson ordered both pieces to continue fire, alternating high-explosive and white phosphorous rounds.

When Gibson started seeing flashes of secondary explosions within the bunker, and thick clouds of smoke pouring from both openings, he ordered his gunners to cease fire. At that the Company E troopers advanced to the bunker's door, encountering no further resistance along the way. Still not taking any chances, a

116

paratrooper tossed a grenade into the bunker, waited for it to detonate, then went in shooting. Seconds later, he came back out to report that all within the bunker were dead.

Gibson took both of his gunners with him and walked through the bunker with the platoon leader, finding the bodies of dead Imperial Marines "lying all over the place." Some of the uniforms on the Japanese were still smoldering from the white phosphorous shell fragments. Between them, Gibson and the paratroop infantry platoon leader counted eighty-five dead. Thanks to the courageous efforts of the artillerymen who had remained out in the open in full view of the enemy while firing at the bunker, not one American life was lost in this action.

Colonel Jones, the Rock Force commander, and Major Melvin R. Knudson, the commander of the 462d Artillery, had witnessed this entire action from Mile-long Barracks. As a result, Gibson and the two Pack 75 gunners were subsequently awarded the Silver Star for having distinguished themselves during the taking of the bunker.

At 8:30 A.M. on this second day of the operation, American aircraft engines could be heard roaring above Corregidor once again as a long skytrain of C-47s from Colonel John Lackey's 317th Troop Carrier Group began passing over the Rock in single file. Seated aboard the C-47s was Major Robert H. "Pug" Woods and his 1st Battalion of the 503d plus Battery A of the 462d Artillery.

In the original battle plan for retaking the Rock, this entire third lift was to have parachuted onto Topside just as the first two lifts had done. However, the jump had been canceled by Colonel Jones the previous night and a coded radio message to that effect had been transmitted to Major Woods back on Mindoro. For some unexplained reason, Woods never received the message until the morning of the seventeenth as he and his men were chuting up for the jump.

The message stated that the entire third lift would be flown from Mindoro to Luzon's San Marcelino Airfield and then taken by ship to Corregidor's Black Beach. Knowing that Postelthwait's infantrymen had already landed over Black Beach, Woods naturally assumed that his amphibious landing would be unopposed.

To save his troopers the trouble of carrying their heavy equipment and ammunition boxes already packed inside padded paradrop bundles all the way from Black Beach up to Topside, Woods formulated a plan with the 317th's commander, Colonel Lackey. It called for the aircraft to pass over the Rock en route to Luzon, dropping all the bundles on Topside's parade field drop zone in the process.

Since much of Corregidor had already been occupied by Rock Force, both Woods and Lackey were confident that their plan for dropping the bundles on Topside was tactically sound. However, as frequently happens with plans that appear workable at conception, this one ran into a few problems during its execution.

Because the paratroopers who had been dropped the previous day were still in such close proximity to the Japanese positions, American bomber and fighter aircraft were unable to provide the usual suppressive fire to protect the incoming troop carriers of the third lift. This resulted in Japanese antiaircraft fire being considerably stronger than it had been during the dropping of the first and second lifts the day before. Sixteen of the forty-four troop carriers passing over the island were holed, thus proving the wisdom of Colonel Jones's decision to have this third lift come in by sea. Casualties aboard the fully loaded C-47s amounted to one dead and five wounded.

As heavy as it was, the Japanese antiaircraft fire did not seriously interfere with the dropping of the third lift's equipment bundles, most of which landed well inside the parade ground target area. All aircraft in the flight continued on to San Marcelino, landing safely without further incident. Waiting ambulances whisked the five wounded troopers to a nearby field hospital.

Within moments after touching down at San Marcelino, Major Woods and his troopers were transported by trucks to the Subic Bay dock area. There they boarded a small fleet of LCMs which shoved off at noon on the first leg of a three-hour voyage south to Corregidor.

Back on the Rock, meanwhile, one of the most important operations of the day—forging a linkup between the paratroopers and infantrymen—was just beginning along the road connecting

Topside and Bottomside. The plan for this operation had been worked out by Major Ernest C. Clark, Rock Force S-3. It called for one company of paratroopers to attack downhill from the west and one infantry company from Lieutenant Colonel Postlethwait's battalion to attack uphill from the east. Knowing that many sections of that two-mile-long stretch of road were still controlled by the Japanese, all of the paratroopers and infantrymen participating in this operation expected they would soon be involved in some hard fighting.

Only fifteen minutes before the linkup operation was to commence, Postlethwait's medical detachment received a radio message from Rock Force headquarters requesting an emergency resupply of plasma and whole blood. Overhearing that message when it came into his command post, Postlethwait decided to send the lifesaving supplies up to Topside in the safest container at his disposal: a Sherman tank.

Two tankers, Sergeant William Hartman of Peoria, Illinois, and Corporal Michael J. Nolan of New York, volunteered their Sherman, nicknamed "Sad Sack," to serve as both an armored spearhead of the uphill attack and as a delivery vehicle for the blood supplies.

Hartman and Nolan loaded the precious cargo aboard the tank themselves, stowing it in the hull's forwardmost compartment where the protective armor was some four inches thick. Moments later, the attack got under way. With a great roar of its engine, Sad Sack surged ahead of the infantrymen who cursed the tankers for leaving behind an enormous cloud of yellow road dust and blue exhaust smoke.

Japanese machine gun bullets were noisily beating against Sad Sack's turret when Sergeant Hartman looked through one of the periscope vision slits and spotted a shell-damaged bridge only fifty yards ahead. The bridge lay slightly askew and there was a jagged gap in its midsection.

Throwing caution to the wind, Hartman yelled down to driver Nolan—who could also see that the bridge was damaged—"Give her the gas, Mike. We've got to chance it. There's lots of wounded jump boys up there on Topside who might die if we don't get through with this stuff!"

Sad Sack weighed thirty-four tons. Either the bridge would hold or it would not. The broad steel caterpillarlike tracks clanked over the jagged gap, overlapping each side of the span by nearly six inches. The bridge groaned loudly several times, but did not collapse.

Safely across, Hartman and Nolan continued guiding the tank past a number of caves from which the Japanese delivered a steady stream of small arms fire against the hull and turret. Fortunately, the enemy troops defending the road had no anti-tank weapons available to them.

The tankers made it all the way to Topside, grinding to a halt in a cloud of dust directly in front of Mile-long Barracks. Paratroopers cheered as Sergeant Hartman threw open the turret hatch and emerged clutching an armful of plasma packets. Grateful medics took the blood supplies and hurried off toward the regimental aid station. Others unloaded a few five-gallon cans of water that Hartman had also thought to bring along.

"I'd be very grateful if you could bring us some more water, sergeant," a paratroop doctor said to Hartman. "We're almost out of it up here."

"Don't worry, sir," replied Hartman. "We'll get you some more right away."

Hartman and Nolan ran the gauntlet again. This time, however, they stopped along the road occasionally to turn the turret and fire point-blank into caves whose occupants had been particularly offensive during the first run.

Returning safely to Bottomside after delivering the water, Hartman and Nolan dismounted and began counting the bullet scars on the hull and turret. When the number reached 200 they stopped counting.

When Postlethwait's infantry company reached the halfway point on the way up to Topside, it suddenly came under fire from Japanese riflemen located in a series of caves overlooking the road. The Americans dropped to the ground and began fire and movement drills aimed at eliminating the enemy force. But when the infantry captain directing this frontal assault saw that he was unable to quickly close on the caves, he sent for Lieutenant William E. Blake. This was the same Lieutenant Blake who, along with most of the 503d's demolition section, jumped on Bataan after one engine of their drop plane had burst into flames the day before. Blake and his paratroopers had arrived on Corregidor by boat only a few hours earlier. On learning that Postlethwait was sending a rifle company to link up with Topside's paratroopers, Blake asked that he and his men be permitted to tag along on the end of that column.

Crouched beside the infantry captain in a roadside ditch, Blake observed six cave openings within a stretch of some twenty yards along an embankment. Because the caves were so close together, Blake decided to attempt neutralizing three of them at once. The infantry captain's men then shifted their automatic weapons fire to the three cave openings on the left while Blake and his troopers went after the first three on the right.

Blake and two of his men, Corporal Willie J. "Andy" Anderson and Private Delbert L. Parsons, belly-crawled to within ten feet of the caves. An Imperial Marine heard them coming and tossed out a grenade which exploded well off to one side, wounding Anderson slightly in both legs. The flamethrower Anderson had strapped to his back was undamaged.

Blake countered by throwing a white phosphorous (WP) grenade squarely into the cave from which the enemy grenade had just come. As white smoke boiled out that entrance, Blake threw a second WP at the cave next door. But this time his aim was bad. It struck beside the opening, bounced backward, and exploded, showering himself and his two men with burning particles of phosphorous.

Undeterred by this minor disaster, and disregarding his own painful leg wounds, Andy Anderson struggled to an upright position. Then he lunged at the first three cave openings, spraying each them with his flamethrower.

Seconds later, a total of nine screaming Japanese came running out of the caves, their bodies aflame from head to foot. They ran straight into Private Parsons, knocking him over. Some of the burning fluid dripping off their bodies fell on Parsons, setting parts of his clothing on fire. He doused it quickly, then turned around and saw the infantrymen who had been supporting his team shoot all nine Japanese as they raced past in flames.

After sealing the first three caves with explosives, Lieutenant Blake and his assistants turned their attention to the remaining three. They had only taken a few steps when a lone Imperial Marine came to the entrance of one the caves slowly waving a badly soiled piece of white cloth. A couple of trigger-happy paratroopers opened fire, driving him back into the cave. But twice more he approached the entrance, sticking out only the hand holding the cloth and shaking it violently. And both times he was driven back inside again by the paratroopers who fired wildly, scoring many hits on the cloth but none on the hand.

Blake became angry with his troopers, ordering them to cease fire. "Knock it off," he shouted. "We need to get our hands on a live prisoner!" Blake then pressed against the hillside just outside the cave entrance where he began hearing angry Japanese voices and the obvious sounds of a scuffle taking place inside. Hearing this, Blake surmised that the lone Imperial Marine was trying to leave the cave and his buddies were attempting to prevent him from doing so.

Suddenly the scuffling sounds ceased and the enemy marine walked out into the daylight. He was in extremely bad condition, bleeding from the mouth, eyes, ears, and nose. On seeing the man's extensive bleeding, Blake concluded that the six caves must lead to a single large underground chamber and that the concussion generated by the sealing of the first three entrances had inflicted these multiple injuries.

A couple of infantrymen led the dazed prisoner away. With murderous expertise, Blake's demolition men set TNT charges around the three remaining cave entrances. Moments later they blew them shut and moved on, leaving the remaining cave occupants to slowly die of asphyxiation. During the next two days, Blake's demo men would seal an additional forty-three caves along the Topside to Bottomside roadway.

It was nearing 1:30 P.M. on the seventeenth when Lieutenant Colonel Postlethwait's infantrymen linked up with the paratroopers advancing downhill from Topside. The meeting took place on Middleside, right where the main road doglegs sharply to the north for a quarter of a mile before turning westward again at the ruins of the Rock's old aboveground hospital.

Upon hearing that the linkup had taken place, Postlethwait dispatched two jeeps to Topside. Each jeep pulled a trailer loaded with five-gallon water cans for the thirsty paratroopers. Rock Force's S-4 (supply officer), Captain Robert M. Atkins, of Miami, Florida, used one jeep and its trailer to retrieve Major Wood's equipment bundles, many of which were still widely scattered across Topside. Colonel Jones hopped aboard the second jeep and went down to Bottomside to shake Postlethwait's hand. As recorded by Jan Valtin, the 34th Infantry Regiment's historian, that meeting was every bit as dramatic as the nineteenth-century meeting between Stanley and Livingston in the African Congo. The meeting between the two commanders lasted only a half-hour, after which Jones returned to his headquarters in Mile-long Barracks.

Light skirmishing was still in progress on Topside when, shortly after 3:00 P.M., the fleet of LCMs bearing Major Wood's battalion began approaching the "fully secure" debarkation points on Black Beach. As the first few LCMs were attempting to push their bows into the sand they were greeted by heavy machine gun fire from caves along the east face of Topside's cliffs. Fortunately, the initial bursts of enemy fire were poorly aimed. Most of the rounds passed over the crowded decks of the LCMs. But still, six paratroopers and one sailor were killed before coxswains aboard the LCMs at the shoreline could hurriedly back their vessels out of harm's way.

When all of the LCMs had pulled back, the destroyer *Claxton* steamed in close to the shoreline and began firing its five-inch guns into the cave mouths with pinpoint accuracy. Several marksmen from the 34th Infantry on Bottomside also took the caves under fire. Finally, the enemy machine guns were silenced, thus enabling the first wave of LCMs to again approach the shoreline.

This second landing attempt was uncontested and, except for three paratroopers who very nearly drowned under the weight of their equipment while wading ashore, was entirely successful. But with the sun already beginning to set, the landing had occurred very far behind schedule.

Due to the lateness of the hour—it was nearing 7:00 P.M.—Colonel Jones instructed Major Woods to form his battalion into a perimeter defense there on Bottomside for the night and move up to Topside in the morning.

By nightfall of the seventeenth, the paratroopers on Topside had been pulled back into a perimeter defensive position slightly larger than the one they had occupied the previous night. Major Caskey's 2d Battalion was now responsible for defending Mile-long Barracks, both drop zones, Senior Officer's Row, plus the prewar administrative buildings and Battery Wheeler. Lieutenant Colonel Erickson's 3d Battalion area had been extended to include all of Morrison Hill, the prewar movie theater and Officer's Club, plus the western half of Middleside.

In addition to having established a ground linkup with Topside this day, Lieutenant Colonel Postlethwait's infantry battalion had been kept very busy consolidating and strengthening its many positions stretching across Bottomside and the top of Malinta Hill.

Over in the North Dock area of Bottomside, two rifle platoons from Company I had spent much of the day locating and closing cave openings. Using the same technique as the paratroopers on Topside, at day's end those two platoons reported that they had blasted shut a total of thirty-one cave openings.

Escorted by a Sherman tank with the words "Murder, Inc." painted across its turret, the soldiers of Company A had conducted a limited reconnaissance patrol along Bottomside's north shore road. As they were moving along the part of the road that curves around the northern base of Malinta Hill, the infantrymen came upon the entrance of a cave that had been carved far into the hillside. Seeing that the entrance was large enough to accommodate a truck, and hearing a lot of shouting within the cave, the infantrymen assumed it must contain a sizable enemy force. So they prudently backed away from the entrance and signaled "Murder, Inc." to come forward.

The tank's gunner stuck the muzzle of the main battle gun just inside the cave entrance and paused for a moment to see if any Japanese would take the hint and come out to surrender. But all he got for his troubles was a blast of rifle fire that bounced harmlessly off the turret's thick skin.

Bullets were still chipping paint when the gunner fired one

round of high explosive, which produced a great deal of screaming and a few shouted orders within the cave but failed to put a stop to the rifle fire.

Convinced that the Japanese had opted to die fighting rather than come out and be taken prisoner, the tank gunner fired two more rounds of high explosive. Each of those rounds set off secondary explosions that violently shook the cave's interior, causing tons of sand and rock to come crashing down from the ceiling and walls. Demolition men completed the job, using TNT to close what little remained of the cave's once large entrance.

While those patrolling and cave-closing operations were taking place on Bottomside, Companies K and L of Postlethwait's infantry battalion continued to occupy their positions spread across the barren crest of Malinta Hill. At a little after noon on the seventeenth, Company L dispatched a ten-man patrol with a supply of TNT to blast shut two cave openings that had been sighted on the eastern slope of the hill. The first cave was unoccupied and rather small, requiring only a few blocks of explosives to seal its entrance.

The patrol moved a little further down the hill to the second cave, which was much larger than the first and also seemed to be unoccupied. At the direction of the patrol leader, all remaining TNT blocks were placed along the sides and top of the entrance. Rather than being sealed shut by the mighty blast that followed, almost the entire cave, plus a small section of the hillside, was blown wide open. Ten badly shaken Imperial Marines staggered out into the open and were shot dead by the Americans perched above them.

Late in the afternoon of the seventeenth, Lieutenant Henry G. Kitnik, the commanding officer of Company K, 34th Infantry, managed to reestablish radio contact with his 3d Platoon riflemen still stranded out on Goal Post Ridge and Little Knob. Under orders to "sit tight" on Malinta Hill, Kitnik could not yet mount a rescue operation. However, through a series of radio transmissions with the platoon sergeant, he learned that his marooned soldiers were still holding their own and that they had killed four Japanese soldiers from Engineer Point who accidentally wandered into their position while searching for drinking water.

Silence had overtaken the island when, a half-hour before midnight on the seventeenth, the Japanese made another desperate attempt to seize control of Malinta Hill. Using all the cunning and stealth they could muster, a company of Imperial Marines managed to climb undetected to within thirty feet of of the American lines atop the hill.

An alert corporal in Company K was the first to hear them coming. He immediately launched a flare which silhouetted nearly 200 Japanese crawling straight up the side of the hill.

For the riflemen of Company K, it was like shooting fish in a barrel. Virtually every bullet they fired stuck one or more of the enemy, who fell away screaming. The Americans gave no quarter during this encounter. As mounds of writhing Japanese wounded began to build at the bottom of the hill, they dropped hand grenades down on top of them.

This surprise night assault ended almost as quickly as it began. Company K suffered twenty-two casualties, one of whom was Lieutenant Kitnik, who had taken command of the company earlier in the day upon the death of Captain Frank Centenni. Kitnik was a native of Broughton, Pennsylvania. He was succeeded as company commander by a fellow Pennsylvanian, Lieutenant Robert R. Fugitti of Philadelphia.

By the light of the moon, Lieutenant Fugitti made his way along the crest of Malinta Hill gathering head counts from his surviving platoon leaders. The final tally was most disturbing: only thirty-eight men and three officers remained. And almost a quarter of those survivors—including Fugitti himself—were walking wounded cases.

At 3:00 A.M., the Japanese made still another attempt to storm Malinta Hill. As had happened during their first two attempts, the full weight of this attack also fell upon the decimated ranks of Company K. Flares were launched, again exposing numerous figures crawling up the steep incline. Undeterred at having been discovered short of their objective once again, a squad of Imperial Marines tried making a frontal assault but they were immediately cut down by machine gun fire. The fighting lasted a full hour before what was left of the Japanese attackers stampeded back down the hill.

Lieutenant Fugitti took another head count, discovering that his company strength had been further reduced to just thirty-three effectives. While medics sorted out the dead and wounded, Fugitti quickly repositioned the battered survivors at several points along the crest of the hill where they could best repel another attack if it should come. When dawn finally broke about an hour later, the infantrymen of Company K looked down on 150 Japanese corpses spread grotesquely along the base of the hill.

During the time that the Japanese were making their unsuccessful midnight attempt to seize Malinta Hill, several paratroopers guarding Topside's Battery Wheeler began hearing suspicious noises in the basement. Before they could go below and investigate, a great explosion shook the entire battery and lit up the sky as if it were midday. Unknown to the paratroopers, a Japanese suicide detachment had used a subterranean passageway to gain entrance to the battery and ignite its main gunpowder magazine.

Terrified by the tremendously loud explosions and the sheets of flame being generated by the burning gunpowder below them, the paratroopers abandoned the battery and ran for cover. While doing so, they literally ran into a squad of Imperial Marines who had infiltrated the American lines and were also running away from the battery in search of safety.

United only in their common desire to escape disaster, the Japanese and Americans continued running side by side. Suddenly a series of pistol shots rang out and the two groups parted company. One American, Private First Class Thomas T. DeLane, was killed; two other paratroopers were seriously wounded. As for the Japanese, they vanished into the darkness that had made it extremely difficult for both sides to distinguish friend from foe during this unusual incident.

Now that every element of Rock Force was ashore, and the second day of fighting had drawn to a close, a clear-cut pattern for reclaiming Corregidor had been established. The island's small size, rugged terrain, and the maze of interconnecting tunnels, caves, and bunkers precluded maneuver by units much larger than a platoon. This meant that the Americans were going to have to conduct a campaign of small-unit assaults using automatic weapons, hand grenades, flamethrowers, all manner of explosive devices, and even point-blank howitzer fire to eliminate the diehard Japanese defenders.

By midnight of the seventeenth, Colonel Jones came to the harsh realization that the Sixth Army intelligence estimates of only 600 Japanese on Corregidor were grossly incorrect. Already, in only two days of fighting, nearly 900 dead Japanese had been counted, with a great many others buried in caves that had been sealed with explosives.

Word of the faulty intelligence estimate and the actual body count totals quickly filtered down to the infantrymen and paratroopers of Rock Force. Such information is impossible to keep from the combat soldiers, for they are the ones who do the actual fighting and provide higher headquarters the counts.

Since their arrival on Corregidor, many of the Americans have already experienced at least one close brush with death. But now they knew the worst part of this battle was yet to come.

9
BANZAI!

Sunday, February 18, the third day of the operation, was very nearly a replay of the previous day's events. At a little after 5:00 A.M. Major Woods and his 1st Battalion of paratroopers, which had landed amphibiously over Black Beach the previous day and spent the night on Bottomside, began the uphill march to Topside. Although the long winding road was by this time officially open, much of it passed through areas still being patrolled by the Japanese. The battalion did encounter some light resistance at a few turns along the way, but all of it was quickly brushed aside. By 7:00 A.M., the battalion's leading company began arriving on Topside. As the last of his perspiration-soaked troopers entered the perimeter a short while later, Woods issued an order for the entire battalion to take a rest break in place. Then he proceeded to the regimental headquarters in Mile-long Barracks to receive his unit's mission.

Now that Colonel Jones finally had all three of his regiment's parachute infantry battalions together on the same piece of real estate he decided to reposition some of the units defending Topside. In this latest tactical arrangement, Major Woods's newly arrived 1st Battalion was designated the regimental reserve and directed to occupy the southern third of the perimeter, overlooking Manila Bay. There Woods deployed his three rifle companies along a curved defensive line that began in the east at Breakwater

129

Point and extended westward through Senior Officers Row to Battery Wheeler.

At Battery Wheeler, Woods tied in by fire with Major Caskey's 2d Battalion, the left flank of which was relocated to the neighboring Battery Cheney. The remainder of Caskey's battalion was strung northward along an arc that fronted the South China Sea and terminated at the head of James Ravine.

At James Ravine, Caskey tied in with Lieutenant Colonel Erickson's 3d Battalion, whose left flank rested atop Morrison Hill. The balance of Erickson's battalion was positioned along a curve that trailed away to the southeast overlooking the distant Bataan Peninsula and Corregidor's Bottomside area. Erickson's right flank terminated just south of Ramsay Ravine. From there he tied in by fire with Major Woods's 1st Battalion troops at Breakwater Point, thus completing Colonel Jones's enlarged circular defensive plan.

During this repositioning of forces a freak accident occurred in the 2d Battalion's area. Private First Class William W. Lee was a rifleman in Company F's 2d Platoon. Like many of his companions, Lee had received a number of bumps and bruises parachuting onto the Rock. But rather than complain about having been injured, he quietly went about his duties knowing that the pain would go away in a few days as it always does after a rough landing. With all of the excitement that took place during the night out at Battery Wheeler, and along Company F's portion of the perimeter, Lee and his companions had gotten very little sleep. So during the initial early morning shifting of forces Lee's platoon was withdrawn to Building 27-D, a bomb-damaged warehouse located well inside the perimeter. There the platoon members were permitted to take a brief rest break before completing the remainder of the move to their new defensive sector. Lee and several members of the platoon walked into an empty room where they each cleared a section of the debris covered floor just large enough to lie down on and take a short nap. Slipping his pack off, Lee let it fall to the floor at the precise spot he selected for it to serve as a pillow. Then he laid down and—referring to the troubled sector of the perimeter his platoon had just left—said, "Boy, am I glad to be out of there!" At that moment a large chunk of concrete fell from the ceiling and struck his head, killing him instantly.

The systematic search for those Japanese forces remaining on Topside and the Rock's lower elevations resumed at 7:30 A.M. when a reinforced platoon of paratroopers from Captain Hudson Hill's Company E began moving down into James Ravine. Leading the platoon was Lieutenant Joseph M. Whitson, a native of Nashville, Tennessee. Today was his twenty-third birthday.

Today, Lieutenant Whitson's platoon was being sent down into the Rock's James Ravine with orders to accomplish three important tasks that had been assigned to Company E: (1) destroy the underground infantry barracks which captured documents revealed the Japanese had recently dug into the ravine's west wall; (2) determine the serviceability of a freshwater pumping station known to have been in use at the bottom of the ravine when Corregidor was surrendered to the Japanese; and (3) destroy an electrical sea mine control system believed to be located somewhere in the ravine.

The third task in Whitson's mission was of great importance to the small fleet of American warships supporting the army's ground operations on the Rock. Skippers aboard the warships noticed that whenever they sailed the waters between the southern tip of the Bataan Peninsula and Corregidor, sea mines were prematurely detonated in their paths. The explosion of those mines led U.S. naval intelligence experts to conclude that Japanese ship spotters and a mine control center were located somewhere in James Ravine.

James Ravine itself was a narrow, precipitious defile that had been carved into Corregidor's sheer northern cliffs during the past several centuries by natural forces. Some 300 feet below Topside the ravine's triangular floor had a large concrete rainwater drainage ditch running through its center. The floor's area was rather large, measuring 300 yards at the shoreline and tapering back to 10 feet at the base of the cut. The only way for foot traffic to move from Topside to the bottom of the ravine was by travelling a narrow unpaved road that had been hewn out of the ravine's near vertical walls by U.S. Army engineer troops in the 1920s. At the base of the ravine's west wall were the entrances to the underground infantry barracks and a powder magazine. The freshwater pumping station was located at the ravine floor's eastern edge, only twenty feet from the shoreline. A concrete pillbox was positioned at the ravine's narrowest point where its occupants could deliver aimed fire all across the shoreline and the roadway coming down from Topside.

Whitson's platoon had advanced only fifty yards along the road leading into the ravine when it received fire from a Nambu machine gun. With an opening three-round adjustment burst from a concealed position somewhere along the ravine floor, the Japanese machine gunner managed to kill the platoon's lead scout, Private First Class James S. Segobia. The enemy gunner quickly shifted his point of aim to Private First Class Edward T. Redfield, the next man in line, and wounded him severely with a second burst of three.

Realizing that they had walked right into the enemy's line of fire, Whitson's men withdrew several yards before hitting the dirt and taking cover along the shoulders of the road. As was his custom during such situations, Whitson rushed forward at a crouch from his position in the middle of the platoon to see exactly what had happened. Arriving at the head of his troops, he dropped to the ground and crawled on all fours until he was within ten feet of where the badly wounded Private Redfield lay motionless in a ditch beside the road. Machine gun bullets were kicking up clods of dirt all around Redfield's partially protected position, making his rescue an impossibility until the enemy gun was silenced. Whitfield slapped a clip of tracer ammo into his carbine and motioned a nearby Browning automatic rifleman, Private Carroll F. Redding, to come forward and join him.

The lieutenant pointed down in the general direction of the machine gun nest then squeezed off three fast tracer rounds to clearly mark its location. He said to Redding, "I'm going to run out and drag Redfield back here where our medic can go to work on him. You keep that machine gunner's head down until I get back in here with Redfield. I'll take off running just as soon as you start shooting."

Enemy riflemen were also beginning to fire on his grounded platoon as Whitson turned toward the wounded trooper and raised himself up, cocking one leg like a runner in the blocks waiting for the starter's pistol shot. Keeping his eyes riveted on the wounded trooper to his front, Whitson waited for his automatic rifleman to start firing. When some thirty seconds had passed and there still was no sound of his covering fire Whitson became annoyed. Turning around, he saw Private Redding slumped dead on top of his weapon. He had been killed by a sniper's bullet.

Seeing what had happened, several riflemen from Whitson's platoon slithered forward on their bellies to the edge of the road where they began banging away at the machine gun nest. Whitson then dashed out to Private Redfield and dragged him back to safety. But this valiant rescue action proved to be in vain as the grievously wounded Redfield died within minutes after being rescued.

With three of his men already killed on this mission, and a heavy volume of enemy rifle and machine gun fire continuing to boil up from the floor of the ravine, Lieutenant Whitson realized that his platoon was heading into the jaws of a meat grinder. Ordering his men to stay put until further notice, Whitson radioed his commander, Captain Hill, to tell him of the situation and request heavy fire support before continuing with the mission. Hill agreed that the time had come to ask for some assistance.

"Pull your platoon back inside the perimeter," said Hill, "I'm going to ask the air controller at Rock Force headquarters to direct an air strike into James Ravine."

Pleased that his platoon would be getting a helping hand, Whitson moved his men, including those who had been killed, back inside the perimeter to await developments. Not quite an hour later, a flight of barrel-chested P-47 Thunderbolts arrived high above Corregidor from their base on Mindoro. Guided by the air controller who had direct radio contact with them, the P-47s swooped down one at a time, dropping napalm pods and 500-pound fragmentation bombs into James Ravine with deadly accuracy.

When the last P-47 had completed its attack, Captain Hill sent Whitson's platoon back down into the ravine. This time the paratroopers made it all the way to the ravine floor unmolested. Numerous small fires were churning out thick clouds of smoke that obscured nearly all of the ravine's terrain features. Nevertheless, Whitson was able to see well enough to discover the location of a large concrete door and several ventilation shafts all of which bore signs of recent construction. Obviously, thought Whitson, this must be the entrance to the underground infantry barracks that was mentioned in recently captured Japanese documents. The charred bodies of eight Japanese lay near the large concrete door, further convincing Whitson that he had found the enemy's hideaway. For a brief moment, Whitson considered opening the door for a look-see. But since it was by then late in the day and the ground smoke was becoming intolerable, Whitson withdrew his platoon to Topside where he reported his discovery to Captain Hill.

Early in the morning of the nineteenth, Captain Hill put in a request to Rock Force headquarters for one of the U.S. Navy's destroyers to fire a few salvos into James Ravine to soften it up for Whitson's platoon. At a little after 9:00 A.M., a destroyer hove into view just off the island's western shoreline and began blasting away at the ravine's lower elevations. This bombardment lasted a full hour, after which Whitson's platoon and its attached engineer demolition section marched unopposed all the way down to the ravine floor.

The first thing Whitson noticed upon reaching the ravine floor was that the eight bodies he had sighted the day before were gone. This aroused his suspicion that something was very wrong. But not as much as what he next came across. There on the ground just outside the entrance to the underground barracks were three machine guns. They had fresh boxes of ammunition stacked beside them and were aimed at the road coming down from Topside. Clearly, thought Whitson, there were a number of combat-ready Japanese still in the ravine and they had literally been caught off guard by his late morning arrival.

Whitson was busy examining the machine guns when he heard muffled Japanese voices coming from inside the underground barracks. Motioning his men to spread out and get ready for action, he silently walked up to the door, and found it to be slightly ajar. Peeking inside, his heart nearly stopped as he looked straight into the eyes of an Imperial Marine who was standing just inside the door. Whitson briskly pulled the door wide open so as to have a wide field of fire. But in so doing, he tripped a booby trap that exploded in his face.

The force of the explosion blew the barracks door off its hinges and knocked Whitson to the ground. During the next few moments he was nearly trampled to death by stampeding Japanese who gushed out of the barracks and ran into the gunsights of the waiting paratroopers. The end result of this encounter was a terrible slaughter. Sixty-five Japanese were killed before they suddenly stopped pouring out into the open. The voices of many more Japanese could be heard inside the barracks but they refused to come out and surrender. Why the Imperial Marines foolishly neglected to keep a guard on duty outside the barracks is something that will forever be known only to them.

The frenzied shooting had just stopped when the platoon's lead scout, Private Elmer L. Kernodle, hurried over to the barracks entrance where Lieutenant Whitson lay under a pile of dead Japanese. Whitson was alive, but just barely. The booby trap's fiery shotgunlike blast had burned his face, singed nearly all the hair off his head, and peppered the front of his body with dozens of steel fragments. A medic succeeded in stopping all the bleeding, then he directed a team of riflemen to carry Whitson up to Topside's regimental aid station.

With Whitson now out of action, command of the platoon passed to his assistant, Lieutenant Lewis B. Crawford, who immediately proceeded to eliminate the remaining Japanese trapped inside the barracks. Crawford instructed a few riflemen to watch the barracks entrance while a team of paratroop demolition men placed explosives around it and the ventilation shafts. Then, to insure destruction of the barracks Crawford had the demolition men pour ten gallons of napalm, which had been brought along for this purpose, into the ventilation shafts. Once those preparations were complete, all but one of the paratroopers slowly backed away from the target area and took cover. On a signal from Crawford, the lone demo man still at the target lit the fuse and ran back to join his companions. The resulting explosion and landslide shook the earth beneath the paratroopers for several minutes, completely sealing the barracks entrance with tons of sand and limestone.

Having destroyed the barracks, Crawford reformed the platoon and set out with it to determine the serviceability of the ravine's freshwater pumping station. Prewar maps of the Rock showed the pumping station to be located on the beach near Morrison Point. With drinking water now in very short supply for all of Rock Force, Colonel Jones had high hopes that the pumps would be found in working condition or, at the very least, in a state that could eventually be repaired. However, the paratroopers found the pumping station to be destroyed beyond any possibility of repair. Crawford at once radioed the bad news to Captain Hill who in turn informed Rock Force headquarters.

The third and final part of the platoon's mission in James Ravine was to find the sea mine control system which naval intelligence strongly suspected was located there. Lieutenant Crawford dispatched squad-size patrols to various parts of the ravine floor with orders to search for cave openings and underground bunkers capable of housing such a device. At about 4:40 that afternoon, one of the patrols reported finding a sizable cave opening and called Crawford over to see it. Before entering the cave, Crawford had a paratrooper toss a grenade in it and hose down its interior with a Thompson submachine gun. As soon as he stepped inside the cave, Crawford saw that naval intelligence had guessed correctly. Arrayed before him on a long table was an elaborate mine control system composed of 100 knife switches connected in series to a power source of six large batteries each the size of a GI footlocker. Electrical leads ran from each switch to an insulated copper cable six inches in diameter. The cable extended to the far end of the cave where it went underground and then out to the mines floating in Corregidor's north shore shipping channel.

It took the paratroop engineer demolition experts only a few minutes to rig the mine system with quarter-pound blocks of TNT and blow it to smithereens. News of its destruction was flashed up the chain of command to naval intelligence.

Even though all three parts of the James Ravine mission had

been accomplished, other platoon-size combat patrols from Captain Hill's Company E continued mop up and cave-closing operations in the ravine for the next three days. During that time, ten paratroopers were killed and another eleven were wounded in skirmishes with Japanese holdouts found hiding in small caves. All told, Hill's men killed 211 Imperial Marines in the ravine by actual body count. And in his after-action report, Hill estimated that another 250 of the enemy died in the nineteen caves that were sealed along the ravine walls. At the conclusion of its operations in James Ravine, the strength of Company E, which had jumped on the Rock with 134 officers and men, was down to only seventy-five effectives.

While Captain Hill's company was busy cleaning out James Ravine from February 18 to 22, the remainder of Rock Force's paratroopers up on Topside were busy with the grim task of clearing their respective zones of action.

At 10:00 A.M. on the eighteenth, Lieutenant William T. Bailey, the commanding officer of Company F, received orders to launch an attack on Battery Smith and Way Hill, both located some 300 yards west of the perimeter. Upon getting those orders, Bailey walked up to the third floor of Mile-long Barracks where he made a detailed visual reconnaissance of the two objectives with his binoculars. From his vantage point, Bailey could see that Battery Smith and Way Hill were separated by Grubbs Ravine, which fell away to the South China Sea, and that the terrain leading out to the objectives was sparsely wooded.

Because of the heavy casualties his company had sustained since its arrival on the Rock, Bailey reorganized its four platoons into two task forces for this mission. To his senior First Platoon Leader, Lieutenant Bill Calhoun, Bailey gave command of one of the task forces and assigned him the job of capturing Battery Smith, which lay on the left flank in the company's zone of attack. Bailey took personal command of the other task force, which was to storm Way Hill on the company's right flank.

As Lieutenant Calhoun sat at the battle map planning his task force's route of advance along the ridge that ran westward from the perimeter out to Battery Smith he saw that in order to reach that objective he would first have to pass through and around Battery Hearn. From the thorough tactical briefings he had received on Mindoro prior to jumping on the Rock, Calhoun knew that Batteries Smith and Hearn were constructed exactly alike. Each consisted of a single twelve-inch gun mounted on an aboveground circular concrete firing pad. The guns themselves were fully exposed to attack from the air, a fact that resulted in their being knocked out of action by Japanese dive-bombers earlier in the war. Directly behind each gun, to the east, was a twenty-five-foot high earthen mound containing hardened ammunition and gunpowder magazines. American intelligence estimated that the magazines of both batteries were now being used by the Japanese as living quarters and storage facilities.

The two Company F task forces jumped off in the attack at 11:30 A.M. on the eighteenth. Lieutenant Calhoun's force advanced at a rather brisk pace due mainly to the aggressive actions of its intrepid lead scout, Private Lloyd McCarter. Unlike the typical scout who advances into enemy territory slowly and as quietly as possible, and much to the consternation of other scouts operating with him, McCarter advanced very rapidly, often at a trot, pausing only occasionally to spray suspicious areas to the front and flanks with his submachine gun.

A little less than a half-hour after departing Topside, Calhoun's task force reached Battery Hearn. Finding it void of enemy troops and equipment, the paratroopers pressed on toward Battery Smith. At a point 200 yards short of Battery Smith's magazine, Private Richard A. Aimers called to a nearby buddy, Private William McDonald, "Look up on that hill, McDonald, there's a Jap observer standing out in the open and he's looking at us through his binoculars!"

"Don't worry about him," replied McDonald. "We'll take care of him in a few minutes when we get up there."

But Aimers, a native of Tennessee and an expert marksman, *was* concerned that his every move was being watched. So much so that he raised him M-1 rifle and took aim at the observer.

"You'll never in a million years be able to hit him from this range," said McDonald.

Undeterred, Aimers squeezed off a single shot. To the utter amazement of McDonald, the observer's head snapped backward and then he fell to the ground still clutching the binoculars.

Turning to McDonald with a wide grin on his face Aimers said, "Those binoculars are mine."

A short while later, the paratroopers scrambled to the top of the magazine. Aimers and McDonald rushed to where the observer had fallen. He was lying face down in the dirt, the back of his skull blown away. Aimers turned him over and removed the binoculars from his hands. It was then that McDonald saw just how incredibly good a marksman Aimers really was. The left eyepiece of the binoculars had a bullet hole drilled clean through its center as did the dead observer's left eyeball.

Aimers did not appear bothered by the damage to his prize. After blowing some particles of sand out of the damaged eyepiece he casually stuffed the binoculars in his baggy trouserleg pocket. Then he and McDonald began looking around for other souvenirs.

Drawn by curiosity, several other members of Calhoun's task force wandered over to take a close look at Battery Smith's enormous twelve-inch gun. None of these paratroopers had ever before seen such a huge weapon and all were fascinated by it. They walked around the big gun marveling at its immense size. Suddenly, a heavy caliber Japanese machine gun off in the distance opened up on the gawking Americans, scoring no hits but sending them running in all directions. Each time the enemy gunner fired the vegetation around him shook, disclosing his location. Seeing this, Private Benedict J. Schilli, a Browning automatic rifleman, ran out to an exposed position next to the twelve-incher and loosed a long burst into the shaking vegetation, knocking the enemy gun out of action. Moments later, another batch of curious paratroopers were gathered around the twelve-inch gun just as if nothing had happened.

The only other resistance encountered at Battery Smith occurred when a paratrooper attempted to enter an open door leading to the fire direction center and was fired upon by its occupants. The paratrooper escaped alive. Moments later he and a few companions tried coaxing the Japanese to come out and

139

surrender, but they were answered by several more rifle shots through the open doorway. The standoff continued as the Americans brought up a flamethrower team. One more attempt was made to persuade the enemy to come out. When that, too, failed the flamethrower operator lit his match and squeezed the trigger, sending a fiendish stream of fire through the doorway. Seconds later, three Japanese came running out, their hair, skin, and clothing burning fiercely. The waiting paratroopers gunned them down.

Company F's other task force, operating under direct control of its commanding officer, Lieutenant Bailey, seized Way Hill without a fight. From documents found there the paratroopers learned that the enemy had hastily abandoned the hill earlier in the day. Some twenty knapsacks containing Imperial Marine uniforms, bath towels, socks, and shaving articles were found scattered about the hill. While rummaging through one of the knapsacks in search of souvenirs, a lucky paratrooper found a special war trophy: a tablecloth-size Japanese battle flag.

His company's two objectives now fully secured, Lieutenant Bailey dispatched several carrying parties from both task forces back to Topside's perimeter with instructions to grab all the ammunition and grenades they could carry and return as soon as possible. Shortly after the carrying parties had left for Topside, Bailey sent word to Calhoun to pull his task force back to Battery Hearn so that it would be located roughly parallel with Way Hill. Both task forces spent the remainder of the day preparing their respective positions for whatever might come their way during the night.

Corregidor's searing tropical heat and its rugged terrain combined to make drinking water one of the more serious supply problems facing the paratroopers, who were kept constantly on the move in search of the enemy. Each trooper had landed on the Rock with two canteens of water. But by the second day of fighting, most of the canteens had been drained dry. Sergeant Bennett M. Guthrie, a former squad leader in Company H, recalls that, "Troopers would suck on pebbles, share a tongue-moistening swallow of water with a buddy, and even shake the canteens of the fallen enemy for water. Tongues would swell and parched lips would crack in thirst."

The water shortage had long been anticipated by Colonel Jones's S-4 (supply officer), Captain Robert M. "Cracker" Atkins of Miami, Florida. A full week prior to the Corregidor parachute assault, Atkins had met on Mindoro with Chief Warrant Officer Lloyd McCullough, the regiment's parachute maintenance officer, to hammer out a plan for daily airdrops of water, ammunition, canned food, and medical supplies. McCullough was one of America's first paratroopers and an expert in aerial resupply matters. His experience with parachutes dated back to the summer of 1940 when he served as a sergeant in the army's legendary Parachute Test Platoon. At the conclusion of their preassault meeting, Atkins and McCullough agreed upon a plan wherein a single C-47 would pass over Corregidor twice each day at irregular time intervals dropping resupply bundles on the parade field drop zone fronting Mile-long Barracks. As worked out by McCullough, a series of color-coded, twenty-four-foot cotton parachutes would be used to identify the contents of each resupply bundle: red for ammunition and demolition materials, blue for water, yellow for food, white for medical supplies, and green for all other classes of supply.

The initial combat resupply mission was flown at 10:00 A.M. on the seventeenth. As the C-47 passed a bare 200 feet above Topside the first door bundle was kicked out by McCullough's assistant, Master Sergeant John Taylor. The waiting ground recovery crew cheered when they saw a blue chute pop open, indicating a load of fresh drinking water. But the cheering abruptly turned to loud cursing when a sudden wind change caught hold of the parachute, driving the load past the DZ and over the cliffs into the ocean. Subsequent resupply drops had to be made at an altitude of only 100 feet to insure a reasonable degree of accuracy. With one exception, the items coming in by parachute survived the hard landings in good condition. That one exception was the metal five-gallon water cans, which had a tendency to burst open at the seams upon impact.

Another problem confronting Rock Force was the increasing

number of flies that were suddenly appearing all over the island and causing almost as much trouble as the Japanese. Big blue flies, corpse-fattened, buzzed and swarmed and stung. "They were so thick," said one paratrooper, "that they showed up in aerial photographs." Initially, although some flies were noticeable on the Rock, they had not been too troublesome for they disappeared at nightfall and were replaced by mosquitoes. But now with hundreds of unburied Japanese bodies scattered across the landscape, the flies were rapidly multiplying in staggering numbers and tormenting the living both day and night. Some members of Rock Force actually stopped trying to eat for it had become impossible to open a K-ration can without dozens of flies instantly darting inside it and contaminating the food.

With the fly problem becoming more serious by the hour, Colonel Jones summoned Captain Atkins to Rock Force headquarters. "Something's got to be done about these damned flies," declared Jones. "Get on it right away, Cracker!"

From the numerous after-action logistical and medical reports he had read concerning battles fought on other islands scattered throughout the Pacific Theater of Operations, Atkins knew that DDT insecticide had provided the Allied forces with one of the more potent weapons used in tropical warfare. Recently published reports mentioned how the Americans had just developed an effective method of spraying DDT from airplanes. Aerial spraying, said the reports, could rapidly kill off flies and mosquitoes, prevent malaria and dengue for from two to four weeks, and aid greatly in keeping down dysentery and diarrhea.

Armed with that information, Atkins contacted his counterpart at XI Corps headquarters. A few hours later, a B-24 bomber modified with external wing tanks filled with DDT insecticide began crisscrossing the Rock. "Within moments after the aircraft's first pass," remembers Atkins with a chuckle, "the flies began dropping like flies." Two days after this first application, the modified bomber again flew back and forth above the Rock, dispensing a fine mist of the insecticide. The fly infestation was thus rapidly eliminated, bringing great relief to all members of Rock Force, and no doubt to the Japanese defenders as well.

About midday on the eighteenth, a four-man team of medics

from the regimental aid station left Mile-long Barracks accompanied by Sergeant Vernon D. Hoover's squad from Company C, 161st Engineers. The medics were carrying a supply of blood plasma to several badly wounded paratroopers being treated in a temporary aid station that had been established below the cliffs south of the parade field. Sergeant Hoover's squad had been sent along to provide protection.

Moments after exiting the perimeter, this group passed six dead Japanese who appeared to have been machine-gunned at close range. Continuing a little further, the group came to another six Japanese who also had been machine-gunned to death. Advancing cautiously, the group suddenly came under enemy fire and was driven back along the trail without suffering any casualties. After a brief pause, Sergeant Hoover selected an alternate route to the temporary aid station and pushed out again. Running into an enemy roadblock this time, Hoover called his machine gunner, Private First Class Jesse S. Castillo, up front to clear a path through it.

Castillo set his machine gun on the lip of a shell crater and proceeded to zero in on the enemy position. He had only gotten off a few short bursts when the gun jammed. Rapidly clearing his weapon, Castillo relayed on the target and squeezed the trigger. Nothing happened. Frustrated, he tried loading a fresh belt of ammo into the weapon but still it would not fire. In his haste to get the gun back into action, Castillo raised his head about three inches to see what was jamming the firing chamber. Just then a Japanese bullet struck the gun's partially upraised latch cover and ricocheted into Castillo's face. Recalling this incident at the 1990 Static Line Awards Festival in Atlanta, Georgia, Castillo said, "It felt as if someone had hit me in the face with a sledgehammer."

Everything turned blank for Castillo, but he remained conscious. "I'm hit!" he yelled. Medics lifted him out of the shell hole while another engineer knelt behind the gun and struggled to get it working. Shortly thereafter, the group fought its way through the roadblock and delivered the badly needed plasma.

Returning to the perimeter later in the day, Sergeant Hoover went straight to the regimental aid station to check on Castillo's condition. The Japanese bullet had sent bone slivers into both of Castillo's eyes, blinding him for life.

Lieutenant Bill Blake, the 503d Parachute Infantry's demolitions expert, was kept very busy during the first several days of fighting on the Rock. Whenever one of the regiment's rifle company commanders came upon a particularly difficult target requiring explosives to neutralize it, Blake and his wrecking crew were called into action. By the third day of the operation, Blake and his men were so busy they barely had time to answer the call of nature.

During the afternoon of the eighteenth, Captain Joseph M. Conway, the commanding officer of Company H, asked Blake to take a look at a large underground bunker his troops were attempting to knock out. The bunker had formerly been an American antiaircraft gun position, but G-2 (intelligence) suspected that the Japanese had converted it into a munitions storage facility. Large double steel doors protected the bunker's entrance. Fresh air entered the underground chamber through a ventilator shaft protruding from the roof. Conway's troopers had blasted the first steel door open with a bazooka. When they went inside to open the second door they were greeted by a Japanese hand grenade thrown from a small air vent above the door. That's when Blake was called in.

Coincidentally, when Blake received Conway's request for assistance he had just finished concocting a new type of demolition device which he dubbed the "Infernal Machine." The odd-looking device consisted of a five-gallon can of napalm with eight white phosphorous grenades taped around its middle. Around all of that, Blake placed six turns of primer cord and two quarter-pound blocks of TNT on each side of the can. He completed the project by attaching a fifteen-minute fuse that led to a blasting cap in the primer cord.

Blake and his demolition crew arrived in Company H's area with the infernal machine in tow. A quick reconnaissance of the target convinced Blake that the surest way of causing the greatest amount of damage to its interior was to drop his explosive device down the ventilation shaft. However, the main problem with that was that the fifteen-minute fuse—which was to allow Blake and his men time to get out of harm's way before detonation—would also provide the Japanese enough time to disarm the device.

Blake planned to solve that problem by using a net made of primer cord to suspend the infernal machine above the shaft and putting a fuse on the net that was three seconds shorter than the one on the can and lighting them at the same time. When the first fuse popped it would disintegrate the primer cord net, dropping the device down the shaft. Then, if all went according to Blake's calculations, the main charge would explode three seconds later.

While Technical Sergeant Charles W. Hill and Staff Sergeant Roy J. King made final adjustments on the infernal machine, Lieutenant Blake climbed up on the bunker's roof to examine the ventilation shaft opening. Blake was clearing a few loose pieces of concrete from around the opening when he was surprised to hear a voice from the shaft speak to him in English: "I wouldn't do that if I were you—there is very much dynamite down here."

Regaining his composure, Blake called back, "Hi ya, Nip."

"Very much dynamite down here. You will blow us all up."

"Okay, Nip."

"Hokay."

At that point in this unusual conversation, Blake's men arrived on the roof with the demolition device. As they were lifting it into place, Blake could hear several Japanese talking excitedly. Suddenly, the voices down below fell silent after which Blake heard the English-speaking Japanese say: "Don't blow us all up."

"Well come on out then," replied Blake.

"I can't come out."

"How much dynamite have you got down there, Nip?"

Blake arched his eyebrows when he heard the response: "Eighty thousand pounds."

"Okay, Nip, if you and your friends won't come out of there then I'm going to send all of you to your ancestors."

"Hokay."

With that Blake ingnited the fuses, then he and his men took off at a full gallop for safer ground. The first sound to be heard coming from the ventilation shaft was the primer cord's faint pop, signaling that the infernal machine had just been dropped down inside the bunker. Then came an ear-splitting roar which lasted for several minutes as huge clouds of black smoke gushed forth from the shaft and all around the steel door. Clearly the underground chamber, and everyone in it, had been destroyed.

The ground around the bunker was still quivering slightly when a wide-eyed Lieutenant Blake remarked to Sergeant Hill, "That Nip sure was right—eighty thousand pounds is one hell of a lot of dynamite!"

Earlier, while the paratroopers were busy expanding their Topside holdings, Lieutenant Colonel Ed Postlethwait's 2d Battalion, 34th Infantry had been hard at work strengthening its grip on Bottomside and Malinta Hill.

On Bottomside proper, Captain Howard G. Fenway's Company I, 34th Infantry, spent most of the day on the eighteenth clearing out the North Dock area for the second time. Japanese Imperial Marine units had infiltrated this area during the night and, even though they became cornered there, refused to surrender. Using the same tactics being employed by the paratroopers, Fenway's infantrymen methodically swept through North Dock, where they killed forty-two Japanese, captured two machine guns, and sealed six cave openings. Company I's only casualty during the sweep was Sergeant Owen Williams. When his rifle squad walked into a grenade ambush, Williams cried a warning. His men ducked down and were saved. But Williams' warning shout had given his position away to an Imperial Marine who killed him with a well-thrown grenade.

The 2d Platoon of Captain Melvin Q. Simpson's Company A successfully maneuvered its way through a gauntlet of sniper fire carrying ammunition and food supplies to the beleaguered infantrymen of K and L companies on top of Malinta Hill. On the way back down to Bottomside, the platoon brought out Company K's casualties of the previous night.

On several occasions throughout the day, Lieutenant Lewis F. Stearns, the commanding officer of Company L, made excel-

lent use of a destroyer's awesome firepower to assist his infantrymen who were sealing cave openings discovered along Malinta
Hill's eastern slopes. With Stearns in direct radio contact with
its gunnery officer, the destroyer steamed to within a quarter-
mile of the shoreline to fire five-inch shells directly into the
caves. The ship's first few salvos uncovered one gigantic fourteen-
inch naval gun and six 155mm howitzers, all of which had been
ferried over from the mainland in recent months by the Japanese.
When informed that all of these heavy caliber artillery pieces
were aimed toward the Rock's eastern flatlands, Colonel Postlethwait was convinced that the defending Japanese had been expecting the Americans to make an amphibious landing
somewhere between Engineer Point and Infantry Point. But as
it was, when the American amphibious forces made their end
run to Black Beach on the Rock's southern shore, the massive
firepower of the Japanese guns could not be used because Malinta
Hill blocked their line of fire.

An air controller working in the 34th Infantry's area called in
an air strike during the afternoon of the eighteenth on a company-
size Japanese force that was observed digging in around Engineer
Point. Even though the bombs were right on target, several
Japanese could still be seen digging in after the planes returned
to base.

Just before dark, Colonel Postlethwait relieved Lieutenant
Fugitti's decimated Company K on Malinta Hill, replacing it
with Captain Fenway's Company I and two heavy machine gun
sections from Company M. At the same time, Postlethwait also
dispatched two more heavy machine gun sections from Company
M to reinforce the firepower of Lieutenant Stearns's Company
L. Up to this point in the battle, Stearns and his men had been
leading charmed lives. Not one member of the company had
been lost. This so impressed the infantrymen of "Love" Company
that they began referring to their outfit as "Lucky" Company.

These tactical moves by Colonel Postlethwait greatly strength-
ened the 34th Infantry's positions spread across the top of Malinta
Hill. They also made a strong impression on the Japanese, for
they did not attempt any large-scale actions against his battalion
for the remainder of the day. The Japanese did, however, fire a

number of mortar shells at Company K's 3d Platoon, which was still marooned out on Malinta Point. The platoon lost two men during the mortar barrage, yet managed to hold on to its isolated position.

Except for an occasional incoming mortar round, the night of the eighteenth would pass quietly for Postlethwait's infantrymen on Bottomside and Malinta Hill. But for the paratroopers defending Topside's enlarged perimeter, that night would be prove to be a living hell.

Unknown to Colonel Jones and his Rock Force staff, the Japanese still had a powerful reserve combat unit hidden away in bombproof shelters that had been secretly dug into the base of the cliffs below Topside's westernmost edge. Known as the Special Naval Landing Force, this reserve unit was composed of 1,300 Imperial Marines all of whom had escaped injury during the tremendous aerial and naval bombardment that preceded the initial American parachute assault. Its commanding officer was twenty-six-year-old Lieutenant Takeji Endo, a native of Yokohama and a 1943 graduate of Japan's Naval Academy. In addition to being the reserve force leader, Endo was the senior surviving Japanese officer on the Rock.

Endo and his men were growing more desperate with every passing hour. Having lost all of their telephone communications facilities to the paratroopers, and with their ground link to other surviving Japanese units severed by Colonel Postlethwait's men holding Bottomside, their destruction was certain unless they could somehow drive the Americans off Topside. Like General Wainwright's defenders three years earlier, Endo's marines desperately needed food, ammunition, and water. In a week or two at most, even if they were left alone by the Americans, many of Endo's men would die of thirst. This water shortage had been brought upon the Japanese by themselves. After they captured Corregidor in 1942, they neglected to repair the island's water purification plant. Instead, they had established only four water points during the occupation. All four of those water points were destroyed by the American preassault bombardment. Entirely cut off from the outside world, the Japanese were literally dying of thirst. In some caves they were existing only on fish boiled in salty sea water, canned juices, and water seepage from the walls.

During the afternoon of the eighteenth, Lieutenant Endo assembled his unit leaders in a bunker near the shoreline to brief them on his plan for attacking Topside that night. Endo began with a rousing five-minute patriotic speech during which he assured the officers that the attack would be successful and urged them to exhibit great personal courage while leading their troops in the charge across Topside. At the conclusion of this pep talk the officers applauded loudly as they repeatedly shouted, "Banzai!" which is generally translated as, "May the Emperor live 10,000 years."

When order was restored a few moments later, Endo announced that the operation would be carried out by two separate attack columns, A and B. Column A would leave the assembly area at 10:30 P.M. to begin its climb up through Grubbs Ravine, where it was to destroy all American forces that might be manning Batteries Smith and Hearn before going on to sweep across the northern half of Topside.

One hour after Column A's departure, continued Endo, he would lead Column B up through Cheney Ravine to make the main attack at Battery Cheney and sweep across Topside's southern half, destroying the American artillery unit based there. The reason for the one-hour delay between columns was to take full advantage of all the confusion that would be created on Topside by Column A's initial attack.

Endo completed the meeting with a question-and-answer session after which his orderly produced a bottle of sake and several small ceremonial cups. The assembled officers drank a toast to their Emperor and another to their homeland. Then one by one they saluted Endo and left the bunker to begin briefing their respective troop units on the plan of attack.

Meanwhile, on Topside Colonel Jones's three paratroop battalions had just ceased offensive actions to begin making defense preparations for the night. In the few hours they had left until darkness, the paratroopers went through the usual day's-end routine of digging in, cleaning and loading individual and crew-served weapons, and placing hand grenades within quick reach around the edges of their foxholes.

Later that night in the War Room of Rock Force Headquarters, Colonel Jones sat discussing the day's events with his S-3 (operations) officer, Major Ernest C. Clark, and his S-2 (intelligence) officer, Captain Francis X. Donovan. The nightly staff briefing had just been concluded and Jones was happy. It had been a good day for Rock Force: 700 more Japanese were reported killed in action. About 10:00 P.M., Jones left the War Room and walked down the hallway to his sleeping quarters. There he removed his boots and slid into what was serving as his bed—two salvaged parachutes laid out on the concrete floor—for a short nap before the nightly Japanese probing attacks began. He would not have long to wait.

The Rock Force commander had been asleep a little more than an hour when, at 11:30 P.M., Endo's Column A troops that had been moving up through Grubbs Ravine collided with Lieutenant Calhoun's task force still defending Battery Hearn. In his after-action report describing this encounter Calhoun wrote:

We heard them coming. They were yelling and shouting as they marched up the road leading into our position. This seemed to be the signal for a U.S. Navy star shell to burst overhead and illuminate the whole area. By the light of the star shell, we could see the Japanese advancing in a column of fours, just as if they were on parade. They seemed to be trying to frighten us by chanting among themselves and occasionally shouting slogans which none of us Americans could understand. This reminded me of stories I had heard about other battles, such as Guadalcanal's Bloody Ridge, where Japanese troops charged the American lines shouting, "Marines you die" and "Blood for the Emperor." When the navy's second star shell popped above us, we could see them more clearly. This was a battalion-size unit: 500 or more men. Some of them were sick and throwing up. We felt they were drunk. The booze was certainly plentiful enough on Corregidor. Our firepower was cutting swaths through their ranks. Groups would crumple from the explosions of our 60mm mortar rounds scoring direct hits on the road. Thanks to our company commander, Lieutenant Bill Bailey, each of our two mortars had forty to fifty rounds of ammunition. He had planned for the worst, as a good company commander should, and had a large amount of ammo carried out to Battery Hearn and Way Hill earlier in the day. We probably would not have survived with less. Bill always did his job well.

Private Lloyd McCarter was in a foxhole near the point where the Japanese chose to launch their attack on Battery Hearn. As a first scout, he was armed with a Thompson submachine gun, a weapon that is deadly accurate at close range but loses its effectiveness against targets beyond a range of fifty yards. Between star shell bursts, McCarter made his way down to a gully right beside the road along which the enemy troops were marching. There he began firing directly into the Japanese column with his weapon. When it overheated, he ran back to his squad's position and grabbed a Browning automatic rifle belonging to Private Benedict J. Schilli, who had just been wounded. Soon it, too, overheated. Out of weapons and ammunition, McCarter crawled to a nearby foxhole, grabbed an M-1 rifle from a dead paratrooper, and continued pouring fire into the enemy ranks.

During the hectic battle being waged all around him, McCarter could be heard yelling and laughing at the enemy. Whenever there was a brief lull in the shooting, he would dash back to his squad's position to obtain more ammunition and grenades. Each time he returned he would ask his fellow squad members, "How are you doing?" Soon the pile of enemy bodies in front of McCarter's advanced position became so high that he had to stand up in search of more targets. By that time, most of the enemy column had melted away into the darkness, leaving McCarter dueling with the few stragglers still milling about Battery Hearn. Eventually, he was felled by a bullet that struck him squarely in the chest but did not kill him.

Private First Class Richard A. Lampman and a couple of medics rushed out and tried to carry McCarter back to safety, but he insisted on staying where he was so that he might continue to warn of approaching enemy troops. In a few seconds he collapsed in a pool of blood. When daylight arrived, McCarter's squad leader, Staff Sergeant Chris W. Johnson counted thirty-five Japanese bodies in front of McCarter's roadside position and 100 more scattered along the road below Battery Hearn.

McCarter did not die. Although he had lost a lot of blood, he retained all of his fighting spirit and wry sense of humor. He was eventually evacuated from the Rock to a field hospital where some wounded Japanese were also being treated. When this one-man gang awoke from the anesthetic, he spied a military policeman guarding the ward door. "Good God, what have I done now?" he asked. In a postwar interview, Rock Force commander George Jones said that this comment, "Rather characterized Private McCarter. . . . He was absolutely fearless in combat, but was often in trouble when we weren't fighting the Japanese." While McCarter was still recovering from his wounds in Letterman Army Hospital in San Francisco, he received a personal letter from President Harry S. Truman asking that he come to the White House to be presented the Congressional Medal of Honor. McCarter was the second, and final, American to win that medal during the battle to reclaim the Rock.

Rifle shots were still being exchanged between the Japanese column A attack force and Lieutenant Calhoun's task force defending Battery Hearn when, at 1:05 A.M. on the nineteenth, the first in what would become a series of disasters to befall the troopers of Major Woods's 1st Battalion (comprising companies A, B, and C) occurred near Breakwater Point. A group of some forty Imperial Marines tried to commit mass suicide by exploding a heavy charge of dynamite in a tunnel beneath the building housing Captain William T. Bossart's Company A command post. The force of the blast was so great that it catapulted a football-size boulder 500 yards inside the perimeter where it fell through the roofless Mile-long Barracks and landed within a few feet of Colonel Jones. Twenty Japanese died in the underground chamber. An equal number of Americans also died as a result of the explosion.

The Imperial Marines who survived the underground blast obviously felt a great sense of failure in the mass suicide attempt. As the dazed Company A paratroopers looked on in total disbelief, the twenty-odd Japanese survivors staggered out of the smoking tunnel, squatted in a circular formation, and began chanting slogans. Then upon a command given by one of their number they pulled pins from grenades they were holding to their chests and blew themselves to pieces.

This suicide act only presaged even greater horrors to be witnessed by the members of Rock Force. It also convinced the Americans that they were facing a far more fanatic enemy than any intelligence source had told them about during the preassault tactical briefings held on Mindoro. Even the hard-bitten paratroopers would become horrified during the next few days by more examples of the enemy's penchant for self-destruction on a grand scale.

An eerie silence returned once more to the embattled Rock as the survivors of the Japanese column A assault force broke contact with the paratroopers defending Battery Hearn and Way Hill and withdrew to the shoreline to regroup and figure out why their attack had failed. On Topside, the paratroopers recovered quickly from the enemy's unorthodox attempt at storming Battery Hearn and the devastating underground blast that wrecked Company A's command post. All three parachute battalions were kept on 100 percent battle alert for a full hour after the Japanese faded away from Battery Hearn. Then word came down from Rock Force headquarters to revert to a 50 percent alert, meaning that half the troopers could now go to sleep.

Many paratroopers had already drifted off into an uneasy sleep when, at 3:30 A.M., Lieutenant Endo and his column B main attack force of some 800 Imperial Marines silently emerged from caves and bunkers far below Topside. Due to the large number of flares that had been fired by U.S. Navy warships during the unexpectedly strong American defense of Battery Hearn, Endo's coordinated attack was running far behind schedule. Nevertheless, Endo and his troops were still very much determined to drive the Americans off Topside or die while trying to achieve that goal. At 4:00 A.M., the column B attack force began to stealthily claw its way up the steep walls of Cheney Ravine on the first leg of its journey to Topside's southwestern quadrant.

Defending Battery Cheney this night was Lieutenant Joseph A. Turinski's Company D, 503d Parachute Infantry. Turinski's men were newly established in the battery, having captured it late in the afternoon of the eighteenth. Because the 2d Battalion's night defense order had not been issued until sundown on the eighteenth, neither Lieutenant Turinski's company, which sat on the south side of Cheney Ravine, nor Lieutenant Bailey's Company F troopers on the ravine's north side had enough time to physically tie in with each other before darkness. As result, the 500-yard gap which separated those two companies had to be covered during the night by artillery and mortar concentrations.

Twenty-year-old Corporal Alan C. Bennett of North Haven, Connecticut, was a member of a security detachment that had been placed forward of Battery Cheney at dusk on the eighteenth to provide early warning of the enemy's approach. Although he had graduated from jump school only a year and a half ago, Bennett already had twenty-one jumps to his credit. Like most young paratroopers, he had always thought of himself as a lucky man. But ever since a Japanese rifleman shot six holes in his parachute while he was descending on the Rock, Bennett sensed that his luck might be running out. At 5:15 A.M. on the nineteenth, Bennett caught a glimpse of five shadowy figures moving below him in the ravine. In keeping with the regiment's shoot-first, ask-questions-later policy, he immediately squeezed off five short bursts with his submachine gun, then emptied the rest of the magazine into another group of dark forms moving straight toward his position. Two of Bennett's companions, Privates William C. Bracklien and William G. Brady, joined in by throwing grenades, which seemed to halt all movement in the area.

For the next few moments there was silence as both Bennett's squad and the Japanese paused to take stock of the situation. But then all hell broke loose when a rain of hand grenades fell on the Americans, killing Bracklein and Brady outright and wounding Bennett in the chest, both arms, and face. Assisted by his friend, Private Ernest Griffen who gave him first aid, Bennett found his Thompson. Then, even though partially blinded by the exploding grenades, he resumed firing, killing eighteen of the enemy in as many seconds.

As valorous as his actions were, Bennett was unable to halt the Japanese onslaught that followed this initial encounter at Battery Cheney. Screaming and shooting furiously as they swept forward like a great tidal wave, the Imperial Marines drove Lieutenant Turinski's 2d and 3d platoons back from their positions around the battery to a separate bunker near Wheeler Point that housed the company command post. During that hectic withdrawal, the Americans could not tell friend from foe so they wisely withheld their fire. On reaching the command bunker, the 2d and 3d platoon survivors banded together with the company's 1st Platoon and Lieutenant John L. Lindgren's Weapons Platoon. Soon the onrushing Japanese mass became intermingled with the paratroopers and a wild shootout erupted at extremely close quarters. Lieutenant Turinski tried to rally his men by climbing on top of the bunker's blast wall and firing his carbine but was quickly killed by rifle fire. All told, thirteen paratroopers were killed and another fifteen wounded during this free-for-all.

Under the command now of the company executive officer, Lieutenant Henry H. "Buck" Buchanan, who was assisted greatly by the wounded Lieutenant Lindgren, the vastly outnumbered paratroopers were able to mass their fire and halt the Japanese, who had made the tactical error of attacking along a narrow trail. Aided by U.S. Navy star shells that cast a flickering, whitish, light across the landscape, the paratroopers continued to pour aimed fire into the enemy column stalled along the trail. It was not until some 250 of his men had been mowed down that the Japanese commander realized the magnitude of his blunder and gave orders for a hasty withdrawal to the depths of Cheney Ravine. There, under cover of heavy jungle vegetation that blocked out the light of the American flares, Lieutenant Endo quickly reorganized his force and set out again for Topside. This time, however, he took a route that bypassed Battery Cheney and Wheeler Point by a wide margin.

By 6:00 A.M., the Japanese column B attack force—still some 550 men strong—had infiltrated and fought its way through the American lines and assembled behind a building that had been

Corregidor's NCO (noncommissioned officers') Club before the war. There Endo called his officers together and detailed their orders. Just before dismissing them he emphasized, "The objective before you must be taken at all costs—to do so every officer and man must give his all for the Emperor." Endo then drew his curved samurai sword and strode briskly to the front of his troops. Meanwhile his officers silently used hand signals to call their men to attention and have them fix bayonets. The supreme moment was at hand for the Imperial Marines.

Many paratroopers on Topside were still in the middle of shaving at 6:15 A.M. on that morning of the nineteenth when they began hearing hundreds of chanting Japanese voices just west of the parade ground drop zone. Seconds later the chanting turned to high-pitched screams of "Banzai! Banzai! Banzai!" Suddenly a great sea of running, screaming Imperial Marines, with Endo at their head, burst out into the open from behind the old NCO Club. Like a herd of stampeding cattle, they ran over everything and everyone in their way.

The Japanese maintained a tightly knit and compact line with a front of some 200 feet as they raced forward bound for glory. One section of the American perimeter was completely overrun before the startled paratroopers could spring into action. In a matter of minutes the air was filled with murderous blasts of counterfire and the Japanese attack began to falter. Most of the paratroopers stayed in their foxholes during the ferocious battle. Unable to load their weapons fast enough, some Americans leaped from their positions to engage the attackers with everything from bayonets to trench knives and hand-to-hand combat.

A few small groups of the charging Japanese managed to penetrate deep inside Topside's perimeter. One squad-size contingent made it all the way to Mile-long Barracks where its members threw hand grenades into a ground-floor room occupied by the Rock Force supply officer, Captain Robert Atkins and several of his men. Atkins escaped the explosions unharmed but four of his men were seriously wounded. Clad only in the T-shirts and undershorts in which they had been sleeping, Atkins and the other survivors grabbed their weapons and returned fire, killing all of the intruders.

Another six-man group of Imperial Marines tried to shoot their way into Rock Force Headquarters but were repelled by a sentinel armed with a carbine. On hearing the shooting taking place at his very doorstep, Colonel Jones drew his pistol, rushed outside, and shot three of the enemy dead. The others fled toward the 462d Parachute Field Artillery's positions on the parade field. Moments after this incident, Private James D. Edgar of the artillery battalion's Battery D had just finished reloading his .50-caliber machine gun when a lone Imperial Marine leapt screaming into his position. Continuing to scream, the marine lunged forward, grabbed the muzzle end of the gun and tried to pull it out of Edgar's hands. Although startled by the sudden appearance of the enemy in his midst, Edgar reflexively pulled the trigger, blasting a grapefruit-size hole in the other man's chest.

Some thirty minutes after it had begun the Japanese attack was over. The end result looked like a movie scene depicting the aftermath of a medieval clash between hordes of opposing foot soldiers. Littered about the battlefield were some 500 dead Imperial Marines, one of whom was Lieutenant Endo.

A quick casualty count gathered by Major Lester H. LeVine, the Rock Force S-1 (personnel) officer, revealed that American losses were moderate by comparison: thirty-three killed and seventy-five wounded.

As early as 8:00 A.M. that morning, it was back to business as usual for the paratroopers. By that time all three of Topside's parachute infantry battalions had patrols out searching for Japanese survivors of the banzai attack. Several Imperial Marines were found hiding in vacant buildings along Topside's western edge. Defiantly adhering to their Bushido warrior's code, none of the survivors permitted the Americans to take them alive.

10
THE FIGHTING CONTINUES

Throughout the remainder of February 19 and for the next few days following the failed banzai attack, the paratroopers and infantrymen of Rock Force continued to destroy small pockets of Japanese whom they flushed out of tunnels, bunkers, and the ruins of buildings with white phosphorous grenades and flamethrowers.

For the paratroopers, mopping up after the attack and counting the enemy dead was extremely dangerous work. Individual Japanese survivors were hiding all over Topside, forcing the Americans to search every building. Others who pretended to be dead would rise up and shoot at the rear of patrols as they passed. One such incident occurred in Company D's area where at midmorning on the nineteenth Sergeant Donald Arbuckle's platoon came upon a cluster of five Japanese bodies all of which had garish wounds and were covered with blood. A large green supply parachute covered the upper half of one of the bodies. Taking no chances, the paratroopers kicked each of the bodies, including the one that was partially hidden by the chute. Getting no responses, they moved on. Seconds later the "dead" Japanese under the supply parachute rose up and shot Sergeant Arbuckle, knocking him to the ground with a serious leg wound. Angry with themselves for having been fooled by the ruse, Arbuckle's men wheeled about and shot the Japanese, and the supply chute he had been hiding under, full of holes.

Moments after that incident, a group of sixteen Imperial Marine survivors located in a huge bomb crater near the top of Grubbs Ravine opened fire on Lieutenant Calhoun's troopers who were still manning Battery Hearn, killing Private First Class Pasquale A. Ruggio and wounding Private Lawrence Ranville. Because most of his riflemen were nearly out of ammunition, Calhoun had them hold their fire while Staff Sergeant Johnnie H. "Red Horse" Phillips's 60mm mortar squad went into action. The first mortar round exploded behind the enemy position and the second fell just short of it. But the third round, fired by Private Burl W. Martin, landed right on target, killing all sixteen of the enemy.

While all that was taking place, Lieutenant Calhoun received a radio call from Lieutenant Daniel J. Doherty, the commanding officer of Battery D, 462d Parachute Field Artillery Battalion. Doherty informed Calhoun that he was standing some 300 yards northeast of Battery Hearn and from his position could see a group of twenty or more men milling about in the depths of Grubbs Ravine. "Are those guys down there friendlies?" asked Doherty. "Heck no," replied Calhoun, "they've got to be part of the gang that attacked us during the night." Doherty then said, "Okay, we'll take care of them for you." Seconds later a pair of heavy .50-caliber machine guns from Doherty's battery opened up and chopped the enemy force to pieces. "The bodies of the dead," wrote Calhoun, "were so heaped up and mutilated by those .50-caliber slugs (each one of which is approximately the size of a man's thumb) that we were unable to determine an exact body count."

The elimination of the enemy force in Grubbs Ravine greatly improved Calhoun's tactical situation. But he and his paratroopers were not yet out of the woods. Things had just returned to normal when Calhoun's troopers came under fire from a Nambu machine gun positioned underneath an old wooden trolley car some 100 yards northwest of the battery. Since his platoon's bazooka gunner still had plenty of ammunition, Calhoun directed him to return the fire. The gunner fired several rockets into the trolley, but the wood was so rotten that they passed through the vehicle without exploding, to detonate harmlessly in the dirt far behind it.

Frustrated by his lack of success, and shaken by the fact that the Nambu was rapidly zeroing in on him, the bazooka gunner was now ready to let someone else try shooting his weapon. Seeing this, Lieutenant Calhoun asked one of his scouts, Private First Class William McDonald, if he thought he could score a hit on the iron rails beneath the trolley. Calhoun knew that McDonald was an excellent marksman with all infantry weapons, but he also knew that this was going to be an extremely difficult shot. "I'll do my best, sir," drawled McDonald. With that, the young paratrooper shouldered the bazooka and proceeded to score a first-round hit on the tracks, knocking the Nambu out of action.

Only one member of the enemy machine gun crew survived. Dazed and bleeding profusely, he staggered out from under the trolley car, sat down on the ground, and crossed his legs. Then he raised both arms above his head and bowed several times toward Battery Hearn. Neither Lieutenant Calhoun nor any of his men could tell if the man before them was asking to surrender or praying. Calhoun radioed his boss, Lieutenant Bailey, advising him of this extremely unusual situation. "Take him alive," said Bailey. "Regiment desperately needs prisoners." Bailey went on to explain that Colonel Jones had recently said that anyone capturing a prisoner would be given a three-day R-and-R (rest and relaxation) vacation. Calhoun dispatched a patrol, passing along Colonel Jones's promise, but warning its members to shoot if the enemy marine made any suspicious moves. As the paratroopers drew to within ten yards of where he was sitting the marine suddenly pulled a grenade from his pocket, but before he could pull its pin a patrol member shot him dead. "Damn!" said the paratrooper who pulled the trigger. "For a while there, I thought I had me a three-day pass."

Shortly thereafter, Privates John E. Bartlet, Perry E. Bandt, and George J. Mikel left Battery Hearn on a mission to retrieve a pair of abandoned enemy machine guns that the returning patrol members had reported seeing near the trolley car. As they were approaching the trolley car, the paratroopers bypassed a large bomb crater containing four Japanese, all of whom appeared to be very dead. Upon reaching their destination, Bartlett and Bandt started looking around for the two machine guns. Meanwhile, Mikel wandered off alone out in back of the trolley looking for souvenirs. Mikel had only been gone a moment or two when he suddenly let out a bloodcurdling scream. Dashing around back to investigate, Bartlett and Bandt saw the four "dead" Japanese grappling with Mikel. As one of them tried to stuff a grenade inside his shirt, Mikel bellowed to his companions, "They're alive! They're alive! Shoot the bastards before they kill me!" Bartlett and Bandt then rushed over to where Mikel was being waltzed around in circles and shot all four of the enemy to death. Not quite half an hour later, the paratroopers returned to Battery Hearn carrying the two machine guns they had set out to retrieve, plus thirteen bolt-action rifles.

During the afternoon of the nineteenth, Lieutenant Bailey received orders from Major Caskey, the 2d Battalion commander, to withdraw his company from its positions at Battery Hearn and Way Hill and pull back to Topside's old post headquarters area. As Bailey's half of the company was forming into a march column at the base of Way Hill one of its members, Private Fred M. Morgan, happened to look inside the entrance of a prewar vintage tunnel that had been dug underneath the hill and was shot dead by an Imperial Marine hiding within. Surprised and infuriated, the paratroopers reacted violently, firing their rifles into the tunnel for the next several minutes. When the shooting subsided, a squad of Bailey's troopers tossed several concussion grenades into the tunnel then charged in seeking revenge. Once inside, they ran down a short concrete corridor that turned sharply to the right and emptied into a large vaultlike room containing twenty-seven Imperial Marines, many of whom had been stunned into a state of incoherence by exploding grenades. Fearing that they might be injured by their own ricocheting bullets, the paratroopers attacked only with trench knives and bayonets, killing all of the enemy. Lieutenant Calhoun and the other half of Company F arrived at the smoking tunnel entrance just as the paratroopers were filing outside. Recalling that meeting after the war, Calhoun wrote: "There seemed to be billions of flies on the Rock by this time. The poor guys in the blood-stained fatigues soon became the targets of enormous hordes of those pesky winged creatures."

With his company reunited, Lieutenant Bailey marched the troopers back inside the perimeter. As they were passing Mile-long Barracks, Bailey declared a thirty-minute rest break during which his men filled their canteens from several water bags they found hanging in the shade of the building's south side. During the rest break, a former member of Company F, Lieutenant Emory N. Ball, happened to walk past and was overjoyed at meeting old friends. When he had been assigned to Company F, Ball served as an assistant rifle platoon leader under Lieutenant Calhoun. His current duty assignment was that of mortar platoon leader in Company E. While chatting with a group of Company F troopers, Ball said he had been worried about them during the terrible fighting that took place out at Battery Hearn and Way Hill. Ball then went on to joke with Lieutenants Bailey and Calhoun about his current duty assignment, saying that as a mortar platoon leader he was "practically a rear-echeloner now" and as such was "out of harm's way for the rest of the war." At the time he made that statement, Ball had two days to live.

Elsewhere on Topside, Lieutenant Charles M. Preston's 2d Platoon from Company D was prowling below Wheeler Point when, at noon on the nineteenth, its point man made a pleasant discovery. Peering into the opening of a small cave, he saw the familiar faces of Privates Calvin C. Martin and Frank B. Keller, both of whom were members of Company D and had been missing since jumping on the Rock three days earlier. They had been blown over the cliffs and landed on a ledge near the beach below Topside. Imperial Marines occupying caves along the face of the cliff had wounded both men with rifle fire and they had responded with submachine guns in an attempt to fight their way up to Topside. But the Japanese fire had been too heavy, and they had crawled into the nearest empty cave, hoping that someone would eventually rescue them.

All during Lieutenant Endo's ferocious banzai attack, the Pack

75 howitzers of the 462d Parachute Field Artillery Battalion had been booming at maximum rates of fire—often at point-blank range—from their hub-to-hub positions on Topside's parade ground. But now that a degree of normalcy had returned to the battleground, some of the artillerymen were busy picking up spent brass shell casings and stacking fresh ammunition beside their guns. Suddenly a concealed Japanese machine gun began firing on a squad of troopers who were out on the parade ground drop zone recovering parachute bundles that had just been dropped by the Mindoro base resupply airplane. Captain Henry W. Gibson was the first one to get a fix on the machine gun's location in a bomb crater only 200 yards south of his Battery B gun emplacements. Since it was impossible for his Pack 75s to effectively fire down into the crater at that close range, Gibson ordered a gun crew to disassemble its howitzer and reassemble it on the second floor porch of a nearby officers' quarters overlooking the enemy position. When the Pack 75 gunner was attempting to sight in on the enemy, it was found that a parachute canopy dangling from the roof was directly in the path of the gun-target line. One artilleryman tried jerking the chute loose but it would not budge. The Japanese machine gun crew noticed the quivering parachute and began firing into the building, sending razor sharp concrete chips buzzing harmlessly through the empty rooms.

As soon as the enemy machine gunner paused to feed a fresh belt into his weapon, Private First Class John P. Prettyman, the howitzer's loader, climbed up on the porch's narrow railing. Holding his arms out to the side like a circus high-wire walker, Prettyman steadied himself before reaching out and grabbing the chute with both hands. Then he gave a mighty pull that tore both the chute and several roof tiles loose. Prettyman was in the act of jumping back down to the porch when he was struck by a long burst of machine gun fire that sent him falling into the courtyard below mortally wounded.

The enraged howitzer crew poured shell after shell into the machine gun nest for some fifteen minutes, after which Captain Gibson ordered them to cease fire. When the artillerymen walked out to examine the destroyed Japanese position it was impossible for them to count the enemy dead because they had all been blown into a pulverized mass of flesh and bones. Private Prettyman was posthumously awarded a Silver Star for gallantry in action.

The grim task of counting the number of enemy dead scattered all over Topside and its approaches was especially irritating to the paratroopers. They preferred to spend their time destroying the Japanese defenders and leaving the counting of shattered bodies to someone else. What upset the paratroopers most of all about the counting process was a Rock Force headquarters-imposed rule that required all counts to be verified by an officer. "What the hell's the problem?" griped one corporal. "Don't those headquarters types think us enlisted men are capable of counting dead bodies that can't get up and move around to screw up the count?"

An example of this resentment surfaced during the afternoon of the nineteenth when a paratrooper in the area being searched by Company G winked at a nearby buddy then called to his platoon leader, "Pardon me, lieutenant, I've got a bunch of assorted body parts over here and I can't quite tell how many bodies they add up to. What do you suggest I do, sir?" The quick-thinking officer—who was well aware of the resentment in the ranks over the count verification issue—replied in a voice tinged with sarcasm, "Just count the arms and divide by two."

In accordance with the administrative portion of Rock Force's detailed plan for retaking Corregidor, the recovered bodies of all dead paratroopers were brought to a makeshift morgue that had been established in Topside's old movie theater. There each body was positively identified, tagged, and made ready to be taken down to Black Beach for pickup by a naval vessel that would transport it to the Philippine mainland for burial.

Meanwhile, the dead Japanese—over 900 by now—had to be left where they had fallen in battle. And so by noontime on the nineteenth the overpowering stench of dead bodies decomposing in the sun was beginning to make many members of Rock Force feel sick to their stomachs. Corregidor's prevailing winds carried the foul-smelling odor out to sea where crewmen aboard the patrolling destroyers and PT boats were nauseated by it. Two bulldozers that had been delivered to the island earlier that morning were put to work digging long, deep trenches on Topside. Then the operators used their huge curved plowblades to push hundreds of corpses into the excavations and cover them with dirt. At one point during this mass burial operation, the paratroopers looked on as the bulldozers pushed as many as fifty corpses over the cliffs of Topside, sending them plunging some 500 feet into the sea.

On the afternoon of the nineteenth the exhausted surgeons of the 503d Parachute Infantry received some much-needed assistance when the 18th Portable Surgical Hospital was delivered to Corregidor aboard an LST. Within minutes after driving ashore in their small caravan of trucks and ambulances the new arrivals headed on up to Topside. There they were given an enthusiastic welcome by Major Thomas Stevens, the 503d's regimental surgeon. Also on hand to greet the newcomers were several paratroop medics who assisted them in setting up shop next to the regimental aid station on the first floor of Mile-long Barracks.

What impressed the paratroop medics most about the recent arrivals was the newness of their vehicles—most of which had been driven less than fifty miles—and their almost limitless supply of state-of-the-art operating room equipment. Prior to the arrival of the 18th Portable Surgical Hospital, Major Stevens and his fellow paratroop doctors worked around the clock performing delicate operations with only the barest essential tools contained in the surgical kits that they had strapped to their bodies when they jumped on the Rock.

While conducting security sweeps across Topside in the aftermath of Lieutenant Endo's banzai attack, the paratroopers captured two wounded Japanese. During their interrogation the prisoners provided Captain Francis X. Donovan, Colonel Jones's S-2, with his first firm information concerning the number of enemy troops who had been on the Rock at the time the initial parachute assault was made on the sixteenth. Slightly more than 3,000 Japanese, the prisoners agreed, had been stationed on Topside and another 2,000 or more were positioned from Malinta Tunnel eastward to the tail of the island. When this information was passed on to Colonel Jones he realized how very vulnerable he and all the other troopers in the initial parachute assault wave had been during the first few hours after jumping on the Rock. Had the Japanese counterattacked during that crucial period when all newly landed parachute units are scattered and trying to get organized, the Imperial Marines more than likely would have succeeded in wiping out the first lift. However, the fierce American preassault bombardment, coupled with the sight of planeloads of paratroopers landing on Topside, had temporarily shocked the defending Japanese forces into a state of inaction.

Under further questioning, one of the Japanese prisoners startled Captain Donovan by telling him that another banzai attack would be made that same night by 1,000 Imperial Marines. Although he suspected that this information might not be accurate, Colonel Jones immediately had it communicated to all members of his command. When the ominous message reached the 503d's Company F, the company clerk philosophically wrote into the daily log book, "If it's true, let them come. We'll get it over with one big banzai."

At 2:00 P.M. on the nineteenth, Captain Joseph M. Conway's Company H was given the mission of knocking out a Japanese stronghold that had just been discovered in a deep ravine north of Bottomside's North Dock area. There the Japanese had converted the Corregidor's prewar ice-making plant into a miniature fortress. Like all of the Rock's American-built structures, the "icehouse" as this building came to be known by the paratroopers, was constructed of reinforced concrete. From this fortress the Japanese could deliver aimed fire on much of the road leading from the beach up to Topside and part of the 34th Infantry's positions atop Malinta Hill.

Captain Conway used the basic infantry assault technique known as "fire and maneuver" to attack the icehouse. The firing element consisted of one platoon that laid a heavy volume of rifle and machine gun fire on the objective's gunports, keeping the enemy fully occupied. Meanwhile the maneuvering element, a second platoon, ran around to the rear of the icehouse. Once there, the paratroopers climbed up on the roof and poured a five-gallon can of napalm down the ventilation shaft. Then they stuffed a gasoline-soaked rubber tire into the shaft's opening and set it ablaze. Moments later, the first globs of burning rubber fell down the shaft, igniting the napalm. In short order, the combination of the flaming tire's noxious smoke and burning napalm forced the Japanese to abandon the icehouse. Twelve Imperial Marines came running out of the building, each one screaming wildly and firing his weapon. The paratroopers gunned them down.

With the icehouse neutralized, Rock Force headquarters declared the road connecting Black Beach and Topside fully secure. Finally, the way was clear for dead and wounded paratroopers to be evacuated by the navy and for the much-needed supplies that had been piling up on the beach to be safely transported up to Topside.

At dusk on the nineteenth, Colonel Jones instructed his front-line battalion commanders to tighten their sections of the perimeter defense in anticipation of a banzai attack. But no attack came that night. The paratroopers had broken the enemy's backbone the morning before when they crushed Lieutenant Endo's attempt to seize control of Topside.

During that night of February 19–20, the tension on Topside became so thick that it could be cut into cubes with a bayonet, said one paratrooper. Nerves were stretched to the breaking point when during the early morning hours of the twentieth another in a series of tragedies for Major Wood's hard-luck 1st Battalion occurred in Company C's sector of the perimeter. A little after 2:00 A.M., an alert trooper in Staff Sergeant Herbert A. Thomas's squad saw a Japanese infiltrator brazenly walk up to the perimeter's edge, trying to bluff his way through the American front lines. Obeying the regiment's shoot-first, ask-questions-afterward policy, the trooper shot the intruder, who screamed and fell to the ground mortally wounded. Awakened out of a sound sleep, Sergeant Thomas jumped to his feet and ran through the darkness toward his squad sector to check on his men. While doing so, he was shot and killed by a paratrooper who mistook him for another infiltrator. Sergeant Thomas's death came as a great shock to all members of Company C. He was one of the outfit's best-liked sergeants. Only two weeks earlier, he had been awarded the Distinguished Service Cross for heroism on Noemfoor Island.

Less than two hours later, an even greater disaster struck the 1st Battalion. Incredibly, this too was in Company C's area. Shortly after 3:30 A.M., Sergeants William M. Newburn, Jr. and D.L. French left the 1st Platoon's command post—which was nothing more than a large hole in the ground containing a radio set and three members of the command section—to check on their men who were deployed along the perimeter's edge. Upon their return to the platoon CP about a half-hour later, the two sergeants were somehow mistaken in the ink-black darkness for Japanese infiltrators. Someone in the CP fired a shot that killed Sergeant French. Survivors of this incident reported that when Sergeant French was shot, Sergeant Newburn—who was standing right beside him—must have assumed that the platoon headquarters area had been seized by the enemy during his brief absence. Newburn lunged forward, firing his submachine gun, and jumped down into the CP where he killed a medic who was reaching for his aid kit and wounded Platoon Sergeant Dempsey Kelly.

Two nearby paratroopers unknowingly compounded this horrible incident by mistaking the still-shooting Sergeant Newburn for an Imperial Marine infiltrator who was bent on wiping out the platoon's command group. Both troopers emptied their rifles into Newburn, killing him instantly.

As soon as the shooting stopped, a third paratrooper, Private Michael Hernandez, asked the two men, "What was all that commotion about?" Still completely unaware of what they had actually done, one proudly replied, "We just killed a Jap infiltrator who was attempting to wipe out our platoon CP group."

When the awful truth became known a few minutes later, the shock was almost too much for the grief-stricken members of Company C. Several of them cursed and slammed their weapons to the ground. Others wept openly.

A few hours later, the first rays of sunlight announced the beginning of another day of suffocating heat and continued skirmishing with the Japanese defenders. Down in the 34th Infantry's area that day, Lieutenant Colonel Postlethwait instructed Lieutenant Lewis F. Stearns, the commander of Company L, to send a squad-size patrol out to Engineer Point to see what the enemy had there. As the patrol was nearing its objective, a passing naval air observer radioed a warning that he could see "at least a platoon of enemy troops" at Engineer Point. The patrol immediately withdrew, permitting the airborne observer to call in fire from a destroyer. Not quite a half-hour later, the observer reported sighting thirty-two enemy bodies lying in the sand.

Elsewhere on the eastern slopes of Malinta Hill, Captain Howard G. Fenway of the 34th's Company I experimented with smoke to see if he could flush the enemy out into the open. Fenway sent one platoon to the eastern entrance of Malinta Tunnel carrying some thirty white phosphorous grenades. His plan was to have all the grenades thrown into the tunnel's small opening. Meanwhile, another of his platoons would block any air vent seen discharging the smoke, thus keeping it in the tunnel to either suffocate the Japanese or force them out in search of fresh air.

On a signal given by Captain Fenway, the platoon at the tunnel's entrance pulled pins and tossed the grenades inside. This produced a lot of shouting within the tunnel but little else. Not one Japanese ran out into the open and not even a wisp of smoke could be seen coming from any of the air vents. Puzzled by the total lack of success with this experiment, Fenway withdrew his troops to their defensive positions west of Malinta Hill.

At the request of Lieutenant Colonel Postlethwait, a pair of destroyers massed their fire on the eastern entrance to Malinta Tunnel a short while after Fenway's withdrawal. The resulting bombardment was so intense that it caused a landslide that sealed the entrance with tons of dirt and stone.

From time to time while they were digging in on Bottomside, Postlethwait's infantrymen uncovered sorrowful reminders of the stand made on Corregidor by General Wainwright and his troops during the dark days of early 1942. Several old soup-plate style steel helmets had already been unearthed around the base of Malinta Hill. Most contained one or more bullet holes.

Out near Black Beach that day, Corporal Joseph W. Sinclair,

of Presque Isle, Maine, made a most unusual discovery. Sinclair had been in the Army since 1938 and had previously pulled a three-year tour of duty on Corregidor, rotating back stateside only one month before the outbreak of the war. As he was digging a foxhole for protection against Imperial Marine snipers still lurking about, Sinclair unearthed a set of dog tags belonging to a buddy with whom he had served on the Rock.

While Corporal Sinclair was making his discovery, a lone Japanese marine was shot and killed near Bottomside's North Dock area. While going through the dead marine's pockets, the infantryman who shot him found a wallet belonging to Private First Class Ned A. Moore, a current member of the 34th Infantry's Company K that had stormed Malinta Hill.

Moore, a twenty-year-old from Linton, Indiana, was called before his company commander, Lieutenant Robert R. Fugitti, to explain how this could have happened. "I was a member of the first wave on D day," Moore said. "When I got about halfway up Malinta Hill, I sprained my ankle and could barely continue on with that big box of ammo that I was carrying. So I removed my heavy pack that contained my wallet, plus most of my other gear, and laid it down intending to go back for it later on. But after getting on top of the hill, my ankle hurt so badly that I forgot all about my pack. When I went to get it later that night, it was gone." As Lieutenant Fugitti handed his wallet back to him, the young soldier smiled nervously and said, "Thank you, sir. I sure am glad to get my wife's picture back."

During the afternoon of the twentieth, Company A of the 34th Infantry was scheduled for an attack up a large ravine located along the northern end of Malinta Hill. In preparation for the attack Lieutenant Oliver K. Smart, the Air Force liaison officer on the ground with the infantrymen, made arrangements for a flight of P-47s to drop incendiary bombs that would burn out the ravine's heavy underbrush and silence a Japanese machine gun in that area. Both Lieutenant Smart and Captain Melvin A. Simpson, Company A's commanding officer, had an excellent observation post in a small trench overlooking the target area. When the planes passed over the Rock on a trial run, a six-foot Imperial Marine jumped out of the underbrush, ran some fifty yards up a narrow trail, and darted back into the underbrush. The Air Force Lieutenant's eyes bulged as he exclaimed, "Hey, I could have nailed that guy if I'd had a rifle!"

Captain Simpson smiled as he borrowed an M-1 from a nearby rifleman and laid it on the parapet. "Okay, there you are," said Simpson. "Now when the first bomb explodes, you keep your eyes open. He'll more than likely flush again."

The bomb dropped near the trail. Out came the Imperial Marine. The lieutenant dropped him in his tracks.

A few minutes later the excited officer realized that he had been neglecting the flight of P-47s orbiting overhead. Picking up the radio receiver, he heard the extremely angry voice of the flight leader who shouted, "What the hell's going on down there? I want to know if that first bomb was on target!"

"Bomb?" gulped the lieutenant, "Oh, yeah, the bomb! Yes sir, it was right on the money. Say, I just shot a Jap!"

Frequently and fortunately, there often were more aircraft available to Rock Force than could be used on close-support targets. Normally, Rock Force would request about four air strikes each day. The Air Force, ever anxious to assist the ground troops, frequently sent enough planes for eight or more strikes.

At Rock Force headquarters the Air Force control officer would say to his S-3 counterpart, "I've got fifteen birds overhead. Any targets?"

"Nothing right now." was the usual reply.

"Okay, they've got two-plus hours of gas. I'll keep them standing by and check in with you when they have about fifteen minutes left on station."

If, at the end of the two-hour period, no close-in targets had become available, the bombs were dropped out on the island's tail and in ravines where naval gunfire could not penetrate. After the bombs had been dropped, the planes would swoop down and strafe any Japanese flushed by the bombing.

For the past two days, a rumor had been circulating throughout Rock Force that the cavernous bowels of Malinta Hill contained enough explosives to blow Corregidor off the face of the earth. Most members of the force considered the rumor too wild to be true; others believed every word of it.

The anxiety felt by believers of the rumor was justified late in the afternoon of the twentieth when Postlethwait's infantrymen found a Japanese document detailing the tremendous quantity of explosive devices stored beneath Malinta Hill. A translation of the document revealed that in the many laterals extending out from the hill's large east–west vehicular traffic tunnel were three tons of TNT, 35,000 artillery shells, 80,000 mortar shells, 93,000 hand grenades, 2,900 antitank mines, and some 2 million rounds of rifle and machine gun ammunition. With the aid of his slide rule, the engineering officer at Rock Force headquarters calculated that the explosives were sufficient, if detonated simultaneously, to blow Malinta Hill and the two rifle companies deployed across its top "sky high." Colonels Jones and Postlethwait kept this alarming discovery to themselves.

Meanwhile, Topside's paratroopers had been fighting a series of brisk skirmishes as they made their way down ravines and cliffsides in pursuit of the elusive Japanese. Early in the morning of the twenty-first, Captain Lyle M. Murphy's Company I of the 503d Parachute Infantry was on reconnaissance in force down through Ramsay Ravine to the shoreline when one patrol discovered five large caves along the water's edge. Hidden away in the caves were nineteen Q boats, the Japanese Navy's equivalent of the kamikaze airplane. Made of plywood, the boats were twenty-five feet long and were powered by an American-manufactured Cadillac automobile engine. A large torpedo-shaped explosive device in the bow of each boat had been rigged to explode upon contact with any solid object.

Earlier, on the night before Rock Force invaded Corregidor, Captain Itagaki had sent thirty of these Q boats under the command of a Lieutenant Commander Koyameda to attack American landing craft anchored in Bataan's Mariveles Harbor. Only twelve of the Q boats succeeded in reaching the harbor. As they were forming into pairs to launch their suicide attacks, the Japanese were discovered and taken under fire. Five boats were quickly sunk, but the others broke through at full throttle and plowed into four American vessels, sinking three and crippling the fourth.

Why Captain Itagaki failed to use more of his fleet of Q boats to destroy the American landing craft neatly lined up in Mariveles Harbor for the next day's invasion will never be known. American naval officers theorize that Itagaki must have been keeping what remained of his fleet in reserve to repel the amphibious attack he expected would soon be launched against his island fortress. However, the ferocity of the American preassualt bombardment, coupled with the surprise of the unexpected parachute attack, prevented use of the Q boats. Since the boats were still seaworthy, Captain Murphy reported their location to Rock Force headquarters who in turn dispatched a squad of engineer troops to disarm the explosive devices. All nineteen boats were eventually turned over to the U.S. Navy.

While Captain Murphy's troopers were examining the Q boats, Lieutenant Calhoun's platoon from Company F was cautiously moving along a trail leading through Grubbs Ravine. Suddenly they came across a number of captured American military trucks and cars that the Japanese had apparently parked there some time ago to move their reserve forces up to Topside and other parts of the the Rock. All of the trucks, and a few of the cars, had been riddled by .50-caliber bullets fired by passing P-47s that regularly strafed this area. As the platoon quietly walked along the line of vehicles, the point man discovered an Imperial Marine sleeping on the bed of a truck. While the point man kept the Japanese covered, a second trooper awoke him and pulled him to the ground. The prisoner walked meekly with the platoon for a short distance and then went berserk, screaming, kicking, and spitting at his captors. Since the platoon was deep in enemy-occupied territory it could ill-afford to have its presence made known. The trooper nearest the prisoner slapped him hard across the face and signaled him to be quiet. When that failed to quiet him, the same trooper shot him to death. The platoon then continued on its way, returning to Topside a short while later without further incident.

On the night of February 21–22, while Lieutenant Colonel Postlethwait's infantrymen were resting quietly above them, the Japanese in Malinta Tunnel busied themselves with final preparations for a suicidal explosion that was to be followed by a giant banzai charge. Since D day, some 2,000 Japanese had been trapped in the many tunnels and laterals beneath Malinta Hill. The preinvasion bombardment and recent shelling by the destroyers had caused great rock slides that sealed the main tunnel's entrance and exit. Some of the Imperial Marines had earlier dug their way out of the tunnel's eastern end to attack Postlethwait's infantrymen deployed across the top of the hill.

Knowing that they were as good as dead anyway, the remaining Japanese trapped inside the tunnel decided to die in style for their Emperor. They planned to use a few hundred pounds of explosives to blast the tunnel entrance open. Then they would charge out and mount one large banzai attack to either kill all the Americans or be killed themselves.

At 11:30 on the night of the twenty-first, a Japanese marine inside the tunnel lit a fuse leading to the explosives stacked against the blocked entrance. A few minutes later there was an explosion of such magnitude that the Americans thought the monster they were sitting on had suddenly come to life. Huge sheets of flame shot from both ends of the tunnel, lighting up the dark sky. Rocks and dirt flew everywhere; large fissures opening along the slopes of Malinta Hill caused massive landslides. Six men from Captain Melvin A. Simpson's Company A were buried alive by one of these slides. Sailors aboard the destroyers could feel the concussion of the blast. While these explosions were occurring, stunned paratroopers on Topside looked down at the tunnel's entrance, which was belching fire and smoke. What in the world, they asked themselves, was going on?

The Japanese plan had quite literally backfired. Flames from the initial explosion had blown deep into the tunnel, setting off the tons of explosives and ammunition stored there. In the ensuing holocaust, all but 600 Imperial Marines crouching in the side laterals were killed before getting out to launch their banzai attack. Confused survivors of the blast ran off toward the tail of the island to await certain death.

In Postlethwait's battalion, casualties from the explosion were heavy. Along with the six men known to have perished in the landslide, many others were still unaccounted for. Throughout the battalion area, medics were hard at work treating whole squads of infantrymen who had been seriously injured by falling debris.

The remainder of the night passed quietly, leaving the paratroopers and infantrymen of Rock Force wondering what awaited them at daylight.

11
DISASTER AT MONKEY POINT

At dawn on Thursday, February 22, Captain Melvin A. Simpson, commanding officer of Company A, 34th Infantry, dispatched a rescue party to the north end of Malinta Hill to see if there were any more survivors of the landslide that had buried six of his men alive the previous night.

This was Simpson's second attempt to find survivors. The first had been made in total darkness immediately after the gigantic blast that shook all of Corregidor. Heading the rescue party was twenty-six-year-old Corporal Maurice K. Hutchins, a rifle squad leader assigned to Company A. When drafted into military service only two years earlier, Hutchins had been teaching mountain climbing and rescue techniques in his hometown of Vail, Colorado. His dogged determination and unique skills as a mountaineer had enabled Hutchins to successfully direct the evacuation of twelve seriously injured infantrymen during the first rescue mission. Working now in broad daylight the rescue party found six more survivors, all unconscious. By 10:30 A.M., those six survivors, plus the bodies of two infantrymen who were found dead among the rubble, had all been extracted from the area of the landslide and the mission was called off.

The tremendous explosion and resulting landslide had been especially damaging to Captain Simpson's Company A. The company no longer had a 3d Platoon. Lieutenant Cornelius S. Hardwick, the platoon leader, and all but six of his riflemen had been either killed or disabled by the landslide. The six who survived unharmed were assigned to the company's other two platoons.

Meanwhile, on Topside the three parachute battalions were once again going about the ugly task of clearing their respective zones of action. At a little after 11:00 that morning, Captain Jean P. Doerr's Company G of the 503d was patrolling down a road leading to Middleside when it flushed an Imperial Marine from a cluster of lantana bushes. In a desperate attempt to escape, the enemy marine ran a short distance without firing the rifle he was carrying. Then he dumbfounded the paratroopers by climbing into the mixing bowl of a large prewar cement mixer rusting by the side of the road. One of Doerr's troopers tossed in a grenade that exploded loudly. The Americans had just resumed the march when they were astonished to see the Imperial Marine crawl out of the cement mixer. Minus his rifle now, and bleeding profusely, the terrified Japanese ran limping toward Bottomside. Even though he was an easy target, no one had the heart to shoot the pathetic-looking figure stumbling down the road. Convinced that the enemy marine would soon bleed to death anyway, the paratroopers let him get away.

During their nearly three-year occupation of Corregidor the metal-hungry Japanese had removed practically all of the island's trolley-car tracks along with many other steel items and shipped them to Japan to be melted down and recast as weapons of war. What used to be trolley-car rights of way were now empty trails that had to be patrolled daily. During the afternoon of the twenty-second, Captain Joseph M. Conway's Company H of the 503d was moving along one such trail between Battery Point and North Dock when a trooper stepped on a land mine that severed one of his legs and mangled the other. Although the company medics did their best to save the severely wounded trooper, he died of shock before a carrying party could deliver him to the hospital in Mile-long Barracks. Because of the many mines in that area, nearly two hours had passed from the time the trooper was wounded until he could be safely carried out on a makeshift stretcher for the long haul up to Topside.

In the meantime, Lieutenant William T. Bailey's Company F

was making final preparations for a sweep that would take them from Topside down through Grubbs Ravine to the island's North Shore Road. Having patrolled this same area only the day before, Bailey's troopers were thoroughly familiar with it.

The plan of attack for today's mission called for the 2d Platoon to operate on the company's left flank, advancing downhill along Grubbs Trail in column formation. The 3d Platoon was to protect the company's right flank by moving down Rock Point Trail, also in column formation. Meanwhile, Lieutenant Bill Calhoun's 1st Platoon would advance straight down the center of the ravine in a line of skirmishers, keeping itself aligned with the two flank platoons. Directly behind Calhoun's platoon would move a strong mobile reserve unit composed of the company's weapons platoon, a light machine gun platoon borrowed from 2d Battalion Headquarters Company, plus three flamethrower teams and one demolitions team from the Regimental Headquarters Company.

It was not quite 2:00 P.M. when Lieutenant Bailey gave the word for his reinforced company to begin moving down into the rough, steeply sloped ravine. During the advance, Lieutenant Calhoun, the 1st Platoon leader, walked in a dry streambed that ran down through the center of the ravine. The streambed had a bank some two feet high. From his central position Calhoun could observe his entire skirmish line as well as the movements of the two flank platoons. Recalling this mission after the war, Calhoun said, "As usual, it was quite hot that day. But I think we were perspiring more than usual because of the tension. We knew for sure that the enemy was down there waiting for us."

After traveling about 100 yards down into the ravine, the line of skirmishers came upon a small wooden building beyond which was a road culvert. Private First Class Stanley Maciborski walked past the building without looking inside the door on the far side of the structure. Seeing this, Calhoun stepped out of the streambed on the left to go take a look. Private George Mikel, the platoon's messenger, who was walking along the right bank, then hopped down into the streambed intending to follow his boss. At that moment an Imperial Marine who was hiding in the culvert fired a shotgun blast that wounded Maciborski, signaling numerous other Japanese to open fire.

178

All hell broke loose. Japanese rifle and machine gun fire seemed to come from everywhere, most of it passing over the heads of the Americans. Only one trooper, Private Paul A. Narrow, was struck down by the enemy's initial volley. A senior aidman, Technical Sergeant Fifth Class William E. Ashton, was shot through both ankles while running to treat Narrow. Disregarding his own painful wounds, Ashton proceeded to crawl through a hail of small arms fire to Narrow's side only to discover that he was dead.

With each minute the volume of Japanese fire seemed to grow stronger. The heaviest concentrations were coming from the area between Grubbs Trail and North Shore Road. Two cave entrances were located there and many Japanese could be seen standing out in the open, firing their weapons. Private Mikel was struck by a bullet that knocked him flat on his back. From his position beside the wooden building, Calhoun looked down at Mikel who was lying motionless upon a bed of large stones. Unable to tell if Mikel was dead or alive, Calhoun shouted to him, "Don't move, Mikel. Just keep laying still and the Japs won't fire at you again. I'm going to get our mortars firing and then we'll get you out of there in a little while."

Next, Calhoun glanced to his far right where he saw Technical Sergeant Philip Todd, his platoon sergeant, crouching behind a tree that was only ten inches in diameter. "Get down on your belly," yelled Calhoun, "that tree trunk is not wide enough to protect you!" Chagrined, Todd plopped to the ground and began looking around for a more reliable form of life insurance.

Leaving Sergeant Todd in charge of his grounded platoon, Calhoun ran through a hail of bullets back to the trailing mortar squads, giving them the firing data they needed to engage the enemy gunners. That accomplished, he rejoined his men just in time to see Private James Wilson throw a white phosphorous grenade into the culvert beyond the wooden building. As soon as it exploded, Wilson jumped down into the streambed and sprayed the culvert area with his Thompson submachine gun, killing eight Imperial Marines. Private Theodore C. Yocum ran to assist Wilson, who had turned away from the culvert to engage other targets of opportunity. But as Yocum drew near the culvert site he was struck by a blast of machine gun fire that instantly killed him.

Amid all this action, Lieutenant Calhoun saw that Mikel was now dead. He had been alive when Calhoun cautioned him to remain still, but just as the lieutenant left to get the mortars in action Mikel sat up despite a loud protest from Sergeant Todd and was killed by several bullets that ripped through his chest.

With mortar shells crashing down on their positions, the Japanese who had been out in the open suddenly ceased firing and withdrew into the caves. Meanwhile, Lieutenant William T. Bailey's 2d and 3d platoons knocked out a pair of machine guns that had been pouring fire in from the flanks. Having thus gained fire superiority, Bailey maneuvered his company down to the cave openings. Several attempts were made to get the Japanese to come out and surrender but they responded by throwing out several grenades that exploded without harming anyone. Privates James Bradley and Mike Natalie then went to work with satchel charges, trying to seal the large entrances. When that failed to produce the desired results, the flamethrower teams were brought forward. While describing what happened next, Private Bradley said, "It must have been pretty awful in those caves because the Japanese finally came running out. Half the poor buggers were on fire as they burst out into the open. I remember Private Richard A. Lampman standing behind a tree, picking them off with his Browning automatic rifle. At the time, I was out of ammo and could not be of assistance to Lampman. That was the only time during the war that I felt any anger toward the Japanese."

When Company F withdrew to Topside a short while later, it left seventy dead Imperial Marines piled up outside the tunnel entrances. Company F's losses were six wounded and three killed.

While Company F was fighting in Grubbs Ravine, word came into Rock Force headquarters that elements of Lieutenant Colonel "Big John" Erickson's 3d Battalion urgently needed some artillery fire support. Erickson's battalion was conducting cave-closing operations down along the shoreline where the 462d

Parachute Field Artillery's Pack 75s could not be brought into play. So Colonel Jones put in an emergency request for some five-inch gunfire from the navy's destroyers. When all the pertinent firing data had been radioed out to the destroyer Jones hurried across Topside and stood at the edge of a cliff directly above the enemy-occupied caves. Five hundred feet below the waters of Manila Bay churned furiously. A few minutes later, the destroyer began firing directly into the cave openings. Because of the unusual curvature of Corregidor's cliffs in that area, Jones could not see the shells exploding some 300 feet beneath him. But he could smell the cordite and feel the ground tremble under his jump boots.

Elsewhere on Topside that same afternoon, Captain Hudson C. Hill was summoned to the 2d Battalion command post in Mile-long Barracks to receive orders for the next day from Major Lawson B. Caskey, the battalion commander. Caskey said: "At 7:30 in the morning you are to pass your company through the 1st Battalion's Company C, which is in position at Searchlight Point, and attack westward with the mission of destroying all enemy forces located between Searchlight Point and Wheeler Point. You can expect to find between 175 to 200 Imperial Marines between those two points. To make your job a little easier tomorrow, regimental headquarters is giving you a heavy weapons platoon and two demolition squads. And, best of all, arrangements have been made with the U.S. Navy for your company to have priority of fires from one of its destroyers throughout the day."

Hill was somewhat worried about the apparent difficulty of the mission but said nothing to Major Caskey. At the conclusion of the briefing, Hill and Lieutenant Larry S. Brown, the battalion S-3 officer, walked to the edge of Topside where the cliffs overlook Wheeler Point. There they made a visual reconnaissance of the 600-plus yards of shoreline between Wheeler and Searchlight Points. In his after-action report, Hill wrote, "It was about 6:00 P.M. and the rapidly setting sun cast an ominous mixture of dark shadows and a red glow over the entire area. The scene below the cliff edge sent a cold chill up my back."

What disturbed Hill most was his observation that there were

181

only two routes along which he was going to be able to maneuver his company during the attack, both of them bad. The first route traced along the curving shoreline's narrow, rock-strewn beach, the other one followed what remained of a bomb-cratered prewar roadway located about halfway up the face of the cliff. Since neither route had any overhead cover, Hill knew that he and his men were going to have to make the attack in full view of enemy troops occupying the caves above them.

Upon completion of his recon, Hill returned to the battalion command post to study several oblique aerial photos that had been taken of his objective area only two days earlier. The heavy preinvasion bombardment had blown away nearly all of the tropical vegetation clinging to the cliffs, so the photos clearly revealed seven cave openings. The largest was at Wheeler Point where a concrete tunnel appeared to lead back into the underground ammunition bunker of Battery Wheeler.

It was dark when Captain Hill gathered his company officers to issue his plan of attack. He opened by announcing that the company was going to attack along two parallel routes, one along the beach and the other along the cliffside roadway. Lieutenant Lewis B. Crawford's 3d Platoon would attack along the beach route. Lieutenant Roscoe Corder's 2nd Platoon would meanwhile attack along the roadway route.

At this point in his briefing, Hill paused to emphatically caution Lieutenants Crawford and Corder that each time their platoons rounded a bend during the mission they probably would run into heavy enemy fire. "Therefore," said Hill, "you will not—repeat, not—move around any points until I give you the order to do so. Any questions on that?" There were no questions.

Hill instructed Lieutenant Emory N. Ball, the company's Weapons Platoon leader, to follow directly behind Corder's platoon: "You are responsible for covering the company's rear and for supporting the leading platoons by fire when called upon to do so." Next came a question-and-answer period after which Hill told his assembled officers that during the attack he would march just behind the leading squad of the 2d Platoon.

There were no attacks along Company E's sector of the perimeter during the night and only one minor attempt at infiltration.

Thus, Hill's troopers managed to get more than the usual amount of sleep. At six o'clock the next morning the company and all of its attached combat support units assembled on the northwest corner of the parade ground. There the paratroopers calibrated their tactical radios and were issued a fresh canteen of water, plus a basic load of ammunition and hand grenades. By seven o'clock the leading platoon arrived in the vicinity of Searchlight Point.

As the rest of his troopers were still closing into the jump-off area, Captain Hill met briefly with Captain John P. Rucker, the commanding officer of Company C. Rucker reported that each time he had tried to move his company around Searchlight Point, the first man had been killed by a heavy volume of small arms fire coming from Unknown Point. Lending stark credence to Rucker's statement was the body of a paratrooper who had been killed not fifteen minutes earlier.

With a half-hour remaining until jump-off time, Hill ordered his company to take a rest break. Meanwhile, he managed to crawl out to the tip of Searchlight Point without getting fired upon. From his vantage point under a clump of bushes, he could see that his initial plan of attack would work satisfactorily. Returning to the jump-off point, Hill held a short conference with his company officers to settle the final details of the attack.

Hill told his officers that he was going to take the company radio and work his way back out to the tip of Searchlight Point for the purpose of registering the destroyer's guns on Unknown Point. Once the ship's guns were registered, he would ask for a five-minute pasting of the target from top to bottom.

Under cover of the destroyer's fire, Lieutenant Corder's roadway platoon would emerge en masse from its covered position at Searchlight Point and advance as far as possible toward Unknown Point. When the ship's fire was lifted, Corder's platoon was to attack all the way to Unknown Point protected by the fire of its attached machine gun section. Also under cover of the destroyer's guns, Lieutenant Crawford's platoon was to move down to the beach and begin clearing all caves it might find along the shoreline.

Having firmed up his initial tactical moves, Hill worked back out to the tip of Searchlight Point where he radioed the destroyer's gunnery officer to ask for a ranging round. Not quite one minute later, the first round exploded halfway up the vertical side of Unknown Point. Hill gave a correction and the second round hit a little lower, but still was not on target. The third round hit the target dead center. Hill was impressed by the floating artillery's speed and accuracy. After the battle he wrote, "The U.S. Navy really can shoot!"

The time was now 7:30 A.M. Hill radioed the destroyer to "go ahead and pile it on" and the ship began firing five-gun salvos with mechanical precision. While Unknown Point was being blanketed by exploding five-inch shells, Lieutenant Crawford double-timed his 3d Platoon down to the beach. Lieutenant Corder meanwhile maneuvered his 2d Platoon around Searchlight Point onto the roadway. Neither platoon suffered any casualties as they rapidly advanced slightly more than halfway to Unknown Point before taking cover from the friendly fire and setting up their machine guns to cover themselves during the remainder of the attack.

As soon as the destroyer lifted its fire, a squad of Japanese hiding in a cave down near the beach took Crawford's platoon under fire. Crawford turned his machine guns on the cave openings but that failed to silence the enemy within. It soon became obvious to Crawford's troopers that the troublesome cave was cut back into the cliff at a sharp angle. This meant that in order to knock it out someone was going to have to cross its front and fire directly into it.

Crawford decided to do this extremely dangerous job himself. He made his way up to the cave's mouth and threw white phosphorsous grenades inside. As the smoke started billowing, he dashed across the front, firing long bursts from his carbine into the opening. Although several shots were fired at Crawford from the interior, he was not injured. But upon reaching the far side, he noticed that his right trouser leg was rapidly becoming soaked. Quickly examining himself for some kind of wound, Crawford discovered that his canteen had a bullet hole drilled through it.

Crawford kept firing into the cave while gradually moving his troopers forward to join him. The cave's occupants continued to resist by throwing out a few grenades, wounding some of Crawford's men. The grenades had no sooner exploded when eleven Imperial Marines charged out of the cave shouting, "Banzai!" Nine of them were instantly gunned down. Of the other two, one was killed when he grabbed the muzzle of a paratrooper's Browning automatic rifle with both hands. The second was knocked down with a butt stroke by one of the riflemen, and his skull crushed with a second blow. This Japanese proved to be the last one alive in that cave.

While examining the cave's interior, Crawford's men found a total of forty-seven dead Japanese, forty-one rifles, and a badly damaged Nambu machine gun. Crawford's casualties amounted to five troopers, all of whom had only been lightly wounded by the exploding grenades.

At this point in his company's mission, Captain Hill received a radio message from battalion headquarters advising him that two of the destroyer's gun turrets had developed electrical problems and that the ship had to depart at once for repairs. Another destroyer would arrive at 12:15 P.M. As further advance without the destroyer's support would be foolhardy, Hill decided to call a halt in place and allow his men to rest and eat an early K-ration lunch.

During this interlude, Captain Hill made a detailed visual recon of Wheeler Point. Then he met with his officers and announced that as soon as the replacement destroyer arrived on station the advance would continue as before, with the beach and roadway platoons leapfrogging forward to the final objective.

The U.S. Navy continued to delight Hill when a destroyer arrived on the scene punctually at 12:15 and quickly registered its guns on Wheeler Point. Hill then asked the destroyer for a ten-minute preparatory barrage during which the troopers continued the march. Some forty-five minutes later, Lieutenant Corder's platoon arrived in the vicinity of Wheeler Tunnel. Continuing to advance cautiously, Corder's troopers received no fire until they were within five yards of the outer waist-high blast wall that sat out in front of the tunnel's huge concrete entrance.

Then nine Imperial Marines charged out, repeatedly yelling "Banzai" as they fired their rifles and threw hand grenades.

Fortunately for the bulk of Corder's men, they had been expecting trouble and all but one of them was in the prone position. The one standing paratrooper was instantly killed.

Apparently the Japanese who had just run out of the dark tunnel were blinded by the bright sunshine. Most of their hand grenades were thrown over the cliff. Also, as they charged straight out into the open, they ran into the blast wall where they bunched up and became confused. As they were still milling around in that area, a paratrooper opened up with his submachine gun. All were killed in a moment's time.

The problem for Corder's platoon did not end there, however. Other Japanese continued firing out of the tunnel. Corder meanwhile kept moving more riflemen around the entrance. Although he soon had his whole platoon ganged up at the large opening, Corder could not gain the upper hand because the enemy force within the tunnel was matching his riflemen bullet for bullet. Desperately trying to gain fire superiority, Corder's men tried tossing several fragmentation grenades into the big tunnel, but that did nothing to change the situation.

Realizing that a stalemate had been reached, Captain Hill proceeded to the tunnel entrance to see if he could do anything to improve the tactical situation. There he gathered three troopers armed with submachine guns and a Browning automatic rifleman. With those men, Hill crawled to the tunnel's blast wall where he had them first throw grenades from the crouching position, then stand and hose down the interior on full automatic fire. This move ended in failure, with one trooper shot dead and a second wounded.

Hill gathered more troopers and set out again for the blast wall. This time he crawled around to each man, personally coaching him to fire low and deep into the tunnel. When everyone had been briefed, Hill raised his carbine, signaling the troopers to throw their grenades. Then they rose as one and poured heavy fire into the tunnel.

The Japanese fire slackened and much shouting could be heard in the tunnel during breaks in the shooting. Suddenly the Japanese stopped firing altogether. This in turn resulted in a slowing down of the paratrooper's fire. Privates William A. Brown and

Howard J. Jandro cautiously began moving toward the entrance. When they were almost to the blast wall, fourteen Imperial Marines armed only with grenades swarmed out of the tunnel. "We had been nicely suckered in," Hill said later.

The Japanese grabbed the two paratroopers and a fierce fist fight ensued. Meanwhile, as a Japanese officer armed only with a samurai sword began hacking at Private Brown, the other troopers standing nearby recovered their senses and moved in firing from the hip. A macabre tug of war then took place between the opposing forces for possession of Brown and Jandro. The hand-to-hand fighting lasted several minutes during which Brown and Jandro were wrestled free and the Japanese killed. Brown was alive, but just barely; he died three days later of his wounds. Jandro was not as seriously injured as Brown, but he did have several facial contusions that the Japanese had inflicted by using his own steel helmet as a bludgeon. Most of the other troopers who took part in this brawl had received a few hard knocks but none serious.

Captain Hill's troopers were still sorting things out when seventeen more Japanese came running out of the tunnel. Their attack was preceded by a shower of hand grenades, most of which had been thrown too hard and went sailing over the cliff. Captain Hill and six of his paratroopers were wounded by grenade splinters, but again the Americans were quick enough to kill all of the attackers before they could do more harm. Neither Hill nor any of his men was injured badly enough to require medical evacuation.

Things had just quieted down when a great many more shots were fired from within the tunnel. Private Jandro, who was just beginning to come to his senses from the beating he had taken, was struck five times and died instantly. Lieutenant Ball was hit twice in the chest and fell mortally wounded.

Medics were still desperately trying to save the lieutenant when a force of twenty-two Imperial Marines stormed out of the tunnel. The wildly screaming Japanese were running with such great speed that most of them were unable to put on the brakes after leaping over the blast wall. Twelve of them ran right off the edge of the cliff and fell to their deaths. Their charge swept

Private Ralph F. Janas along with them, but he managed to grab hold of a strong bush at the edge of the cliff and save himself. An enemy marine kept himself from going over the cliff by grabbing on to Private Gerald G. Kirkpatrick who promptly stabbed him to death with his World War I vintage trench knife. The rest of the Japanese were killed by small arms fire.

It was now 3:34 in the afternoon and most of Captain Hill's paratroopers were out of ammunition. So he asked for and received permission to withdraw his company to Topside. While granting the withdrawal request, battalion headquarters informed Hill that an LCM (landing craft, medium) would pick his company up at Searchlight Point and deliver it to Bottomside's Black Beach.

Hill ordered his radio operator, along with Lieutenant Corder's platoon, to beat a hasty withdrawal. Then he fired what remained of his last clip of ammunition into the tunnel and took off running after Corder's men who had already disappeared around the bend.

During its withdrawal, Lieutenant Corder's platoon carried Privates Brown and McBride, both of whom had been seriously wounded. Because of the speed with which the withdrawal had to be made, the bodies of Lieutenant Ball and Private Jandro could not be evacuated from Wheeler Point. Sometime during the night of February 23–24, the Japanese removed their dead as well as the remains of the two Americans. Subsequent patrols into this area failed to find a trace of them.

News of Company E's difficult, day-long fight had reached the other 2d Battalion companies on Topside. As the company was marching back across the parade ground in column formation, it was met by small clusters of paratroopers who offered cigarettes, or a canteen of water, or to lift a trooper's weapon from his shoulder and carry it for him. Hill recalled: "Some tried to help the tired men along, but were firmly shaken off. It was a proud company. Although tired beyond all reason, they held their heads high."

Earlier that morning Captain Joe Conway's Company H of the 503d was pressing east toward the ruins of the island's prewar power plant when a Japanese flushed from the lantana bushes ran toward the nearby opening of a large cave. Lieutenant Bonnell H. Stone, the officer in charge of the leading platoon, chased after the fleeing enemy, snapping off a shot as he was entering the cave. Stone's bullet missed the Japanese and traveled on into the cave where it ignited a tremendous explosion. A blast of flame shot out like a huge blowtorch, incinerating Lieutenant Stone before the horrified eyes of Sergeant Bennett M. Guthrie. Meanwhile the whole hillside exploded, knocking the paratroopers to their knees. Four Company H men were killed by the landslide. Frantic digging by several troopers uncovered Staff Sergeant Dominic C. Dimascio, whose arm was seen protruding from the rubble. Dimascio had lost an eye and his face, wrote Sergeant Guthrie, "resembled raw beefsteak." The bodies of two dead paratroopers were recovered from the debris. But those of Privates Albert C. Lovinguth and James R. Moore were never located.

Elsewhere on the Rock this day, Lieutenant Colonel Postlethwait's infantry battalion undertook an operation aimed at opening Bottomside's North Shore Road in preparation for Rock Force's pending thrust out to the monster's tail section. At seven o'clock that morning, the battalion's 81mm mortar platoon fired several concentrations on the small knob above the old Enlisted Men's Bathing Beach at Engineer Cove. The last mortar shell was still in the air when a spearheading Sherman tank clanked on down the road followed by a rifle platoon from Captain Simpson's Company A.

Arriving at Malinta Hill's hospital tunnel portal, the tank commander stuck his main battle gun inside and loosed a pair of high explosive rounds. Twenty-one Japanese banzaied out of the tunnel only to be mowed down by the infantrymen who were set up and waiting for them. Demolition crews then blew the entrance shut, after which the tank–infantry team pushed on to link up with Company K's 3d Platoon, which had been isolated out at Malinta Point for the past seven days.

Now that Company F paratroopers had cleared Topside's Grubbs Ravine, and Company E had neutralized Wheeler Point, Rock Force Commander Jones decided the time had come for him to proceed with phase four of the plan to recapture the Rock:

destruction of enemy forces east of Malinta Hill. Colonel Jones knew that some small pockets of enemy resistance remained on and about Topside and that he would have to leave part of his force behind to clear them up while the majority of his combat units were pushing toward the tail section.

At 4:00 P.M. on the twenty-third, Colonel Jones met with his battalion commanders at a company command post atop Malinta Hill to issue orders for the attack that was to begin the next day. From that lofty point the officers had an excellent view of the entire eastern half of Corregidor. Jones opened by saying that Major Pug Woods's 1st Battalion would jump off at 7:30 in the morning, spearheading the attack down both sides of the narrow tail, with Lieutenant Colonel Big John Erickson's 3d Battalion following behind as a ready reserve force. Meanwhile, Lieutenant Colonel Postlethwait's infantry battalion would continue to maintain its blocking positions across the island's waist section and Major Caskey's 2d Battalion of the 503d would remain on Topside to clean up the few pockets of enemy resistance remaining there. Jones closed the briefing by reminding his battalion commanders that throughout this final phase of the operation the U.S. Navy's floating artillery would be standing by to blast targets of opportunity and Air Corps dive bombers would be on station ready to pounce upon the enemy with bombs, napalm, and .50-caliber bullets.

Less than an hour after Jones had dismissed his officers, Captain Henry Gibson of the 462d Parachute Field Artillery was dispatched to the top of Malinta Hill by his battalion's fire direction center (FDC). Gibson was to set up an observation post (OP) from which he could register the battalion's Pack 75s and concentrate their fire where necessary as they supported the infantry's advance in the morning. The infantrymen atop the hill gave Gibson and his radio operator a warm welcome, assigning them a large vacant foxhole to use as an OP. Gibson quickly established radio contact with the FDC, then he and the radio operator settled in for what they thought was going to be a restful night among the hospitable infantrymen.

Back up on Topside, Major Ernest C. Clark, Rock Force's

operations officer, handed Colonel Jones the S-3 section's periodic report number 8. It read as follows:

Reporting Period: From 1800 hours 22 February 1945 to 1800 hours 23 February 1945.
Map: Corregidor Island: 1/12,500.
1. Our operations:
    a. Infantry: Mopping up proceeding in the Wheeler Point and Searchlight Point areas has nearly cleared western sector of the island of enemy forces. Our forces are in position to initiate assault on eastern sector beginning 0730 hours 24 February. Combined air, naval, artillery, and ground action will be utilized. Softening up of the area continues today.
    b. Aviation: Our planes bombed and strafed the area east of Malinta Hill to Airstrip. Thirty-one P-47s used in morning strike, expending 4,000 gallons napalm, thirty-eight 500-pound bombs, 31,000 rounds of .50-caliber ammo. Area adjacent to Engineer Point was bombed and P-47s continue to strafe.
2. Casualties:
    a. American: To date: 118 killed, 314 wounded, 10 missing.
    b. Enemy: To date: 2,486 killed, 2 prisoners.

At 3:30 A.M. on February 24, only four hours before the tail assault was to begin, seven separate explosions rocked Malinta Hill. Fire and smoke shot out from the many air vents protruding from the hillside, convincing everyone there that the hill was about to burst apart at the seams. The 34th Infantry's historian later wrote:

During the night of 23–24 February, the enemy made his most serious attempt to demolish Malinta Hill. In the early morning hours, seven explosions, all in quick succession, threatened to tear the hill asunder. Foxholes crumbled, flames belched from every hole in the central and northern portions of the hill, and with it belched parties of Japs—either corpses

191

blown out by the blast, or men driven out into American fire and death.

It was devastation—stark, awe-inspiring, terrifying. But for the Jap—not for the intended victim.

Columns of black smoke were still flowing from several openings along the sides of Malinta Hill when at 7:30 A.M., precisely on time, Major Woods led his 1st Battalion paratroopers across the line of departure behind a pair of Sherman tanks borrowed from Lieutenant Colonel Postlethwait's infantry battalion. Meanwhile a rolling barrage of artillery shells being fired by the massed Pack 75 howitzers of the 462d Parachute Field Artillery Battalion whistled overhead. On reaching Malinta Hill, Woods sent Captain William T. Bossert's Company A around its southern flank with orders to attack toward Camp Point. Then he sent the two tanks, plus Captain Wert R. Cates's Company B and Captain John P. Rucker's Company C, around the hill's northern flank to attack toward Infantry Point.

As its northern column was bypassing the Malinta Hill hospital tunnel portal, which had been reopened during the night by the industrious Japanese, disaster struck the hard-luck 1st Battalion once again. An entire squad of Imperial Marines suddenly made a banzai charge out of the tunnel, causing panic among the startled Americans. In a wild shootout the leading tank's gunner tried to help by opening up with his machine gun. But he accidentally killed four paratroopers who had become intermingled with the Japanese. Seeing this, the tank commander ordered his driver to back up and pivot the vehicle into a safer firing angle. The driver promptly complied, crushing to death a fifth paratrooper who had been lying behind the tank firing at the enemy.

The melee ended a few minutes later when all of the surviving Japanese suddenly bolted back toward the tunnel. The second tank clanked after them, firing two high-explosive rounds into the tunnel. Then the tank commander blocked the entrance with his huge machine, allowing the paratroopers to safely pass by. A demolition team placed several satchel charges around what remained of the opening, blasting it shut in a matter of seconds.

Companies B and C advanced the next 800 yards unopposed.

But upon arriving in the vicinity of Infantry Point, they came under machine gun fire. With bullets kicking up dirt all around his grounded squad, Technical Sergeant Robert W. Heyer of Company B leapt to his feet and charged the enemy gun, knocking it out of action. Heyer was killed during this action, for which he was posthumously awarded a Silver Star.

Meanwhile, over on the other side of the island's tail, Captain Bossert's Company A was advancing rapidly against light opposition. There the enemy defenders were in small caves, most of which were located along the shoreline and could safely be approached from the rear. Several of the caves were blown apart by shipboard gunners who expertly aimed their five-inch shells. "It was an exhilarating luxury," said Bossert, "to have a destroyer attached to a rifle company."

Bossert's paratroopers had just finished counting 101 enemy dead along their route when a Japanese officer dashed out of a cave brandishing a samurai sword. Seconds later he was joined by a squad of grim-faced Imperial Marines who fell in behind him and stood stiffly at attention with their rifles at their sides. The officer shouted a command at the marines who then dutifully surged forward over the rubble directly into the aimed fire of the astonished paratroopers.

Bossert's company then pushed on to Camp Point. Just before nightfall, Bossert tried moving his 2d Platoon to the top of Water Tank Hill. Despite strong prepatory fires delivered by the 462d Parachute Artillery, the platoon was unable to take the hill. Less than a half-hour after jumping off in the attack, the paratroopers returned carrying their wounded. Major Woods then called a halt to the advance, ordering all companies to dig in for the night.

As the sun started to set in the west, Colonel Jones visited Major Woods's forward command post in a huge bomb crater. In the crater with Jones and Woods was Technical Sergeant James L. McMillen, the battalion sergeant major; Sergeant Matthew J. Dallas, Major Woods's communications chief; Corporal Peter Fieden, the battalion clerk; Corporal Richard W. Dews of the intelligence section; and Privates Glen R. Knapp and Roy E. Marston, both radio operators.

The Rock Force commander had been up front with the attacking 1st Battalion throughout most of the day. He was well pleased by their performance and told Woods as much. Woods then briefed Jones on his plan for renewing the attack at dawn, after which the Rock Force commander said he must be getting back to his headquarters on Topside.

"No need to rush off, Colonel," said the young major. "You can spend the night here with us. Then you'll be able to jump off with us in the morning."

"Thanks, Pug," said Jones with a smile, "but I really must go. One of General MacArthur's senior aides landed on Topside just a short while ago in a Piper Cub and I'm told he's been acting rather mysteriously. I've got to get back to the store and see what he's up to." (Jones would later learn that Major General William F. Marquat had arrived to make arrangements for an impending visit by General MacArthur.)

"You might not get back alive, Colonel," cautioned Woods. "It's already starting to get dark, and if a Jap straggler doesn't shoot you, one of our own troopers just might accidentally do you in."

"Well, Pug," Jones replied with a shrug, "that's a chance I'm going to have to take."

Jones climbed out of the bomb crater and headed for Topside. It was a decision that would save the Rock Force commander's life within the hour. Unknown to Jones, enemy mortar crews were about to bombard the 1st Battalion's positions in preparation for a mighty banzai charge by some 500 Imperial Marines located in bunkers beneath Water Tank Hill.

True to the fight-to-the-death Bushido code, the surviving Japanese commander had decided to ignore the lopsided odds he was facing and launch a suicidal counterattack intended to drive the Americans off Topside.

Jones and his aide had just departed for Topside when Pug Woods summoned his company commanders and staff to the CP to issue his attack order for the early morning continuation of the attack. Captain Rucker of Company C was the only company commander who had arrived at the CP when, shortly after 9:00 P.M., the first enemy ranging round exploded fifty yards short. Not quite two minutes later a second mortar shell landed fifty yards behind the CP, causing Sergeant McMillen, an old mortarman, to whisper to Corporal Fieden, who was sitting next to him, "Now they've got us bracketed. The next one's going to land on our heads."

"Well, then, what should we do?" asked Fiedel nervously.

"Get out of this hole, that's what," replied McMillen.

Two minutes later the unmistakable thump-whoosh sound of a mortar launch echoed through the darkness. McMillan and Fieden had just rolled out of the huge crater when the incoming mortar shell exploded in the CP.

The blast instantly killed Major Woods, Corporal Dews, and Privates Knapp and Marston. Captain Rucker was still alive, but one of his arms had been nearly severed at the elbow. Sergeant Dallas, who had been sitting next to Major Woods, survived without a scratch.

With the death of Major Woods, command of the 1st Battalion passed to Major John N. Davis, formerly the battalion executive officer who happened to be just a short distance away from the CP when the mortar shell exploded. While medics frantically tried to save Captain Rucker who was "bleeding like a stuck hog," Davis put in a call to the 462d's Fire Direction Center on Topside, asking the artillerymen to search for the offending mortar. As later reported by a prisoner, the resulting torrent of Pack 75 shells caught the Japanese at the worst possible moment as nearly 500 of them were assembling out in the open to launch a banzai attack down Water Tank Hill.

As the American shells continued to explode throughout his positions, the Japanese commander stubbornly refused to permit his men to take cover. Instead, he kept yelling at them to assemble into attack formation. As a result, approximately half his force was knocked out of action before the attack could get underway.

Despite his frightful losses, the Japanese commander regrouped his battered troop units and at 3:30 A.M. personally led them in a wild banzai charge straight toward the 1st Battalion positions. Savage fighting raged in the darkness for the next hour, during which the dug-in paratroopers did not yield an inch and the Japanese ranks were ripped by exploding artillery shells and withering blasts of rifle and machine gun fire. With dawn approaching, the Japanese broke off their attack. The survivors, about 165 Imperial Marines, withdrew eastward toward the tip of the island carrying their wounded with them.

Despite their horrendous casualties, the Japanese continued to put up stiff resistance when, at 10:45 A.M. on the twenty-fifth the 1st Battalion—now led by Major Davis—jumped off to attack Water Tank Hill. Only seconds into the attack, Private John C. Pace was killed and two of his fellow squad members were seriously wounded.

Fortunately for his exhausted paratroopers, who had gotten practically no sleep the previous night, Major Davis had wisely decided against making a frontal attack up the steep slopes of Water Tank Hill. Rather, he relied upon the navy's destroyers and the 462d Parachute Field Artillery to deliver a series of crushing bombardments on top of the hill while he maneuvered two companies around its flank mopping up dazed survivors. By 4:30 P.M. Davis's troopers had fought their way forward some 700 yards to a rocky knoll located just short of Kindley Field, the island's small airstrip. From that vantage point, Major Davis could see the end of Corregidor. But since only a few hours of daylight remained, he called a halt to the attack, ordering his troops to dig in for the night. By the onset of darkness, the 1st Battalion's companies were stretched across the island from Cavalry Point on the north shore to Ordnance Point on the south shore, a distance of 550 yards.

Earlier in the day, while the 1st Battalion was pushing eastward, Big John Erickson's trailing 3d Battalion companies were clearing bypassed pockets of resistance. While doing so they encountered several Imperial Marines who, rather than disgrace themselves by surrendering, committed suicide by either exploding grenades held against their heads, shooting themselves, or in a few cases, hanging themselves.

Captain Joe Conway's Company H from Erickson's battalion was patrolling along the northern shoreline that morning when it flushed out an Imperial Marine who ran a short distance down the beach then took refuge under a cliff that projected into the water. A bazooka shell forced him out into the open, dazed and bleeding. As a couple of paratroopers were leading him to the rear, a rifle shot was fired by a third paratrooper standing on the hillside above. The bullet tore into the captive's upper right shoulder and exited through the lower left abdomen, fatally wounding him.

What happened next horrified the battle-hardened paratroopers, all of whom by this late part of the war thought they had already seen the absolute worst cases of Japanese self-destruction. The mortally wounded enemy marine got to his feet and staggered over to the water's edge where he picked up an empty five-gallon gasoline can that had been washed ashore. Placing the can on the sand before him, he plopped down on his knees, removed his long cloth ceremonial tiger marine belt and neatly laid it on the can. Next, he removed a pouch of prayer sticks from around his neck and placed it atop his belt. Taking a prayer stick, he bowed to the west toward Japan and chanted for a moment or two. Then he briskly sat upright and pulled several feet of intestines from the gaping hole in his abdomen. He repeated this incredible act several times during which a number of paratroopers turned away and vomited. Finally, a paratrooper who was unable to stand the sight of the enemy marine torturing himself any longer, stepped forward and shot him through the head, ending this grisly melodrama.

Also on the twenty-fifth, Lieutenant Colonel Postlethwait's 3d Battalion of the 34th Infantry Regiment left the island aboard a small fleet of LCM's. The 34th Infantry's parent outfit, the 24th Infantry Division, had been ordered to Mindanao to participate in other combat operations aimed at liberating the southern Philippines. During the ten days it spent on the Rock, Postlethwait's tough little battalion lost forty-two men killed in action and 163 wounded and was credited with killing over 800 of the enemy. Postlewait's battalion was replaced by the 38th Division's 2d Battalion, 151st Infantry Regiment, whose members occupied the existing foxholes just vacated by the departing infantrymen.

Against sixteen paratroopers killed on the twenty-fifth, the defending Japanese had lost over 500 men. The day's fighting had raised the total number of Japanese dead to 3,703 by actual body count. After a blanket of darkness enveloped Corregidor that night, the noticeable absence of the customary infiltration attempts and mortar attacks confirmed that the Japanese were in serious trouble.

At 8:00 A.M. on the twenty-sixth, Major Davis's 1st Battalion began advancing on a broad front toward Kindley Field behind a rolling barrage of artillery and mortar fire. The attack continued without incident until the battalion's right flank was nearing Monkey Point. There it came under heavy automatic weapons fire most of which seemed to be coming from the entrance of a large tunnel located beneath a knoll at Monkey Point. Major Davis promptly changed the direction of the attack by moving two companies of paratroopers to deal with this newest threat. By 11:05 A.M., Captain Bill Bossert's Company A—the same company that had lost twenty men on Topside when the Japanese detonated an explosive device beneath its CP—was positioned squarely on top of the knoll at Monkey Point. Meanwhile Captain Cates's Company B guarded the western approach to Monkey Point and Company C—now led by its new commanding officer, Lieutenant George Kish—was deployed along a line facing Kindley Field.

Unknown to Major Davis and his paratroopers, the Japanese had stored many tons of TNT and ammunition in an extensive tunnel complex located beneath Monkey Point. In recent days they had been using the tunnels as air raid shelters. But by now they had converted them into a minifortress and were prepared to die defending it. At 11:15 a paratrooper was shot dead as he attempted to place a shaped charge against the tunnel's big steel door. Rather than risk losing any more of his footsoldiers, Major Davis ordered one of the Sherman tanks to roll up to the tunnel and blast the door off its hinges.

The tank commander complied, firing a single armor-piercing round that penetrated the door and continued on inside the tunnel where it touched off an explosion far greater than the ones that had occurred under Malinta Hill.

The initial colossal explosion was quickly followed by four others that sent scores of bodies, both American and Japanese, rocketing into the sky. For the next several minutes, boulders, chunks of concrete, and dirt rained down from the sky, further injuring numerous men lying scattered about the blast area moaning with burns and ghastly wounds. The explosions completely obliterated the knoll that had been at Monkey Point and left in its place a giant smoking crater 130 feet long, 70 feet wide, and 30 feet deep.

The thirty-five-ton tank that fired the fatal round was flipped end over end like a child's toy a distance of fifty feet. It came to rest upside down with the crew trapped inside. Rescuers later heard a man's voice in the tank. An acetylene cutting torch was quickly borrowed from a destroyer and he was rescued. All other members of the tank crew were dead. A 2d Battalion trooper a mile and a half away up on Topside was seriously injured by a large chunk of falling stone. Another huge stone struck the deck of a destroyer located 1,000 yards offshore.

Private Carl G. Bratle of Company C was standing some 500 feet away from Monkey Point at the time of the initial blast. Although he had no visible wounds, blood was oozing from the young trooper's nose, ears, and eyes. Wiping the blood from his eyes, the first thing Bratle saw was a dead American officer who had been torn in half at the waistline. While trying to find his squad leader a few moments later, Bratle was horrified to come across a paratrooper's jump boot with a foot still in it.

Elsewhere in Company C's area, Private Leo Shirley laid on his stomach hugging the ground as debris rained down upon him. Because he was wearing a steel helmet and back pack, Shirley felt they would protect him from serious harm. When the debris finally stopped falling, Shirley rolled over and sat up. That's when he saw his right leg had been mangled and a long section of gleaming white bone was protruding from the wound.

Captain Bossert, who was standing at ground zero, was knocked flat by the blast with such force that two of his ribs were broken and his chest crushed. Major Davis was catapulted through the air like a human cannonball. He came to earth some thirty feet down range, stunned and gasping for air.

Although badly shaken, Davis was able to continue with his duties as battalion commander a few minutes later when his head stopped spinning. But he found little left to command. Disaster had finally disabled the 1st Battalion as a fighting machine. The explosions had inflicted 196 casualties on his battalion, including fifty-two killed. By "counting arms and dividing by two" the paratroopers calculated that the enemy forces had lost 150 men at Monkey Point that day.

Two days prior to this catastrophic event, Captain William C. McClain, the 1st Battalion surgeon, had borrowed two brand new ambulances from Topside's 18th Portable Surgical Hospital unit for use during the push to the tail. "Make sure you don't take them too close to the fighting," admonished the lending officer.

"Not to worry," replied McClain, "I'll bring them back still looking like new."

When the blasts occurred, McClain and his medics were only fifty yards from Monkey Point. Both ambulances survived the initial explosion with only minor paint damage. But one was subsequently totaled when a chunk of stone "as big as my desk," remembers McClain, landed on its roof. The ambulance driver survived unharmed.

Colonel Jones had been on Topside when the blasts occurred. He immediately ordered all available medical support forward to aid the crippled 1st Battalion. Then he rushed out to Monkey Point, finding several paratroopers frantically digging out buddies who were buried beneath dirt and debris but were still alive.

The Rock Force commander did not allow the calamity to shake his military judgment. He quickly ordered Big John Erickson's 3d Battalion to pass through what remained of the 1st Battalion and continue the attack down the tail while the enemy forces were also still recovering from the shock.

The 3d Battalion pushed out immediately with Company I in the lead, Company G protecting the north flank, and Company H guarding the south flank. Quickly brushing aside light resistance, the paratroopers reached Kindley Field just before sundown. There Erickson had his men clear the airstrip of mines and booby traps. Then he formed them into a perimeter defense and made preparations to continue the advance in the morning.

Meanwhile, back in the devastated Monkey Point area it had taken scores of medical personnel over two hours to evacuate all casualties up to Topside's hospital facilities. Graves registration teams spent an equal amount of time gathering the American dead for delivery to the embarkation point at Black Beach. The dead were neatly wrapped in ponchos and laid along both sides of the dusty South Shore Road. Sergeant Bennett M. Guthrie vividly remembers seeing them along that road, "perhaps an arm's length apart, their feet pointing toward the tracks of the roadway. The line of bodies probably extended more than a hundred feet."

When the last ambulance load of casualties had pulled away toward Topside, and all of his dead had been transported to Black Beach, Major Davis led what remained of the hard-luck 1st Battalion back to a perimeter defense position near Water Tank Hill for the night.

12

"I SEE THE OLD FLAGPOLE STILL STANDS"

The night of February 26–27 passed without incident. A peaceful silence had once more descended across the war-torn Rock. Only a few rifle shots punctuated the quiet of the night, all of them fired by itchy-fingered paratroopers who suspected that the wily enemy still had something up his sleeve. The lingering memory of the gigantic explosions and catastrophe at Monkey Point prompted one of the paratroopers on guard duty at Kindley Field to ask a fellow squad member the question that was uppermost in the minds of all members of Rock Force: "How many more tons of explosives do you suppose the Japanese have waiting underground for us?"

At 7:00 A.M. on the twenty-seventh, Lieutenant Colonel Erickson's 3d Battalion resumed its attack toward the tip of the island. From its jump-off point at Kindley Field, the 3d Battalion still had just over one mile to go before it would reach East Point, the geographical eastern end of Corregidor.

As he had done during yesterday's advance on Kindley Field, Erickson maneuvered his paratroopers forward on a broad three-company front. Captain Jean P. Doerr's Company G advanced on the battalion's left flank where it swept the area north of the airstrip all the way down to the water's edge at Cavalry Point before turning due east. On the right flank Captain Joe Conway's Company H had the mission of clearing the area south of the airstrip all the way to Monkey Point. Meanwhile, Captain Lyle M. Murphy's Company I was in the middle of the zone of action, marching east along a rocky ridgeline running down the center of the island's tail.

The advance proceeded smoothly for a few hundred yards before Company I was halted by a burst of machine gun fire from a cave opening on the right side of the ridge's tree-lined pathway. While three members of his platoon kept the cave's occupants hemmed in with rifle fire, Staff Sergeant Ernest J. Debruycker crawled up to the cave entrance intending to smoke the enemy out into the open. Standing off to one side of the opening, he pulled the pin on a white phosphorous grenade and quickly tossed it deep into the cave. There it was caught by an alert Imperial Marine who instantly threw it back outside where it exploded, seriously injuring Debruycker. Disregarding his painful wounds and the choking cloud of white smoke billowing around him, Debruycker took another grenade from his belt, this time a more lethal fragmentation grenade. To prevent a repeat performance by the enemy's star catcher, Debruycker next did what all combat infantrymen do before throwing a frag at a close-in target. Knowing that frags have a three-second fuse, he pulled the pin and held onto the grenade, allowing it to "cook off" for one second. Then he hurled it into the cave, this time making sure it struck a wall and skidded uncontrollably along the floor. There was some shouting in the cave after the grenade exploded, but then its occupants fell silent. A flamethrower team was called forward to hose down the interior for good measure. Meanwhile, a medic began treating Debruycker's numerous wounds, most which still contained particles of burning phosphorous. As soon as the flamethrower operator backed away from the cave entrance a demolitions team moved in and blew it shut. Company I then continued on its way minus the services of Sergeant Debruycker, who had to be evacuated to the rear to receive additional medical treatment.

As Lieutenant Colonel Erickson's parachute battalion steamrolled eastward along the ever-narrowing tail section it gradually became compressed into a cone-shaped formation with Captain Murphy's Company I at the point. Eventually, the tail narrowed to a width of only 100 yards. There Erickson halted all forward movement by his two flanking units, companies G and I, ordering them to patrol back along their routes of advance to check for possible bypassed cave openings.

Meanwhile, he instructed Company I to press on alone toward East Point. Murphy's troopers became engaged in some skirmishing along the way. During one encounter twenty-year-old Private First Class Stanley C. Crawford was mortally wounded as he single-handedly killed six Imperial Marines while knocking out a machine gun nest that was holding up his platoon's advance. Crawford was posthumously awarded a Silver Star for his gallantry in action.

A little after 4:30 P.M., Murphy's company reached the end of the ridgeline and descended unopposed onto the small fifty-foot-wide plain that was East Point. There the paratroopers began wildly cheering and clapping, celebrating the fact that they were finally standing on the very tip of Corregidor's tail.

When all of the shouting and applause came to a halt, several troopers walked on down to the shoreline where they quietly stood gazing out at the swirling waters of Manila Bay. The silence was overwhelming. A few minutes passed, after which one trooper removed his helmet and filled it with seawater. Then he slipped around behind his sergeant and gave him a good dousing. Soon everyone else was doing the same thing and water was flying everywhere.

The paratroopers were still cavorting at the seashore when four quick rifle shots cracked over their heads, sending everyone sprawling on the ground in search of cover. It was not until the fourth bullet that the troopers were able to determine that they were being fired upon from Hooker Point, a small islet some 100 yards east of East Point. Incredibly, a small party of diehard Japanese had waded out to that narrow spit of land earlier in the day at low tide and established a defensive position there.

With time on his side, Murphy had his troopers keep the enemy on Hooker Point pinned down with occasional bursts of machine gun and rifle fire until low tide occurred again at 6:37 P.M. Then he sent a full rifle platoon and two flamethrower teams wading out to the islet. As that small detachment was preparing to step ashore at Hooker Point it was greeted by an overthrown grenade that exploded in the water without doing any damage. The paratroopers then surged forward like a tidal wave, firing their weapons on full automatic. This small but ferocious assault killed four Imperial Marines who were found crouched behind a pile of boulders.

Even though Corregidor had been combed from end to end by February twenty-seventh, Rock Force still had a lot to do. The Americans had expended over seventeen tons of explosives while closing a total of 468 caves. Yet even as Murphy's platoon was wading back to East Point from Hooker Point new caves were being dug elsewhere on the Rock by surviving Japanese units.

For the next few days, Colonel Jones had Rock Force conduct vigorous mopping-up activities with each battalion assigned a specific zone of action. During this phase of the operation Major Lawson B. Caskey's 2d Battalion was given the responsibility of continuing daily sweeps across Topside and of making occasional forays down through the lower elevations to the shoreline. Topside's Wheeler Battery continued to be a great source of difficulty to the 2d Battalion. It was one of the favorite hideouts of the Japanese. On six occasions during the twenty-seventh and twenty-eighth, paratroop flamethrower teams had to be called in from Rock Force headquarters to burn enemy troops out of the battery's ruins.

Morrison Point also proved to be a difficult spot to mop up. As the 3d Platoon from Captain Hudson Hill's Company E was patrolling in that area on the twenty-seventh it was fired upon by a small party of Japanese holed up in a freshly dug cave. During a brisk firefight the paratroopers worked their way up to the entrance, killing seven Imperial Marines in the cave. The platoon then backed off a short distance to allow its accompanying demolition crew sufficient room to march forward and rig TNT charges around the cave opening. As he was approaching the entrance to provide security for the demo crew while they were setting the charges in place, Private William L. Edwards was shot through the right shoulder by an enemy marine still concealed within the depths of the cave. The demo men immediately dived for cover and the paratroopers loosed a fusillade of rifle fire into the cave opening. Meanwhile, the platoon's medic rushed forward, dragging Edwards off to one side and out of the line of fire. Although his single wound did not appear to be serious at first glance, Edwards had in fact been severely injured. The enemy bullet had shattered upon striking his collar bone, causing considerable internal bleeding. Several of Edwards's fellow platoon members carried him all the way up to Topside's hospital on the double, but he died in the operating room.

In an attack made on the twenty-eighth down along the shoreline in the vicinity of Wheeler Point, the 2d Battalion's Company D had its withdrawal route to Topside cut off by a platoon of Imperial Marines. A fierce skirmish erupted during which Company D lost three troopers killed in action and five more wounded. When it became apparent that the company might not be able to fight its way back up to Topside before dark, the U.S. Navy was called upon. As the sun was setting, two LCIs nudged into the shoreline below Topside and dropped their ramps. Shipboard gunners kept the enemy force pinned down with .50-caliber machine gun fire as the troopers scrambled aboard and made good their escape. During this dramatic rescue mission, Company D was commanded by Lieutenant James P. Gifford, Jr. He was the third officer to command that company since it had parachuted onto the Rock twelve days earlier. Gifford had replaced Lieutenant Henry H. "Buck" Buchanan who had been injured during a freak accident in which a grenade he threw at the enemy rolled back downhill and exploded near him. Fortunately for those paratroopers who were near him at the time, Buchanan was the only one injured by that grenade.

While Company D's troopers had been skirmishing in the vicinity of Wheeler Point on the twenty-eighth, Lieutenant Bill Bailey's Company F was methodically searching through a number of underground bunkers that had just been discovered some 100 yards northeast of Mile-long Barracks. There Bailey's troopers uncovered a huge cache of civilian clothing plus several hundred cases of American whiskey and Japanese sake. While describing this and subsequent incidents in his personal wartime journal, Lieutenant William Calhoun, Bailey's 1st Platoon leader, wrote:

We were still doing a little patrolling, but enemy activity was lessening every day. Our company found a large supply of men's civilian clothing. There were blue cotton slacks and cotton short-sleeve shirts of every color of the rainbow. Most of the shirts were a bright shade of yellow. Someone, I believe it was Major General Marquat who had just recently arrived on Corregidor, said that the Japanese had looted most of the merchandise out of the department stores in Manila and brought it out here for storage. This seems to be the reason for the large amounts of alcoholic beverages we've been finding lately. By this time, our battle fatigues were unbelievably filthy. During our earlier campaigning on Noemfoor Island our fatigues had become sour and moldy. But now they were stiff as boards from all the dirt that had been ground into them and heavily crusted with salt from our dried perspiration. So when we returned to the perimeter from our patrolling activities we put on some of the brand-new civilian clothes to lounge around in. It was so nice to get out of the hot and dirty combat fatigues we were wearing. But then someone wore one of those bright yellow shirts on patrol. The patrol moved out across the parade ground and was seen by someone in regimental headquarters. Orders came out immediately thereafter, threatening the most dire consequences for anyone caught wearing civilian clothing. I guess headquarters was correct in making such a threat. Combat parachutists just didn't look dressed for the part attired in a steel helmet, jump boots, web suspenders with eight-round bullet clips and frag grenades hanging from them, plus civilian blue trousers and a bright yellow shirt.

Elsewhere during the mop-up phase, Big John Erickson's 3d Battalion continued to roust Japanese hideaways out of newly dug caves found out on the tail section. Simultaneously, the newly arrived 2d Battalion of the 151st Infantry probed along the base of Malinta Hill and Bottomside where the pickings were slim. Meanwhile, Major Davis's decimated 1st Battalion was recalled to Topside where it became Rock Force's ready reserve unit and was assigned a very small section of the perimeter to defend. When this hard-luck battalion's casualty figures were tallied, it was discovered that Company A—now commanded by First Sergeant Willie G. Jetton, who had replaced Captain Bill Bossert when he was badly injured at Monkey Point—was down to only forty-two enlisted men and no officers. Company A suffered the greatest number of casualties of any company that fought to reclaim Corregidor. When it waded ashore on February 17, D-plus-1, Company A had an assigned strength of six officers and 132 men. If this same company had parachuted onto the Rock, its strength figures would have been even more deplorable by this stage of the battle.

By February 28, the Japanese survivors seemed to finally realize that they had lost Corregidor. Only the day before, the crew of a PT boat patrolling in the north channel had spotted an Imperial Marine attempting to escape to the Bataan Peninsula by swimming through the nearly three miles of shark-infested water clinging to the trunk of a palm tree. The boat's skipper ordered the coxswain to pull alongside the swimmer. As the boat reached him, the bobbing escapee pulled a pistol from a hollowed-out section of the tree trunk and fired a shot that just barely missed hitting one of the sailors reaching down to help him aboard. The rescue ended then and there. As the boat sped away, its .50-caliber gunner shot the still swimming Japanese to pieces.

Late that same night, a group of eleven survivors silently made their way down to the shoreline and attempted to swim to Bataan. At about the midway point they were discovered by another patrolling PT boat whose skipper ordered a star shell fired to illuminate the scene. Mindful of what had happened during the other boat's rescue attempt, the crew of this one cautiously approached the escapees, three of whom gladly climbed aboard. But all of the other Japanese in this group staunchly refused to be rescued. Each time the boat approached them they shouted something unintelligible and swam away into the darkness. After making several additional unsuccessful attempts to convince the remaining swimmers to come aboard, the skipper ordered the .50-caliber gunner to open up on them.

In spite of the great distance involved, the swift-flowing tides, and the sharks, dozens of Japanese continued to attempt swimming to the Bataan Peninsula from Corregidor. Nearly all of the escape attempts were made under the cover of darkness for obvious reasons. But occasionally a few desperate souls made a break for it during broad daylight.

Captain Henry Gibson was sitting in his artillery observation post atop Malinta Hill one afternoon when he saw a lone Japanese swimmer clinging to a small makeshift raft. As Gibson watched through his binoculars, an American machine gunner fired several long bursts, all of which splashed harmlessly off to one side of the swimmer. Motivated by all the unwanted attention he was getting, the escapee turned on a burst of speed that soon put him out of range of the machine gun. At that point, Captain Gibson contacted his fire direction center up on Topside, requesting permission to fire one round at the furiously swimming Japanese who had become caught in the channel's swift-flowing currents and was getting nowhere fast. The request was approved. Gibson then fired one round of high explosive which landed in the water with a great splash but no explosion. As he slowly raised the radio speaker to order a second shell, Gibson was overcome with a sense of compassion for the enemy marine who was making a valient attempt to escape and fight another day. "Aw hell, captain, why not let the poor bastard go?" suggested a nearby infantryman. That was all the prompting Gibson needed to make up his mind. He then pressed the microphone to his lips and canceled the fire mission. Barely a few moments later, a lone P-47 that had been circling overhead spotted the swimmer and swooped down on him with its .50-caliber guns blazing. Water boiled all around the raft for the next several seconds, after which the swimmer vanished into thin air.

As more swimmers were sighted later that same day, Lieutenant James R. Thomas, the flamboyant pilot of the 462d Parachute Field Artillery Battalion's Piper Cub observation airplane, took to the air from Topside's rough airstrip to join in the hunt. Flying his two-seater aircraft with one hand and clutching a submachine gun in the other, Thomas skimmed up and down Corregidor's shoreline blasting away at escapees. When gunners aboard a destroyer tried to horn in on his private air war, Thomas protested by buzzing the vessel at mast level, wig-wagging the Cub's wings. The destroyer took the hint and moved on to other hunting grounds. But not before its skipper fired off a blistering message to Rock Force headquarters that resulted in Thomas getting his tail feathers chewed off when he landed.

Shortly after noon on the twenty-eighth, U.S. Navy PT 376, *Spirit of '76*, pulled alongside Corregidor's North Dock to deliver a few prisoners it had just plucked out of the north channel. This same boat had earlier rescued several misdropped paratroopers who landed in Manila Bay on D day. After the prisoners had been turned over to an army guard detachment the boat's skipper permitted half the crew to go ashore for a few hours. Two sailors, Gunners Mates 3d Class Norman H. Smith of Fulton, New York, and John Collins of Elmira, New York, made their way up to Topside's Mile-long Barracks. There they were given a hearty welcome by several paratroopers who vigorously thanked them for the part they and their boat had played on D day. Describing his exciting though brief shore leave, after the war Smith wrote:

We visited with the paratroopers for awhile and when we told them about our rescue mission during the D day jumps they gave us some souvenirs. I remember getting a large piece of camouflage parachute, part of which I had made into pajamas after I came home. I still have one of the small chutes that pop out first and pull out the emergency reserve parachute. I used to entertain my children by attaching one of their toy soldiers to it and throwing it as high as I could.

The most exciting part of that day, though, came when about eight or nine paratroopers who were going out on patrol offered to take me along and show me some of the sights. The sights were not pretty; the ones I remember anyway. But that patrol did show me something. My war, up to that point had been one of shadows, barges, and rafts barely seen in the night or in the half-light of a star shell from our mortar. We never stayed around to see the results. Here was the stark and sickening reality of war. No longer the Hollywood version. For a twenty-year-old who thought the Charge of the Light Brigade was the way to go, this was, indeed, the moment of truth.

Like I've said many times over the years since World War II, those of us aboard the PT boats had a ringside seat for the retaking of Corregidor, a panoramic view of the whole bloody, glorious spectacle. We also had time to think about what was happening that day while the paratroopers were jumping on the Rock. That, I'm sure . . . time to think . . . was a luxury those brave boys were denied. Their view, though it may have begun high in the sky as a panorama, was soon shrunken to a small, hot, sweaty, noisy world where thought, conscious thought, was indeed a luxury they did not have time for. Training, a mighty tough job to do, a will to survive, and some good old Yankee ingenuity was all they had that day and it made for them a place in history and hopefully a place in the hearts of all Americans forever.

With Colonel Jones's paratroop and infantry battalions now operating all across Corregidor's length and breadth, it had become too risky for Rock Force headquarters to call in supporting air strikes. There was always the very real danger that a well-intentioned dive-bomber pilot might mistakenly drop his bombs on one of the many American combat units roaming through the Rock's numerous wooded ravines and gullies. Rock Force did, however, continue to use the pinpoint accuracy of the U.S. Navy's destroyer gunfire throughout the mop-up phase.

Having worked themselves out of a job at Corregidor, the American air units were now focusing much of their attention on the tiny Japanese-occupied island of Caballo some three miles southeast of the Rock. The daily bombing attacks made on that half-mile-long island were a source of considerable amusement for the members of Rock Force. The paratroop battalions up on Topside had the best view of "the Caballo Show" as it came to be called. From their elevated positions the troopers could watch the bombing mission from start to finish: the attack planes swiftly approaching the target from their airbase back on Mindoro; the dropping of the bombs; and the aircraft slowly disappearing from view as they flew back to base to be rearmed for the next show.

Topside's finest seats for the Caballo Show belonged to Lieutenant Bill Bailey's Company F, part of which was quartered in and around the old Spanish lighthouse whose battered tower was still standing. After watching a few of the air strikes, Lieutenant Bill Calhoun, Bailey's 1st Platoon leader, made the following entry in his journal:

> The top of the lighthouse is a great place for observing the aerial bombardment of Caballo Island. Our P-47 Thunderbolts worked it over daily. Soon some of the twin-boomed P-38 Lightnings also joined the attacking formations. The really spectacular attacks, though, were made by two P-51 Mustangs, a new type of aircraft that none of us over here in the Pacific Theater of Operations had ever seen before. We had only heard about this new fighter being used in Europe, and we didn't really expect to see them here. The most modern military equipment always seems to be sent over to Europe. Some Army Air Corps people had said that the Mustangs would never be able to operate off the dusty airstrips we have here in the Pacific because of the big air scoop positioned in front of the P-51's engine. Nonetheless, two P-51s had shown up at Mindoro and were being given a thorough workout. Their bombing attacks were really something to behold. They would come in flying very high over Caballo Island, looking as though they were going to continue straight on toward Manila. But then they would suddenly fall off on one wing and go into a near vertical dive on the island. At a very low altitude, they would drop their bombs then pull out of the dive and gracefully climb back up into the heavens. Also during the day we could usually see two or three destroyers steaming around Caballo, firing at a slow and deliberate rate with their five-inch guns.

With a great many recently killed Japanese still out in the hot tropical sun, the once troublesome fly problem returned to haunt Rock Force. But this time the flies rapidly became so numerous and aggressive that Rock Force soldiers had to cover themselves with a poncho before attempting to eat a K-ration meal so as to keep the insects out of their food. The worsening situation resulted in another hurried call to the Air Corps for its insecticide-spreading aircraft to give the Rock a good dousing. During the afternoon of the twenty-eighth a lone C-47 flew back and forth across the island with someone shoveling a powdery yellow substance out its cargo door. Within a matter of minutes of the aircraft's first pass, the flies again began dropping like flies.

When the last shovel-load of insecticide had been tossed out into its prop blast, the C-47 pilot guided his aircraft to the far western end of Topside. Upon reaching the edge of the cliffs he dropped the big plane out of sight, descending to an altitude of only 200 feet above the water where he began flying along the shoreline. As the C-47 was approaching a ground combat patrol being led by Lieutenant John E. Mara of Company D, one of its aircrew members mistook the Americans for Japanese and fired upon them from the open door with a Thompson submachine gun. Fortunately for all concerned, the airman's marksmanship skills were poor and his bullets landed wide of the mark.

Down on the shoreline, meanwhile, Mara and his paratroopers were livid. Shaking his clenched fist at the airplane, a paratrooper shouted, "You stupid son of a bitch, I'm gonna get you for that!" Another trooper grabbed the radio set and screamed a death threat at the Air Corps liaison officer up at Rock Force headquarters: "You tell the dumb bastard who's flying that C-47 that if he makes another pass over our patrol we're going to shoot his ass out of the sky!" That was the last time a C-47 was ever seen anywhere near Corregidor.

By sundown of February 28, D-plus-15, all organized enemy resistance on Corregidor had ceased. Rock Force headquarters reported 4,506 Japanese counted dead and twenty prisoners. Additionally, many more were known to have perished when they were sealed inside caves blown shut by explosives. Countless others had literally been blown to pieces in the suicidal explosions beneath Malinta Hill and elsewhere. Numerous uncounted enemy dead bodies had been pushed off Topside's cliffs by bulldozers, and an estimated 100 more had been shot while

213

attempting to swim across to the Bataan Peninsula. Altogether, over 5,000 Japanese had died defending the Rock, a figure dramatically larger than the original 600 enemy troops Sixth Army intelligence officers had estimated were defending the island fortress. Rock Force's battle casualties totaled 1,005 men. Of that number, 455 had been killed in action.

General of the Army Douglas MacArthur, the sixty-five-year-old Supreme Commander of the Southwest Pacific Area, made his triumphant return to Corregidor on March 2, 1945. With his keen sense of recent history, and a flair for the dramatic, MacArthur elected to return to the Rock with his entire staff in exactly the same manner they had all been forced to leave it just nine days short of three years ago—aboard a quartet of PT boats. At a little after eight o'clock that morning General MacArthur stepped aboard PT 373 from Dock 2 in Manila wearing a starched khaki uniform, sunglasses, and his trademark crushed officer's hat with tarnished gold braid on its visor. After casually greeting all hands he remarked, "So this is the 373. I left on John Bulkeley's 41."

The skipper of the 373, Lieutenant Joseph A. Roberts, USNR, backed his boat out into the harbor, turned her about, and set her speed at the customary thirty-five knots. Meanwhile, General MacArthur stood on the bow talking with Vice Admiral Daniel E. "Uncle Dan" Barbey, Lieutenant Generals Walter Krueger and Richard K. Sutherland, Brigadier General Carlos Romulo, and others of his party. Astern, the other three PT boats jockeyed themselves into a port echelon formation, carrying other members of MacArthur's entourage who had endured the Bataan-Corregidor nightmare of 1942 and who had escaped with him from the Rock. Throughout most of the thirty-mile voyage out of the island, MacArthur was very talkative. But when Corregidor's shimmering outline first came into view he fell silent and just stood there staring at it. It was not until the echelon swung in toward the shattered North Dock area below Malinta Hill that the general broke his silence by saying, "Well, gentlemen, we are finally back to Corregidor!"

As MacArthur stepped ashore he was greeted by Colonel Jones and a detachment of paratroopers under the command of Lieutenant Charlie T. Horton of Battery C, 462d Parachute Field Artillery, who were guarding the entire North Dock reception area with .50-caliber machine guns. Colonel Jones had assembled a small convoy of jeeps to transport the distinguished visitors up to Topside. At MacArthur's request, the procession of vehicles first drove on out toward the island's tail section where it briefly halted at the partially blocked east entrance to Malinta Tunnel. There the general dismounted and walked several feet into the darkened tunnel alone. Meanwhile, all of the paratroop escorts held their breath expecting a shot to ring out. But nothing happened and MacArthur casually walked back out a few minutes later to the waiting jeeps. Spotting several dead Japanese near the exit who had been burned to death by flamethrowers, he said in a voice devoid of emotion, "It was bad enough for us when we were here, but it has been far worse for them."

The motorcade continued on out to Monkey Point, scene of the disastrous explosions that very nearly wiped out Colonel Jones's 1st Battalion of paratroopers. From there, Jones led the column of jeeps back through Bottomside and on up toward Topside, passing the icehouse, the bombed-out remains of Middleside's troop barracks, the hospital, post exchange building, and finally the old movie theater that was still serving as a morgue. At that point, MacArthur asked the Rock Force commander to escort him across Topside so that he might visit what was left of Wheeler Battery. There the general got out of his jeep, driven by paratroop Corporal Sims H. Smith, thrust his hands into his back pockets, and silenty looked out over the South China Sea and then across to the cloud-covered mountains of the Bataan Peninsula. Again, the paratroop escorts held their breath. Only yesterday, several Japanese had been found and killed inside the battery. A few minutes passed after which the general climbed back into the jeep without uttering a word. Then the motor cavalcade proceeded to the parade ground, arriving there promptly at 11:00 A.M.

Standing on the parade field were 366 members of Rock Force, including Lieutenant Colonel Postlethwait and a contingent of 34th Infantry troops, all of whom had been returned to the Rock for this special ceremony. The Rock Force troops were formed up in a rectangular block with the regimental staff officers in a line in front of the formation. The distinguished visitors dismounted from their jeeps and were aligned by their aides in a separate formation on the other side of the flagpole, facing the Rock Force troops. Fluttering in the trees at the edge of the parade ground were several parachutes that had been left hanging there by their passengers on D day.

As General MacArthur stepped in front of him, Colonel Jones called his troops to attention, saluted smartly, and said, "Sir, I present you Fortress Corregidor." The general returned the salute, then proceeded to congratulate the troops on their heroic achievement of reclaiming the island.

His talk completed, MacArthur glanced up at the bent but unbroken flagpole behind him and said, "I see the old flagpole still stands. Have your troops hoist the colors to its peak and let no enemy ever haul them down." At that, twenty-two-year-old paratroop Corporal Donald G. Bauer of Dayton, Ohio, briskly hoisted Old Glory to the top of the pole.

With a big assist from Colonel Jones and his Rock Force, history had repeated itself.

The entire poignant flag-raising ceremony, emotional and historic as it was, lasted only seven and one-half minutes. At its conclusion, MacArthur and his entourage climbed back into their jeeps and were delivered to North Dock where they reboarded the waiting PT boats. On a prearranged signal given by Lieutenant H. Stillman Taylor, USNR, the PT boat squadron's commanding officer, all four boats cranked engines simultaneously. A flurry of formal salutes were exchanged, after which the boats slowly backed away and set course for Manila, leaving Colonel Jones and his paratroopers standing at attention on the dock.

As his boat was still backing away from North Dock, General MacArthur doffed his famous hat to the paratroopers and, with tears welling in his eyes, placed the hat over his heart and continued to hold it there as he said something that was unintelligible over the roar of the PT boat engines. But a sharp-eyed trooper in the dockside honor guard detachment read his lips. The general had said, "Thank you."

The PT boats were just beginning to disappear from view when a rifleman from the 151st Infantry shot and killed a sniper lurking in the brush at the base of Malinta Hill.

Only one unpleasant incident marred the otherwise successful flag-raising ceremony and visit by the VIPs. It had to do with parachutes. Lieutenant Bill Calhoun explained the incident in his journal:

> Parachutes were still hanging all over the place. We had been instructed not to pick any of them up and also warned not to cut them up for souvenirs. After the ceremony was over some of the visiting officers and their aides were seen gathering up as many parachutes as they could carry and putting them in their jeeps to carry back as their own. This naturally burned us paratroopers up. We had busted our bottoms jumping on the roughest DZs of World War II and were told not to touch the chutes. Then these rear echelon commandos come over to the Rock and walk off with as many chutes as they can carry. As far as I know, after this happened not one company commander in our outfit ever saw a man cutting up a chute. In fact, it's hard to see someone else doing exactly what you're doing.

For the next few days, Rock Force continued to scour Corregidor's shoreline and many ravines, searching for enemy holdouts. Lively skirmishing continued between March second and seventh, during which an additional 118 Imperial Marines were shot to death and four more paratroopers were killed in action.

While the mopping up continued unabated, the majority of Colonel Jones's 503d Parachute Regimental Combat Team made preparations to return to its base camp back on Mindoro. Excess artillery and mortar shells were hurriedly fired off at suspicious target areas, gear was packed up, and the few remaining wounded were evacuated to army field hospitals on Luzon and Leyte.

Early on the morning of March eighth, D day-plus-21, a small fleet of LCIs arrived at Black Beach and began embarking the entire 503d Parachute Regimental Combat Team, plus all of its weapons and equipment. The 2d Battalion of the 151st Infantry remained behind to garrison the island and hunt down remaining survivors.

At 5:00 P.M. the LCIs pulled away from the beach bound for Mindoro. With the coming of darkness the winds grew strong and the sea became extremely rough as the convoy was overtaken by a passing tropical storm. Several of the small LCIs seemed to stand on end in the rough waters and many troopers were injured by loose equipment that had been improperly stowed for sea travel. But the convoy continued on through the night, finally reaching Mindoro intact at noon the following day.

As the paratroopers were wading ashore they passed a large sign that read: "Beware! Panama Jones and his 3,000 thieves return today."

EPILOGUE

Upon their return to the Mindoro Island base camp on March 9, 1945, the exhausted paratroopers of Colonel Jones's 503d Parachute Regimental Combat Team were given a few days of rest and relaxation. During that time the combat team received several hundred new teenage replacements, all of whom had just recently graduated from the U.S. Army Parachute School at Fort Benning, Georgia. Also during that R-and-R period, many of the outfit's veteran troopers who had been lightly wounded and injured on Corregidor were returned to their respective companies and batteries from field hospitals on Luzon.

Despite the infusion of new blood from Fort Benning and the return of its walking wounded, the combat team was still not quite back up to full strength when it received marching orders in mid-March for yet another mission. General MacArthur was not satisfied with halting offensive operations after liberating Leyte, Samar, and Luzon. He felt obligated to eject the enemy from the entire Philippine archipelago so that he might complete the blockade of the South China Sea and simultaneously secure new airbases from which Allied aircraft could support the impending invasions of the Dutch East Indies and Borneo. His plan for doing that had been formulated in February while Rock Force was still fighting to secure Corregidor. It called for the liberation of Mindanao, the huge southernmost island in the archipelago, and the Visayas, an island group comprised of Panay, Negros, Cebu, Bohol, Guimaras, and a number of smaller islands. The military forces would be Vice Admiral Thomas C. Kinkaid's Seventh Fleet; Lieutenant General Robert L. Eichelberger's Eighth Army; and Filipino guerrilla units commanded by Colonel Arcario L. Peralta and Lieutenant Colonel Salvador Abecede.

The 503d Parachute Regimental Combat Team's mission during this newest grand offensive called for the troopers to assist U.S. Army Major General Rapp Brush's 40th Infantry "Grizzly" Division in the liberation of Negros, which is about the same size as the American state of Rhode Island.

On April 8 and 9, 1945, Jones's combat team (less its 1st Battalion, which was left on Mindoro to complete reorganization and combat training) was airlifted to the port city of Iloilo on the island of Panay by Colonel John Lackey's 317th Troop Carrier Group, the same air unit that had dropped it on Corregidor. By that time, most of the eastern portion of Panay had been cleared of Japanese forces. From Iloilo the paratroopers were delivered aboard LCIs to Negros where, on April ninth, they went ashore at Bacalod, a west coast town previously secured by 40th Infantry Division troops. Later that same day they began pushing inland toward the fog-covered mountains of the island's interior in pursuit of Japanese Major General Takeo Manjome's 102d Infantry Division troops, all of whom were well fed and equipped. On April 23, Major Davis's 1st Battalion arrived on Negros from Mindoro. It immediately marched inland, joining up with the other two paratroop battalions that were locked in combat with Manjome's forces. By this time, the paratroop battalions were being resupplied in their forward positions by airdrops of everything from beans to bullets. The enemy forces were meanwhile fighting with great skill and tenacity as they fell back on their mountain supply bases, many of which had been established at elevations in excess of 8,000 feet.

By the middle of May, stiffening Japanese resistance and the island's inhospitable terrain and climate had combined to reduce the 503d Parachute Combat Team's fighting effectiveness to half-strength. About this same time, another few hundred replacements arrived from Fort Benning's Parachute School to fill out the combat team's rapidly thinning ranks. On June 16, the paratroop battalions began to be relieved in their frontline positions by elements of Lieutenant Colonel Abecede's Filipino guerrilla army. By this time, nearly 14,000 guerrillas on Negros had been armed and equipped by the Americans and were controlling nearly two-thirds of the island.

The paratroopers were still conducting patrolling activities on

Negros when, on August 6, 1945, they were stunned by the announcement that a lone American B-29 Superfortress had dropped a single atomic bomb on the Japanese city of Hiroshima, virtually wiping it off the face of the map. Most of the troopers found it difficult to believe that there was a bomb more powerful than the gigantic underground explosions that had caused so much death and destruction on Corregidor. Despite Hiroshima's ruin, and the death of over 100,000 of its citizens, Japan refused to capitulate. When the Hiroshima bomb failed to bring about an immediate surrender, the United States launched a second nuclear strike on August 9. The target this time was Nagasaki where another 39,000 Japanese perished in a matter of seconds and thousands more eventually died of radiation sickness. At midday on August 15, forty-four-year-old Emperor Hirohito broadcast to his shocked nation and to the world the message of Japan's surrender. A few days after the Emperor's stunning announcement, General Kono and 6,150 of his soldiers came marching down out of the mountains of Negros and formally surrendered to the 503d Parachute Regimental Combat Team.

A bare two weeks after Japan's capitulation, the 503d was unceremoniously deactivated on Negros, scene of its last battle. Oldtimers in the regiment were sent home for discharge, and the newer members were reassigned to Major General Joe Swing's 11th Airborne Division that was still in the Philippines preparing to be airlifted to Japan for occupation duty.

In September 1945 a U.S. Army survey team headed by Colonel Reingold Melberg arrived on Corregidor to inspect the island from end to end and determine what might be salvaged from the $150 million worth of hardware the U.S. government had poured into the Rock's prewar coastal defense system. At the conclusion of his three-day tour of the Rock, Colonel Melberg reported that "absolutely nothing" was worth salvaging.

During its inspection tour of Corregidor, Colonel Melberg's team was hosted by a rifle company from the U.S. Army's 6th "Sightseeing Sixth" Infantry Division, which had been providing security for a graves registration detachment that was searching for American dead of the two campaigns. Incredibly, on New Year's Day 1946, Sergeant James M. "Moon" Mullens of the

221

graves registration detachment was startled to see a formation consisting of twenty smartly uniformed Japanese marching at right shoulder arms straight across Topside's parade field toward him. With Mullens still staring in disbelief, the Japanese lieutenant in charge of the formation halted the troops a few feet in front of him. Then the officer shouted a command, bringing his soldiers to present arms (a formal rifle salute) after which he bowed and presented his sword to Sergeant Mullens.

Upon later questioning by the Rock's American infantry commander, the Japanese lieutenant said that he and his men had just learned of their country's capitulation in an old American newspaper they had found down along the shoreline two nights earlier during their nocturnal searches for food and water.

General Jonathan M. Wainwright, the officer who was left in command of United States and Philippine forces, and who was eventually forced to suffer the humiliation of surrendering the islands to the invading Japanese, remained a prisoner of war until 1945. At MacArthur's request he assisted in the signing of the Japanese surrender aboard the *U.S.S. Missouri* in Tokyo Bay on September 2, 1945. He retired at four-star rank in 1947 and died in 1953.

General Masaharu Homma, the officer who accepted General Wainwright's surrender in 1942, and who was himself relieved of command and forced into an early retirement in Japan for failing to gain a quick victory in the Philippines, was brought back to Manila in 1945 for trial as a war criminal. Held responsible for the brutal sixty-mile-long Bataan Death March, during which 10,000 of the starved American and Filipino defenders of Bataan perished while marching to prison camps, Homma was executed by a firing squad in 1946.

General Homma's successor, General Tomoyuki Yamashita, the Tiger of Malaya, was taken to Baguio on September 2, 1945, to sign the formal surrender of all Japanese forces in the Philippines. On December 7, 1945—the fourth anniversary of Japan's devastating surprise attack on Pearl Harbor, Hawaii—a military court in Manila sentenced Yamashita to death for the numerous atrocities committed by troops under his command. On February 23, 1946, he was hanged at Los Banos, a former Japanese prison camp south of Manila. Even to the present time, Yamashita's trial and execution remains a matter of great controversy among historians and legal scholars.

Corregidor was ceded by the United States to the Philippine government in 1946 and subsequently turned into a national shrine of the Pacific War. Yearly, thousands of Americans, Filipinos, and Japanese, many of them veterans of the war in the islands, board a Hovercraft in Manila's harbor that carries them out to the now peaceful, and nearly abandoned, island.

Upon reaching the Rock, visitors are taken on a two-hour bus tour of gun positions, many now nearly concealed by lush growths of ipil-ipil, acacia, and palm trees. Still, many reminders of the terrible battles fought there have been preserved. One of the tour's first stops is Malinta Tunnel, part of which has been reopened. Inside Lateral No. 3, now empty and restored, visitors cannot help but imagine the agonizing days and nights when General MacArthur pleaded in vain with Washington to send reinforcements to save the beleaguered Philippines.

From Malinta Tunnel, the tour proceeds along a modern paved road that leads up through Middleside to Topside. There visitors can survey the old parade field where Corregidor's prewar garrison troops once proudly marched to stirring martial music and the paratroopers jumped to begin the Rock's liberation.

Topside's roofless Mile-long Barracks still stands along the parade field's northern flank. Around and within the giant three-story concrete ruins thick jungle growth obliterates all signs of former human habitation. A ghostly desolation prevails where thousands of American coast artillerymen once lived in the 1930s, and where Rock Force had its headquarters during the 1945 liberation battle, and also where paratroop doctors performed surgery around the clock, saving the lives of severely wounded American and Japanese soldiers.

The tour's high point is the Pacific War Memorial, which was built in 1968 and is located along the parade field's eastern flank. A striking contrast to the many ruins surrounding it, this white marble complex features a domed museum containing Corregidor memorabilia. It connects to a long, marble-paved walk that is hemmed in on either side by four-feet-high walls memorializing crucial battles that were fought throughout the Pacific Theater of Operations. At the far end of the walk stands an impressive abstract steel sculpture, the Eternal Flame of Freedom. Just beyond the sculpture can be seen the old flagpole that flew the Spanish, American, Japanese, and now Philippine flags.

The tour of the Rock ends where it begins, on a wooden pier at Bottomside's North Dock area.

Due to a shortage of funds to properly maintain it, Corregidor's Pacific War Memorial fell into a state of disrepair during the mid 1980s. The dome was cracked during a severe storm and the bronze tablets along the walkway were overgrown with leafy vines. During that same period, scrap dealers illegally began cutting up some of the giant American artillery pieces that once defended the Rock and selling them on the mainland for profit. But beginning in 1988, the American and Philippine governments launched a joint effort to restore the memorial to like-new status. A team of U.S. Navy Seabees and Filipino forces repaired and painted the dome, cleared away vegetation, and scrubbed the commemorative tablets clean. Additional restoration work is still in progress on many parts of the Rock. Philippine security guards are on duty to prevent further acts of vandalism.

In 1951, the U.S. Army reactivated the 503d Parachute Infantry Regiment and assigned it to the 11th Airborne Division based at Fort Campbell, Kentucky. The 503d went to the 11th Airborne to fill a gap that had been created the previous year when that division sent its 187th Parachute Infantry to fight in the Korean War.

Upon my return from the Korean War in 1953, I was assigned to the 503d Parachute Infantry and spent the next four and a half years as a sergeant in its Company A. When I first reported for duty with the regiment, I was impressed at seeing in the lobby of the headquarters building a footlocker-size chunk of stone that had been shipped from Corregidor to the regiment upon its reactivation. That venerable piece of the Rock occupied a place of honor atop a well-lacquered wooden pedestal positioned directly across from the desk of the regimental sergeant major.

It was regimental policy that each newly assigned officer and enlisted man be brought to the CP to see—but never to touch—

that piece of Corregidor. Whenever visitors came into the headquarters building, the sergeant major would position himself directly beside The Rock as it was called, giving a brief lecture on its historical significance, and guarding it as if it were one of his daughters. He was never bashful about forcefully telling anyone, regardless of rank, who even *looked* as if he might be going to reach out and touch The Rock to keep his hands to himself.

George Madison Jones, the rugged, no-nonsense combat commander of the 503d Parachute Regimental Combat Team is still remembered by those who served with him as the General Patton of the Pacific who often was up front with his troops in the thick of the fighting. He remained on active duty after World War II and was promoted to the rank of brigadier general in 1962. It was my honor to serve as a company commander in the 3d Infantry Division's 7th Infantry when General Jones was the assistant division commander in Germany. After completing thirty-three years of active duty, General Jones retired from military service. He currently resides in Tucson, Arizona.

Lieutenant Colonel Edward M. Postlethwait, the commanding officer of the 3d Battalion, 34th Infantry that was a part of Rock Force on Corregidor, also remained on active duty after the war. At age forty-two, and at the rank of colonel, he graduated from Fort Benning's Parachute School. In 1956, he commanded the 503d Parachute Infantry Regiment while I was serving with it as a sergeant in Munich, Germany. He retired in 1967 as a colonel and died in 1985 in Fayetteville, North Carolina, home of the 82d Airborne Division.

A number of paratroopers who fought, and nearly died, on Corregidor went on to see additional combat service in the Korean War, which began in 1950. A very few others survived Korea and also fought in Vietnam. One of those hard-core, professional combat paratroopers is Command Sergeant Major Lewis E. Brown, who was born in Florence, Alabama. At age seventeen in 1940, he enlisted in the U.S. Army, later becoming a member of the 501st Parachute Battalion in Panama. He remained with the 501st when it became a part of the 503d Parachute Infantry and was shipped to Australia. While with the regiment during

World War II, Brown rose to the rank of technical sergeant; won a Silver Star medal; was twice wounded; and made combat jumps at Nadzab airstrip in New Guinea, and Noemfoor and Corregidor islands. During the Korean War (1950–1953), Brown served with the 187th Airborne Regimental Combat Team, rising to the rank of master sergeant and making two more combat jumps behind enemy lines at Sukchon and Munson-ni. Later, in 1963, he became a Special Forces (Green Beret) trooper and joined an A Team as a weapons specialist. While with Special Forces, he attained the rank of command sergeant major (the highest enlisted rank) and served three combat tours in Vietnam, where he was wounded in action for the third time. He retired in 1976 after completing thirty-five years and four months of military service and currently resides in Fayetteville, North Carolina.

John H. "Smiling Jack" Tolson, a 1937 West Point classmate of Colonel Postlethwait, also remained on active duty after World War II. During the Vietnam War he commanded the 1st Cavalry Division with great distinction and retired in 1973 as a lieutenant general. He now resides in Raleigh, North Carolina.

World War II had been over for some twelve years when, on February 2, 1957, at the Bath Iron Works in Maine, the mother of Watertender Second Class Elmer Charles Bigelow christened a destroyer named in honor of her son who died of injuries sustained while saving his ship, the *U.S.S. Fletcher*, in the waters off Corregidor. By the time of that christening ceremony, the mortal remains of Watertender Bigelow had been brought home to the United States and reinterred at Hebron, Illinois, where his mother still resides.

Later, in 1974, the U.S. Navy further honored the intrepid Bigelow by naming a building after him at the Naval Amphibious Base located at Norfolk, Virginia. The *U.S.S. Bigelow* remained a part of the active fleet until 1982 when she was decommissioned and placed in the inactive reserve fleet docked at the Philadelphia Naval Shipyard.

Fourteen years after the christening of the *U.S.S. Bigelow*, the first reunion of shipmates who had served aboard the *Fletcher* was held in the Pocono Mountains of Pennsylvania. One of the chief organizers of that reunion was Keith E. Snyder, who had lost most of his left arm aboard the *Fletcher*. Today, Snyder is still serving as secretary of the *Fletcher* Association.

By coincidence, the *Fletcher* had earned thirteen battle stars during World War II and thirteen former crewmembers attended that first reunion. Today, well over 300 of the *Fletcher's* World War II crew attend its reunions that are held every other year. The guest of honor at each reunion is Mrs. Verna Perry, mother of Watertender Bigelow.

The *U.S.S. Fletcher*—the ship that was saved by Bigelow—subsequently saw additional combat service during the Korean War. It took part in the epic Inchon landings masterminded and personally supervised by General MacArthur, who was then serving as commander of all United States and United Nations forces in Korea. Subsequent to those landings, the *Fletcher* remained in Korean waters providing fire support to United Nations ground forces up and down the coastline throughout the war.

The *Fletcher* remained a part of the active fleet until 1969 when she was decommissioned and sold for scrap after twenty-seven years of service. In 1980, a second U.S. Naval destroyer was christened the *U.S.S. Fletcher*. This state-of-the-art warship is armed with two Mark 45 lightweight guns, two triple-barreled MK 32 torpedo launchers, plus an antisubmarine rocket launcher. She also is outfitted with facilities for embarkation of subhunting helicopters. The original *Fletcher's* ship's bell and wheel are both on board the new ship.

The paratroopers who fought on Corregidor hold annual reunions. In 1965 a few former members of the 503d Parachute Infantry gathered for the first time since the war to remember their fallen comrades in arms. Since then the regimental association has grown to over 5,000 members.

On February 16, 1979, the thirty-fourth anniversary of the Corregidor jump, General Jones and some sixty veterans who had parachuted on to the Rock with him returned there to dedicate a memorial to the men and women who defended and recaptured the island. The memorial itself was designed by Harry J. Drews, formerly of the regiment's Company D, who lost a leg as a result of severe wounds sustained during heavy skirmishing on the shoreline below Battery Wheeler.

One of the veteran troopers attending that 1979 return to Corregidor was Preston McArthur of Pensacola, Florida. In 1971, at the age of fifty-seven, McArthur took up the dangerous sport of sky diving and later became licensed as a demonstration jumper by the United States Parachute Association.

By the time he returned to Corregidor, Preston McArthur had logged over 1,000 free-fall parachute jumps and was a past master at landing in hard-to-reach drop zones. To celebrate his return to the Rock, he planned to make a parachute jump on Topside immediately following the unveiling of the association's monument in front of Mile-long Barracks. But when he was advised that his wartime commanding officer, General Jones, was not in favor of the jump because it might take away from the solemnity of the occasion, he decided to postpone his leap until the following day, February 17, 1979.

On that day, McArthur left his hotel in Manila carrying the parachute he had brought along in his luggage. Hailing a cab, he proceeded to the Manila International airport where he boarded a waiting helicopter that he had hired to make his leap. Arriving over Corregidor a short while later, he had the chopper pilot land on Topside so that he might take precise readings of the prevailing wind speeds and direction. After making a few quick calculations and holding a final flight plan conference, McArthur had the pilot take him up to an altitude of 4,000 feet above sea level at a distance of one-quarter mile upwind of the Rock. There, with an Associated Press reporter and photographer recording the proceedings, he stepped out into space and fell to 3,500 feet before opening his chute. The rest of the jump, reports McArthur, "was a piece of cake."

Due to a number of tragic occurrences in their personal lives after World War II, some veterans of the 503d Parachute Regimental Combat Team never were able to attend one of the annual reunions. In the fall of 1947, two former members of the hard-luck 1st Battalion, Captain Neil Taylor and Lieutenant George Kish, along with Lieutenant William E. "Red Dog" LaVanchure of Company F, were killed in a plane crash while en route from Fort Benning, Georgia, to the annual Army-Navy football classic. Five years later, another former 1st Battalion officer, Captain John R. Richmond, was killed in a plane crash at Fort Bragg, North Carolina.

Private Lloyd G. McCarter, the 503d Parachute Infantry's one-man gang who was awarded the Medal of Honor for heroism on Corregidor, was medically discharged in 1946 with a Japanese bullet still lodged next to his heart. Surgeons choose not to attempt removing the bullet, fearing that the extensive surgery required to do so would result in the death of McCarter. Upon his return to civilian life in 1946, McCarter was employed by the Veterans Administration as a contact representative in Idaho. He married in 1948 but lost his wife four years later due to illness. In February 1956—eleven years after he had jumped on Corregidor—while deeply despondent over the death of his wife, and suffering greatly from his war wounds, McCarter did what the Japanese never were able to do during the war: He took his own life. He was survived by his twin sister Lillian, and his younger brother William.

Private Jesse S. Castillo, the combat paratroop engineer who was totally blinded while firing a machine gun on Corregidor, regulary attends the annual regimental reunions. In 1945 he married his fiancée, Ruth, and went on to became successful in real estate and as a restaurateur. In 1987, Jesse and Ruth moved from their home in Pamona, California, to Tahelquah, Oklahoma, where they still reside. As the couple was preparing for the move to Oklahoma, Ruth jokingly told Jesse that he'd "better start looking for a seeing eye horse" to ride over the forty acres at their new home.

In 1987, three former members of the 503d Parachute Infantry returned to Corregidor and spent ten days walking through the many battlefields and ravines where their lives very nearly ended abruptly in 1945. The trio consisted of Carl G. Bratle of Southold, New York, who had served as a Private First Class in Company C; Donald E. Abbott of Santa Rosa, California, formerly the executive officer of Company E on Corregidor and the commanding officer of Company A on Negros; and John L.

Lindgren of Laguna Hills, California, who had been Company D's 4th Platoon leader during Lieutenant Endo's ferocious banzai attack. Lindgren remained in the service after World War II and later served in Vietnam as a military advisor; he subsequently retired as a lieutenant colonel. During their revisit to the Rock, the three ex-paratroopers stayed at the Corregidor Inn, a small, four-room guest house that had been built on Bottomside and has since been destroyed by a storm. A large twenty-room hotel is currently under construction on the island.

Two years after their ten-day visit to the Rock, Lindgren and Abbott returned again, spending an entire month retracing their respective company's every move during the 1945 battle to recapture Corregidor. Both men were then in their mid-sixties and had physically prepared themselves for the rigors of climbing up, down, and all around the Rock by participating in extensive exercise drills for several weeks prior to the long flight back to Manila.

In 1990, Don Abbott returned alone to the Rock for a third time, spending another three weeks hiking and climbing all over the island. During that visit he discovered several lengths of nylon parachute suspension lines wrapped around some rubble in the empty swimming pool beside the ruins of Topside's prewar Officers Club. The parachute lines had been lying there, untouched, since 1945.

Since it was by then D-day-plus-forty-five years, Abbott didn't feel the least bit guilty when he cut the lines and stuffed them in his pocket.

APPENDIX A

The President of the United States takes pride in presenting the MEDAL OF HONOR posthumously to

ELMER CHARLES BIGELOW,
WATERTENDER SECOND CLASS
UNITED STATES NAVAL RESERVE

for service as set forth in the following

CITATION:

For conspicuous gallantry and intrepidity at the risk of his life above and beyond the call of duty while serving on board the U.S.S. FLETCHER during action against enemy Japanese forces off Corregidor Island in the Philippines, February 14, 1945. Standing topside when an enemy shell struck the FLETCHER, BIGELOW, acting instantly as the deadly projectile exploded into fragments which penetrated the No. 1 gun magazine and set fire to several powder cases, picked up a pair of fire extinguishers and rushed below in a resolute attempt to quell the raging flames. Refusing to waste the precious time required to don rescue breathing apparatus, he plunged through the smoke billowing out of the magazine hatch and dropped into the blazing compartment. Despite the acrid, burning powder smoke which seared his lungs with every agonizing breath, he worked rapidly and with instinctive sureness and succeeded in quickly extinguishing the fires and in cooling the cases and bulkheads, thereby preventing further damage to the stricken ship. Although he succumbed to his injuries on the following day, BIGELOW, by his dauntless valor, unfaltering skill and prompt action in the critical emergency, had averted a magazine explosion

231

which undoubtedly would have left his ship wallowing at the mercy of the furiously pounding Japanese guns on Corregidor. His heroic self-sacrifice in the face of almost certain death enhanced and sustained the highest traditions of the United States Naval Service. He gallantly gave his life in the service of his country.

HARRY S. TRUMAN

APPENDIX B

THE WHITE HOUSE
WASHINGTON

The President of the United States takes pride in presenting the MEDAL OF HONOR to

LLOYD G. McCARTER, PRIVATE
UNITED STATES ARMY

for service as set forth in the following

CITATION

He was a scout with the regiment that seized the fortress of Corregidor, Philippine Islands. Shortly after the initial parachute assault on 16 February 1945, he crossed thirty yards of open ground under intense enemy fire and at point-blank range silenced a machine gun with hand grenades. On the afternoon of 18 February, he killed six snipers. That evening, when a large force attempted to bypass his company, he voluntarily moved to an exposed area and opened fire. The enemy attacked his position repeatedly throughout the night and was repulsed each time. By 0200 hours, all the men about him had been wounded. Shouting encouragement to his comrades and defiance at the enemy, he continued to bear the brunt of the attack, fearlessly exposing himself to locate the enemy soldiers and then pouring heavy fire on them. He repeatedly crawled back to the American line to secure more ammunition. When his submachine gun would no longer operate, he seized an automatic rifle and continued to inflict heavy casualties. This weapon, in turn, became too hot to use and, discarding it, he continued with an M-1 rifle. At dawn the enemy attacked with renewed intensity. Exposing himself to hostile fire, he stood erect to locate the most dangerous enemy positions. He was seriously wounded; but although he had killed more than thirty of the enemy, he refused to evacuate until he had pointed out immediate objectives for the attack. Through his sustained and outstanding heroism in the face of grave and obvious danger, Private McCarter made a significant contribution to the success of his company and the recapture of Corregidor.

HARRY S. TRUMAN

APPENDIX C

X-BATTLE HONORS. As authorized by Executive Order 9396 (Sec. I, WD Bul. 22, 1943), superseding Executive Order 9075 (Sec. III, WD Bul. 11, 1942), the following unit is cited by the War Department under the provisions of Section IV, WD, Circular 333, 1943, in the name of the President of the United States as public evidence of deserved honor and distinction. The citation reads as follows:

The 503d Parachute Infantry Regiment, with the following attached units:
462 Parachute Field Artillery Battalion
3d Battalion, 34th Infantry Regiment
Company "C" 161st Parchute Engineer Battalion
(Now 161st Airborne Engineer Company)
18th Portable Surgical Hospital (Reinforced)
3d Platoon, Antitank Company, 34th Infantry Regiment
3d Platoon, Cannon Company, 34th Infantry Regiment
3d Platoon, Company "C" 3d Engineer Battalion
Company "A" 34th Infantry Regiment
3d Platoon, Company "C," 24th Medical Battalion
Detachment, Service Company, 34th Infantry Regiment
Battery "A," 950th AAA (AW) Battalion
174th Ordnance Service Detachment (Bomb Disposal Squad)
Detachment, 592d Engineer Boat and Shore Regiment
Detachment, 98th Signal Battalion
Detachment, 1st Platoon, 603d Tank Company
Detachment, 592d Joint Assault Signal Company
Detachment, 6th Support Air Party
Combat Photo Unit "A," GHQ Signal Section
Combat Photo Unit "Q," GHQ Signal Section

Appendix C

These units, organized as a task force, distinguished themselves by extraordinary heroism and outstanding performance of duty in action against the enemy from 16 to 28 February 1945. This force was directed to seize the enemy held island fortress of Corregidor, one of the most difficult missions of the Pacific War. A long prepared and fanatical enemy, strongly entrenched in numerous tunnels, caves, dugouts, and crevices, awaited the assault in commanding and extensively fortified positions. The small dropping area for the parachutists was bordered extensively by sheer cliffs, with resultant variable air currents and eddies; and previous bombings and naval gunfire had cut trees and shrubs close above ground, creating hazardous stakes which threatened to impale descending troops. The approach by sea, through shallow water known to be mined, led to a beach protected by land mines. At 0830 on 16 February, the initial assault was made by parachute drop on terrain littered with debris and rubble. Heavy casualties were sustained. Two hours later the amphibious elements advanced by sea through the mine field to the beach; and, though many lives were lost and much equipment destroyed by exploding mines, this element moved rapidly inland and under heavy enemy fire seized Malinta Hill. Meanwhile, the Airborne element though subjected to intense enemy fire and suffering increasing casualties, were organized into an aggressive fighting force as a result of the initiative of commanders of small units. Advancing doggedly against fanatical resistance, they had by nightfall, secured "The Top of the Rock," their initial objective. On the following morning, the entire task force began a systematic reduction of enemy positions and the annihilation of defending forces. Innumerable enemy tunnels and caves were sealed by demolitions after hand to hand fighting, only to have the enemy emerge elsewhere through an intricate system of inter-connecting passageways. Direct fire of our supporting weapons, employed to seal tunnels and caves, often resulted in the explosion of enemy emplaced demolitions and ammunition dumps, causing heavy casualties to our troops. Under increasing pressure, the enemy, cut off from reinforcements, exploded demolitions in tunnels, destroying themselves as well as elements of our task force. At the completion of this desperate and violent struggle, 4,509 enemy dead were counted. Prisoners totalled nineteen. Throughout the operation all elements of the task force, combat and service troops alike, displayed heroism of the highest

Appendix C

degree. Parachuting to earth or landing on mined beaches, they attacked savagely against a numerically superior enemy, defeated him completely, and seized the fortress. Their magnificent courage, tenacity, and gallantry, avenged the victims of Corregidor of 1942, and achieved a significant victory for the United States Army.

OFFICIAL:
    EDWARD F. WITSELL
    Major General
    Acting The Adjutant General

    G.C. Marshall
    Chief of Staff

APPENDIX D

COAT OF ARMS

Shield: Argent, a fort voided azure, pierced to the center by a pile of the second counterchanged with the fort and bearing three parachutes of the first, two and one.

Crest: None.

Motto: The Rock

Symbolism: The colors, blue and white, are the current and old colors of infantry. The inverted triangle terminating in the broken fort symbolizes the drop on Corregidor during the Luzon campaign, whereas the three parachutes represent the three other campaigns of the organization in World War II.

Distinctive Insignia
The distinctive insignia is the shield and motto of the coat of arms.

LINEAGE

Constituted 24 February 1942 in the army of the United States as the 503d Parachute Infantry (concurrently), First Battalion consolidated with the 503d Parachute Battalion (constituted 14 March 1941 and activated 22 August 1941 at Fort Benning, Georgia) and Second Battalion consolidated with the 504th Parachute Battalion (constituted 14 March 1941 and activated 5 October 1941 at Fort Benning, Georgia) and consolidated units designated as the First and Second Battalions, 503d Parachute Infantry.

Regiment (less First, Second, and Third Battalions) activated 2 March 1942 at Fort Benning, Georgia. Third Battalion activated 8 June 1942 at Fort Bragg, North Carolina. (Second Battalion reorganized and redesignated 2 November 1942 as the Second Battalion, 509th Parachute Infantry, hereafter separate lineage; concurrently, new Second Battalion, 503d Infantry, activated in Australia.) Regiment inactivated 24 December 1945 at Camp Anza, California. Redesignated 1 February 1951 as the 503d Airborne Infanty; concurrently, allotted to the regular army and assigned to the Eleventh Airborne Division. Activated 2 March 1951 at Fort Campbell, Kentucky.

Relieved 1 March 1957 from assignment to the Eleventh Airborne Division; concurrently, reorganized and redesignated as the 503d Infantry, a parent regiment under the Combat Arms Regimental System.

CAMPAIGN PARTICIPATION CREDIT

World War II
New Guinea
Leyte
Luzon (with arrowhead)
Southern Philippines

Vietnam
Defense
Counteroffensive
Counteroffensive, Phase II
 (with arrowhead)
Counteroffensive, Phass III
Tet Counteroffensive
Counteroffensive, Phase IV

Appendix D

Vietnam
Counteroffensive, Phase V
Counteroffensive, Phase VI
Tet 69 Counteroffensive
Summer-Fall 1969
Winter-Spring 1970
Sanctuary Counteroffensive
Counteroffensive, Phase VII
Consolidation I

DECORATIONS

Presidential Unit Citation (Army), Streamer embroidered *Corregidor* (503d Parachute Infantry cited: WD GO 53, 1945).

Presidential Unit Citation (Army), Streamer embroidered *Bien Hoa* (First Battalion, 503d Infantry cited: DA GO 40, 1966).

Presidential Unit Citation (Army), Streamer embroidered *Phouc Vinh* (Second Battalion, 503d Infantry cited: DA GO 40, 1967).

Presidential Unit Citation (Army), Streamer embroidered *Dat To* (173d Airborne Brigade (less Third Battalion, 503d Infantry) cited: DA GO 42, 1969).

Presidential Unit Citation (Navy), Streamer embroidered *Vietnam 1966* (Fourth Battalion, 503d Infantry cited: DA GO 32, 1973).

Philippine Presidential Unit Citation, Streamer embroidered *17 October 1944 to 4 July 1945* (503d Parachute Infantry cited: DO GO 47, 1950).

Meritorious Unit Commendation. Streamer embroidered *Vietnam 1965–1967* (First, Second, and Fourth Battalions, 503d Infantry cited: DA GO 48, 1968).

Vietnamese Cross of Gallantry with Palm. Steamer embroidered *Vietnam 1965–1970* cited: DA GO 51, 1971 (inclusive dates: 5 May 1965–27 September 1970.)

Vietnamese Civic Actions Medal Unit Citation. Streamer embroidered *Vietnam 1969–1971*, cited: DA GO 5, 1973. Inclusive dates: 15 April 1969–16 March 1971.

APPENDIX E

1. Main (back) parachute
2. Demolition kit containing blasting caps, detonation cord, and eighteen blocks of TNT each weighing ¼ pound.
3. Reserve (chest) parachute
4. Thompson .45 caliber submachine gun
5. Mosquito netting for head area
6. Leather gloves
7. Jump rope—for use in climbing down out of trees
8. Two extra pistol magazines, each containing seven bullets
9. Ammo pouch for submachine gun. This pouch contains 250 bullets
10. Machete
11. Trench knife with brass knuckles
12. Load-carrying suspenders
13. Compass
14. Flash light
15. Condensed food rations
16. Hand grenade
17. Water canteen
18. First aid packet
19. Colt .45 caliber pistol
20. Notebook
21. Pencil
22. Pocket knife
23. Waterproof container for matches
24. Sulphur bandage
25. Lubrication oil for weapons
26. Water purification tablets
27. Salt tablets
28. Tooth brush for cleaning weapons
29. Spoon
30. Anti-fungus foot powder

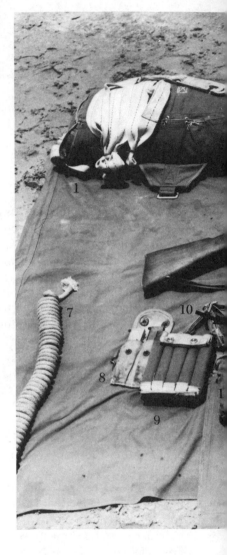

American World War II paratroopers often jumped into battle carrying upwards of eighty pounds of equipment and supplies. This photo shows a typical combat load carried by a demolition man of the 503d Parachute Infantry Regiment in the Pacific. Identical equipment was carried by paratroopers fighting in Europe. The following other items—not displayed here—were also carried: steel helmet, binoculars, map, soap, razor, toothbrush, towel, dogtags, cigarettes, and extra socks. Because of his heavy weapon and equipment load, the paratrooper didn't have room for comfort

Appendix E

items such as a raincoat or blanket. As a result he spent many wet and cold nights in combat. The submachine gun shown here is fitted with an ammunition drum containing fifty bullets. Later versions of this weapon were fitted with a straight, vertical-feed magazine containing thirty bullets. Though it contained fewer bullets, the latter magazine enabled the paratrooper to reload his weapon far more quickly than he formerly could with the drum magazine. *(U.S. Army)*

243

BIBLIOGRAPHY

Baker, A.J. *Yamashita*. New York: Ballantine Books, 1973.

Barbey, Vice Admiral Daniel E., U.S.N. *MacArthur's Amphibious Navy*. Annapolis, MD: United States Naval Institute, 1969.

Barnes, Maj. Gen. G.M. *Weapons of WW II*. New York: D. Van Nostrand, 1947.

Bashore, Boyd T. *Sword of Silk, Part 1*. Fort Benning, GA: Infantry School Quarterly, 1956.

Beck, John J. *MacArthur and Wainwright, Sacrifice of the Philippines*. Albuquerque: University of New Mexico Press, 1974.

Belote, James H., and William M. Belote. *Corregidor: The Saga of a Fortress*. New York: Harper and Row, 1967.

Blair, Clay, Jr. *MacArthur*. New York: Doubleday, 1977.

Bourne, Edward G. *The Philippine Islands*. Cleveland: Arthur H. Clark, 1935.

Brereton, Lt. Gen. Lewis H. *The Brereton Diaries*. New York: Century Croft, 1951.

Breuer, William B. *Retaking the Philippines*. New York: St. Martin's Press, 1986.

Buckley, Capt. Robert J., Jr., U.S.N.R. *At Close Quarters*. Washington, DC: Government Printing Office, 1962.

Cannon, M. Hamlin. *The U.S. Army in WW II: Leyte: The Return to the Philippines*. Washington, DC: Government Printing Office, 1954.

Craven, Wesley F., and James L. Cate. *The Army Air Force in WW II: The Pacific—Guadalcanal to Saipan*. Chicago: University of Chicago Press, 1950.

Dupuy, Col. R. Ernest, and Trevor N. Dupuy. *Military Heritage of America*. New York: McGraw-Hill Book, 1956.

Falk, Stanley L. *Decision at Leyte*. New York: W.W. Norton, 1966.

Flanagan, Lt. Gen. Edward M. *Corregidor: The Rock Force Assault*. Navoto, CA: Presidio Press, 1988.

Bibliography

Gavin, Lt. Gen. James M. *Airborne Warfare.* Washington, DC: Infantry Journal Press, 1947.

Guthrie, Bennett, M. *Three Winds of Death.* Chicago: Adams Press, 1985.

Huston, James A. *Out of the Blue.* West LaFayette, IN: Purdue University Studies, 1972.

Japanese Parachute Troops Special Series No. 32. Washington, DC: Military Intelligence Service. U.S. War Department, 1944.

Kenney, Gen. George C. *General Kenney Reports.* New York: Duell, Sloan and Pierce, 1949.

Krueger, Gen. Walter *From Down Under to Nippon: The Story of the Sixth Army in World War II.* Washington, DC: Combat Forces Press, 1953.

Kusman, Michael. *Register of Graduates and Former Cadets of the U.S. Military Academy.* West Point, NY: Association of Graduates of U.S.M.A., 1975.

Liddell-Hart, B.H. *History of the Second World War.* New York: Putnam, 1971.

Lightfoot, Keith. *The Philippines.* New York: Praeger, 1973.

(MacArthur, Douglas) *Reports of General MacArthur.* Vol. 1. *The Campaigns of MacArthur in the Pacific.* Prepared by his General Staff. Washington, DC: U.S. Government Printing Office, 1960.

Mahon, John K., and Roman A. Danysh. *Army Lineage Series, Infantry.* Part I. Washington, DC: Office of the Chief of Military History, Dept. of the Army, 1972.

Manchester, William. *American Caesar.* Boston: Little, Brown, 1978.

Morison, Samuel Eliot. *The Two-Ocean War.* Boston: Little, Brown, 1963.

Morton, Louis. *U.S. Army in World War II: The Fall of the Philippines.* Washington, DC: Office of the Chief of Military History, Dept. of the Army, 1953.

Parr, Charles M. *So Noble a Captain, The Life and Times of Ferdinand Magellan.* New York: Thomas Y. Crowell, 1953.

Smith, Joseph H. *Small Arms of the World.* Harrisburg, PA: Stackpole, 1976.

Smith, Robert R. *The Approach to the Philippines.* U.S. Army in World War II. Washington, DC: Government Printing Office, 1953.

Bibliography

————. *Triumph in the Philippines. U.S. Army in World War II.* Washington, DC: Office of the Chief of Military History, Dept. of the Army, 1961.

Toland, John. *The Rising Sun: The Decline and Fall of the Japanese Empire 1936–1945.* 2 vols. New York: Random House, 1970.

Young, Brig. Gen. Gordon R. *The Army Almanac.* Harrisburg, PA: Stackpole, 1959.

REPORTS

Blair, Maj. John H., III. *Operations of the 3d Battalion, 503d Parachute Infantry Regiment in the Landing on Corregidor, P.I., 16 February–2 March 1945. Personal Experiences of a Battalion Staff Officer.* Fort Benning, GA: The Infantry School, 1949.

Helding, Maj. James J. *Combined Assault—Corregidor.* Fort Leavenworth, KS: U.S. Army Command and General Staff College, 1971.

Hill, Capt. Hudson C. *The Operations of Company E, 503d Parachute Infantry Regiment at Wheeler Point, Island of Corregidor, Philippine Islands, 23 February 1945. Personal Experiences of a Company Commander.* Fort Benning, GA: The Infantry School, 1947.

Lackey, Lt. Col. John H. *The Rock Operation.* Air Staff College, 1946.

LeVine, Maj. Lester H. *The Operations of the 503d Parachute Infantry Regiment in the Attack on Corregidor Island, 16 February–2 March 1945. Personal Experiences of a Regimental Adjutant.* Fort Benning, GA: The Infantry School, 1947.

Smith, Capt. Magnus L. *Operations of the Rock Force (503d RCT Reinforced) in the Recapture of Corregidor Island, 16 February–8 March 1945. Personal Experiences of an Assistant Regimental Operations Officer.* Fort Benning, GA: The Infantry School, 1949.

United States Army Forces in the Far East Board Report No. 308. *Corregidor Island Operations, 16 February–8 March 1945.* Headquarters, USAFFE, May 16, 1945.

INDEX

Index

Index

Gifford, James P., Jr., 114, 115, 206
Goal Post Ridge, 71, 92, 97, 98, 102, 125
Gort, Lord, 19
Gridley, Charles V., 4
Griffen, Ernest, 154
Grubbs Ravine, 137, 149, 159, 179–180
Grubbs Trail, 178–179
Guam, 5, 13
Guimaras, 219
Gulsvick, Edward, 81
Guthrie, Bennett M., 140, 189, 201

H

Handlon, Glen E., 88
Hardwick, Cornelius S., 176–177
Harley, Richard, 60
Harp, Willard, 100
Harris, Richard G., 69
Hartman, William, 119–120
Herb, Robert E., 55–56
Hernandez, Michael, 168
Heyer, Robert W., 193
Hill Airfield, 44
Hill, Charles W., 145
Hill, Hudson C., 80–81, 82, 116, 131, 133, 134, 137, 181–182, 183–184, 185, 186, 187, 188, 205
Hirohito, Emperor, 221
Hiroshima, bombing of, 221
Holland, 3
Hollandia, New Guinea, 30, 64

Homma, Masaharu, 15–16, 17, 19, 21, 22, 222
Hong Kong, 4, 13, 18
Hooker Point, 204–205
Hoover, Vernon D., 143–144
Hopewell U.S.S., 42, 43
Horton, Charlie T., 215
Howard, Samuel L., 22
Hoyt, Charles H., 97, 109
Huff, Delby A., 78, 88, 89
Hughart, Paul A., 114
Hutchins, Maurice K., 176

I

Iloilo, Panay, 220
Impson, Amazon B., Jr., 54
Impson, Jack, 54
Infantry Point, 192, 193
Itagaki, Ikira, 35, 58, 74, 75, 173

J

James Ravine, 75, 90, 131–137
Janas, Ralph F., 188
Jandro, Howard S., 187, 188
Japan
    1st Infantry Division of, 65
    Bushido Code, 74–75, 194
    Hiroshima/Nagasaki bombing in, 221
    invasion of Philippines, 14–16, 19–22
    in Mindoro assault, 34–35
    occupation of Philippines, 17, 22–23
    Pacific War strategy of, 13

254

Index

Pearl Harbor attack by, 13–14
surrender of, 221, 222
See also Corregidor, recapture of
Japanese-Americans, in United States armed forces, 47–48
Jetton, Willie G., 208
Johnson, Chris W., 79, 152
Joint Assault Signal Company (JASCO), 47
Jones, George Madison, 30, 33, 34, 57, 61, 227, 228
attack order by, 38
background of, 27
Corregidor command, 50, 52–53, 59, 73–74, 85–86, 90, 95, 105, 117, 123, 128, 129, 136, 150, 152, 157, 160, 166, 189–90, 193–194, 35, 200, 205, 214, 215, 216
and Noemfoor jump, 31, 32
plan for Corregidor assault, 36, 37, 39
postwar duty, 225
Jones, Gertus, 81–82

K

Kambakumis, Angelos ("Greek"), 110–111
Kamiri Airdrome, 31–32, 33
Keller, Frank B., 162
Kelly, Dempsey, 168
Kenney, George, 30
Kernodle, Elmer, 135
Kettle Hill, 4
Kindley Field, 8, 9, 196, 200, 202, 204–204

King, Ernest J., 24
King, Roy J., 145
Kinkaid, Thomas C., 219
Kinsler, Kenneth H., 27, 30
Kirkpatrick, Gerald G., 188
Kish, George, 198, 228–229
Kitnik, Henry G. ("Hank"), 102, 125, 126
Kline, Arlais E., 33
Knapp, Glen R., 193, 195
Knox, Cameron, 32
Knudson, Melvin R., 117
Komer, Peter J., 83, 90–91
Krueger, Walter, 26, 76, 214

L

Lackey, John H., 39, 50, 117, 118, 220
Lae, New Guinea, 30
Lampman, Richard A., 87, 88, 151, 180
LaVanchure, William E. ("Red Dog"), 228–229
Lee, William W., 130–131
LeVine, Lester H., 157
Leyte, 1, 12, 25, 34, 65
Leyte Gulf, 2
Lindgren, John L., 155, 229–230
Lingayen Gulf, 14, 15, 16
Little Knob, 71, 92, 97, 98, 102, 125
Lopez, Anthony D., 110
Lopez de Villalobos, Ruy, 2
Lovinguth, Albert C., 189
Luzon, 1, 13, 14, 15, 22–23, 25, 27, 35, 65

Index

Index

Index

ABOUT THE AUTHOR

Gerard M. Devlin enlisted in the U.S. Army in 1950 and served as a paratrooper in the Korean War.

After attaining the rank of sergeant first class he attended Infantry Officer Candidate School and was commissioned a second lieutenant in 1958. During the Vietnam War he was trained to speak Vietnamese and assigned as chief advisor to Vietnam's famous "Black Tiger" 44th Ranger Battalion. While with the rangers he received wounds requiring a year's hospitalization. He later returned to Vietnam, completing a second combat tour with the 25th Infantry Division.

In 1970, Devlin retired from the U.S. Army at the rank of major. He is a graduate of the Command and General Staff College, and his decorations include the Distinguished Service Cross, five Bronze Stars, the Purple Heart, two Vietnamese Crosses of Gallantry, and the Combat Infantryman Badge with star. He lives in Hilton Head, South Carolina.